May God bless al......................concerning their prayers and .... this publication. I................................ goodness and mercy, may He bestow endless graces upon all who will read and share this book. "So ask the master of the harvest to send out laborers for his harvest" (Mt 9:38).

While Mary's "yes'" given at the Annunciation continues in so many ways, one of the most glowing is that of joyful, generous, faithful, consecrated women religious! As Pope Francis said here at Saint Patrick's Cathedral, "Where would the Church be without our religious Sisters!"

—Timothy Cardinal Dolan
Archbishop of New York City, New York

The witness and encouragement of religious Sisters was indispensable to my own journey to the priesthood. I know that amidst so much unhappiness and confusion in the world today, the Church needs all the more the witness and wisdom of women who have come to know the joy of living in trusting dependence on the Lord, and who will respond to the call of Jesus to give their lives completely to helping others know that happiness which comes from trusting and following Him.

—Most Rev. Allen H. Vigneron
Archbishop of Detroit, Michigan

God invites certain men and women to choose consecrated life. Religious life is, without question, a gift to the Church and our world that gives witness to the power of prayer, communal life, and service to others. We are blessed in our time by a steady influx of young and culturally diverse women who respond as Our Blessed Mother did: *Fiat!*—"May it be done to me according to Your word." May the women of our Church continue to have the courage of Mary to respond *"Fiat!"* to Our Lord's call to religious life. And may we continue to support them through our prayers and encouragement!

—**Most Rev. James F. Checchio**
Bishop of Metuchen, New Jersey

God the Father continues to call women to be spiritual mothers and brides of Christ, to give their lives in love of God for the sanctification of His Church and the salvation of souls. There is no better choice to make than to say "Yes" to the Lord and follow the Lamb wherever He goes. This true love for humanity is seen in the vocation of women religious as they pray and serve those whom the Lord Jesus Christ so dearly loves. May this book inspire many women to consider God's call for their lives to make His love and mercy known.

—**Most Rev. Thomas J. Olmsted**
Bishop of Phoenix, Arizona

Throughout my life and ministry, I have been blessed by the presence and influence of many women religious, including my aunt, Sister M. Clotine Siegel, OSF, who was a Joliet Franciscan for over 60 years. In my interactions with these Sisters, I was enriched greatly by their faith, wisdom, and example. It is my hope and prayer that people today, young and old alike, might  have the same opportunities I had to encounter women religious in the classroom and in parish life. More than ever, we need to continue to pray for and support our Sisters and those in formation, as well as encourage girls and young women to open their hearts to the Lord's call to a vocation to consecrated life.

—Most Rev. Joseph M. Siegel
Bishop of Evansville, Indiana

The beauty of women committing their lives to Jesus Christ in consecrated life is of immeasurable value in today's troubled world. Women religious echo the "Yes" of the Blessed Virgin Mary to the will of God in ways that challenge modern assumptions about how women can flourish today. The Church rejoices profoundly when modern women promise their lives in service to the Gospel by vows of chastity, poverty, and obedience. We celebrate the joy in Christ that these women radiate and share with the world.

—Most Rev. Joseph E. Strickland
Bishop of Tyler, Texas

Meeting a Sister of Mary, Mother of the Eucharist or getting to spend time in one of their convents, you instantly realize that these young women are living out Pope Saint John Paul II's description of religious women as "dispensers of mercy, heralds of Christ's return, living signs of the Resurrection and of its treasures of virginity, poverty and obedience" (Vita Consecrata §111). Behind every vocation story, there is a unique history, a personal path, a struggle, and a surrender. These pages accordingly present to the world more than one hundred and fifty consecrated religious whose "Yes" years ago and each day continues to make real in this fallen world the face, heart, and hands of Mary, Mother of Our Eucharistic Lord.

—Father David V. Meconi, SJ
Editor of *Homiletic & Pastoral Review*
Director of Catholic Studies Centre at St. Louis University

I was educated in the late 1950s at a Catholic parochial school staffed by Dominican Sisters. Their discipline and commitment to faith changed my life and caused me to become a daily communicate in fourth grade! Today, sixty years later, the Dominican Sisters of Mary, Mother of the Eucharist in Ann Arbor form a replica of the Sisters who taught me. These Sisters now staff JSerra Catholic School in San Juan Capistrano, California. Their relevance to the coed students is a critical example to inspire young men and women to the important religious vocation of dedicating their lives to the Lord.

—Tim Busch
Founder of Napa Institute

The real beauty of religious life is found in the *"Fiat"* of those who trust Our Lord and Our Lady just enough to peek into the unknown and serve Him. We are each called to give our whole lives to Jesus; some are called to serve Him as religious Sisters, who become  beacons of hope witnessing to each of us how best to turn away from the darkness and distractions of life and instead focus our lives solely on the love and mercy of Jesus Christ. If you are reading this book, perhaps you are asking yourself if God is calling you to be a Sister. Or perhaps your daughter or sister or friend is discerning and you are not sure to which vocation God is calling her. Know this: the easiest way to heaven is to say yes to your vocation. If you want a true guide, be sure to follow the Sisters as they are often the closest to Jesus, Mary, and the saints.

—**Rosemary C. Sullivan**
Executive Director,
National Conference of Diocesan Vocation Directors

Seventy years ago, many—if not most—of the parishes in the United States would also have had a convent attached to it with Sisters teaching in the parish school or working in local hospitals. Much like a biological family with both father and mother present, so a spiritual family is fullest when it has the examples of both spiritual fathers and mothers (Sisters)! As a Dominican, it affects me personally that our Order needs more authentic, spiritual mothers. But hope is on the way! When I entered the novitiate twenty years ago, the Dominican Sisters of Mary, Mother of the Eucharist were establishing a new convent in California. Today, our brothers have built beautiful relationships with these amazing women who encourage us men to be better

religious, to be more zealous in our preaching, and above all, to be more holy! We need our Sisters now more than ever! The feminine genius brings something we priests just cannot give. Let us pray for this new springtime of religious women to re-populate our parishes and help us with the urgent task of the new evangelization!

—**Father James Junipero Moore, OP**
Oakland, California

From the contemplative Carmelites and Pink Sisters in my hometown, whose chapels of Eucharistic Adoration fostered my desire for contemplation, to the joyful witness of the Sisters who cared for and prayed with my grandparents during their last days in their nursing homes, to the teaching Sisters with whom I worked who showed me the importance of teaching the Faith in truth and love, women religious helped stir up my vocation initially and have helped to sustain it through their prayers and support.

The witness of faithful women religious inspires and encourages all in the Church to live their vocations with joy and holiness. Theirs is an especially vital witness to the power of Christ's love in a world where indifference and isolation are sadly so prevalent.

—**Father Patrick Hyde, OP**
Pastor and Director of Campus Ministry
Indiana University

Holy Mother Church has an urgent need of women who by vow share her bridal love for Christ. Such love brings healing and new life to the whole Mystical Body.

—Father John Saward
Dominican Tertiary; Fellow of Blackfriars Hall, Oxford;
Priest-in-charge, Saints Gregory and Augustine Parish, Oxford

Women religious in this country and throughout the world have played a crucial role in healing and educating the Body of Christ. Following in the footsteps of Jesus, religious women have taught our poor and cured our sick. Always seeking the spiritual, these heroic women understood that the flame of Christ's love burned for every human person created in the divine image. They saw the poor, the orphan, the immigrant, and the person of color not as the "other" but as a brother and a sister with the same heavenly Father. It is my fervent hope that this volume will rekindle a fervor in our hearts—a warmth that nourished the work of religious women who, in imitation of the Blessed Mother and emissaries of the heart of the Church, always said yes to promoting the Kingdom of Christ among the poor.

—Father Michael Maher, SJ
Associate Professor of History and Pastoral Minister,
Marquette University

The importance of women religious in the Church and in the world cannot be overstated. Not only is their work and their prayer of great effect, but by their very being they reveal the love of the heart of the Savior, Spouse and Lover of our souls. A second volume from these particular women religious, the Dominican Sisters of Mary, Mother of the Eucharist, is a compelling witness to the happiness that is found in union with God and fidelity to the Church. One hopes that there will continue to be material for many more volumes to come!

—Father Sebastian White, OP
Editor-in-Chief, Magnificat

It is essential for our Church, our world, our families and our children to have as many women's religious vocations as

possible. These holy women pray for our priests and us daily. Their prayers are clearly heard, as they have consecrated and dedicated their life to the most Holy Trinity. They are an inspiration to our children and us, as we see them in their wedding dress daily.

—Julian Heron
Lay Dominican, Lawyer, and
Lobbyist in Washington, D.C.

There is nothing more beautiful in the world than consecrated virginity! Lord, send more!

—Dr. Ralph Martin, STD
Director of Graduate Theology in the New Evangelization
Sacred Heart Seminary, Archdiocese of Detroit, Michigan

In the darkening days and daze of modernity's disintegration, the courageous witness of faithful religious Sisters, such as the indomitable and always inspirational Dominican Sisters of Mary, Mother of the Eucharist, are like beacons of divine light in the diabolical gloom. Their courage encourages the rest of us to fight at their side in the service of Christ and in the battle for souls.

—**Joseph Pearce**
Catholic Author,
Editor of the *St. Austin Review*

Since the time of Christ, there have been faithful virgins who have dedicated themselves as living witnesses of the spousal love between Jesus and His Church. We have an unprecedented need and opportunity to support women who prayerfully consider giving themselves to Christ in this way. We must do all that we can—and above all, I invite you to join me in prayer, fasting, and almsgiving—to help these wonderful women listen for the call of Jesus Christ to give themselves entirely in this life that many more may be with Him in the next life.

—**Curtis A. Martin**
Founder and CEO
Fellowship of Catholic University Students (FOCUS)

The Sisters possess something modern man longs for, but cannot purchase and more often than not does not have - joy. Sisters are vital to our world because they are a living, breathing example of radiant, pure joy that bursts forth from a disciplined religious life - and it is a discipline impelled by love for Jesus Christ. Sisters show us that heavenly joy is possible here and now, even as we make our way through this valley of tears.

—**Father John Eckert**
Pastor, Sacred Heart Church
Salisbury, NC

 Shortly after the Incarnation, Mary, carrying Jesus in her womb, went off to visit Elizabeth, thereby setting up a way of behavior that motivates us today. The closer one is to Jesus, the more one wants to bring Him to others. Such was the motivation of those Mary-like religious women who had, through the years, made Catholic schools so distinctive. Today, however, demographers tell us that only thirty percent of those raised Catholic practice their faith. Could one reason be the lack of Mary-like religious women in our Catholic schools? Today, Mary is prompting young women to be more open to the presence of Jesus within them, so that they can know and do His will and bring Him to young people.

—**Father Cornelius Buckley, SJ**
Thomas Aquinas College
Santa Paula, California

Seeing Sisters in habits is a beautiful sight and demonstrates again that there is more to life than the world offers. Women who dedicate their lives to God in such an unselfish and authentic manner remind us all that heaven is what matters, and we should live our lives in preparation to be saints. God bless all the women religious who make our world a better place and help us prepare for the world to come.

—**Steve Ray**
CatholicConvert.com

Our world is in crisis in so many ways. As a university professor, I have seen firsthand the terrible effects of these crises in our youth, including those who have grown up in the Catholic Faith. Perhaps one of the greatest counter-forces against these trends is the presence of religious orders on our campus. This is of paramount importance for young women, who are urged by our society to find fulfillment in a variety of ways, at the exclusion of the only true path to fulfillment: union with Our Lord. We need religious vocations, and we need women religious in particular to set a luminous example as brides of Christ, beacons of purity, hope, and virtue. This also I have seen firsthand, as religious women have taken my classes, and as some of my students have discerned religious vocations. Let all women be icons of Mary, but let us pray for those who fulfill this calling in a special way, in religious life!

—**Dr. Sara M. Pecknold**
Clinical Assistant Professor of Sacred Music
Catholic University of America

The Sister is a most powerful witness of the ability of a soul to respond and be transformed by the One who must be our all-in-all. We need Sisters now more than ever before; humanity needs to know Jesus, and Sisters aid the hungry, thirsty, desiring soul in becoming one with Christ. The Dominican Sisters of Mary, Mother of the Eucharist offer to each of us a most noble opportunity to know Jesus, and in response to His love for us, they give witness so as to best know how to love Him in response.

—**Father Stash Dailey**
Vicar for Religious, Diocese of Columbus

Religious women who are contemplatives in action go directly to the wounds of the world and insert Christ's presence. They do so following the example of Our Lady, with the heart of a mother. Their prayers bathe the world with impenetrable layers of spiritual protection, defending it from evil. It is because of these prayers that the world is not worse off. Religious women are the superheroes of all time. They do war in *kairos* time accepting the blows of poverty, contempt, and humility, responding with weapons of love, faith and charity. These hard-earned wins endure for eternity. The powerful,  selfless examples of religious women inspire me in my meager efforts to evangelize here and now. Thank you for letting the Lord use your life to invite others to His eternal goodness.

—**Bernie Neal, CA**
Friend of the Sisters

If our broken world needs priests to make present the merciful love of our Heavenly Father, even more does it need the witness of women religious to make present the virginal love of Our Lady. People have an openness to women religious that makes them willing to pour out their hearts in a way they are often hesitant to do with priests. And like Mary did at the wedding at Cana, women religious bring the pains and struggles others have shared with them to her Son.

—**Father Bryce Sibley**
Chaplain at the University of Louisiana at Lafayette

Saint John Paul II spoke of the consecrated life as not only a help and support for the Church in the past, but also "a precious and necessary gift for the present and future of the people of God, since it is an intimate part of her life, her holiness, and her mission" (Vita Consecrata, §3). The Dominican Sisters of Mary, Mother of the Eucharist are a living embodiment of the Marian dimension of the Church that echoes the "Yes" pronounced by the Blessed Virgin, when she spoke "in place of all human nature" (S. Th., *Summa Theologiae* III q. 30 a.1). Mary's "Yes" continues in a most profound way in consecrated women like the Dominican Sisters of Mary, Mother of the Eucharist. They are an intimate part of the life, mission, and call to holiness of the Catholic Church today.

—Dr. Robert Fastiggi
Professor of Systematic Theology
Sacred Heart Major Seminary, Detroit, Michigan

Women religious image the holiness of the Church as bride. They manifest that we are loved by God, and that we are called to love

Him in return. The primacy of this call is easily forgotten in our focus on doing the works of God. Love is to be our motivation, and the feminine heart naturally focuses on the person of Christ, as we see in the lives of so many women saints. What a consolation to God Himself our women religious must be!

—Father Mark Mary, MFVA
Superior, Franciscan Missionaries of the Eternal Word

We need more holy Sisters, more holy priests, and more holy layfolk. We are trying to change the world. Each one has a part.

—Father Richard Zang, CSC
Chaplain of the Dominican Sisters of Mary, Mother of the Eucharist

The world desperately needs the witness of joyful, holy, and faithful young Sisters, who have given themselves completely to Jesus Christ in religious life. Having grown up with religious Sisters in my Catholic school, I can testify to the difference the witness and *love* of these Sisters can make, impacting the lives of so many. I pray for *many* more loving Sisters to transform our world and direct our gaze back to Christ!

—Father Joseph Kirkconnell
Native of Cayman Islands, ordained for the Archdiocese of Detroit

The Trinitarian life of consecrated religious is so needed in our day and age. As icons of Our Lady—Daughter of the Father, Mother of the Son, and Spouse of the Holy Spirit—they bear unique witness to the "one needed thing" in this valley of tears.

—Father Tom Hoisington
Saint Francis of Assisi Catholic Church, Wichita, KS

The importance of the witness of women religious as spiritual mothers in our Church and world today cannot be underestimated. As RCIA Director at UND, I value the women religious with whom I have been blessed to collaborate. They model a unique and beautiful way to live out the grace of Baptism in a free, fruitful, and joy-filled way. Espoused to the Body of Christ, the sign of their religious habit speaks of a radical availability; these spiritual moms are here for every soul throughout the world, to remind us of God's eternal love for all of His children. Above all, I think Sisters educate in the classroom of joy: the joy of a Sister whose heart is set on fire for love of Jesus and souls is contagious! May Our Lord set even more hearts ablaze, that more women will consider the beautiful, joyful vocation of religious life in the Church!

—Brett Perkins
Assistant Director for Evangelization & Religious Education
Campus Ministry, University of Notre Dame, Indiana

Religious women are God's gift to the Church and to the world. They bring to life the Blessed Virgin Mary's motherly love and care for the mystical body of the Son of God. Consecrated women serve the needs of their brothers and sisters through daily prayer, community life, and apostolate driven by deep love for their Spouse who loved them first. May God richly bless them.

—Father Nicholas Sseggobe Kiruma
Kampala, Uganda

When I say "Sisters", my mind goes directly to those who I call "the white angels", the Dominican Sisters of Mary, Mother of the Eucharist. I had the privilege to be their chaplain at the Motherhouse in Ann Arbor for more than two years. God's call is the most precious gift to a person, given to us freely. We need Sisters who not only consecrate their lives for the love of Christ and His Church, but also are mothers to us all. They educate new generations, nourish the broken-hearted, and by Christ's grace can work the harvest tirelessly to let the people love Christ through them.

—Father John Paul Bassil, OMM
Superior of Saint John Paul II Monastery
Ryde, New South Wales, Australia

And Mary's 'Yes' Continues Afresh!

Religious Vocations in the New Millennium
Volume II

Dominican Sisters of Mary, Mother of the Eucharist

Except where noted, scripture texts in this work are taken from the New American Bible, revised edition © 2010, 1991, 1986, 1970 Confraternity of Christian Doctrine, Washington, D.C.

Copyright © 2021 Dominican Sisters of Mary, Mother of the Eucharist

All rights reserved. No part of this publication may be reproduced or transmitted in any form or means, electronic or mechanical, including photocopy, recording, or information storage and retrieval system, without the permission in writing from the publisher.

Lumen Ecclesiae Press
4101 East Joy Road
Ann Arbor, Michigan 48105

ISBN: 978-1-7347684-4-2

General Editor: Sister Joseph Andrew Bogdanowicz, OP
Copy Editor: Rebecca W. Martin
Cover Design and Interior Design: Allison Barrick
Book Layout: Lauren Stefanov
Interior Artwork: Dominican Sisters of Mary, Mother of the Eucharist

First Printing

Printed in the United States of America

Dedication

For eight hundred years, the Virgin of the Salve Regina has come to all faithful Dominican men and women, in the evening of their lives, to draw them under her mantle. In both the dawning and the evening of the writing of these books, the Dominican Sisters of Mary, Mother of the Eucharist wish to dedicate each volume to Mary, Mother of all Vocations, under whose protection the Sisters are able, by gift of their Dominican vocation, to consecrate all the days of their lives to Jesus through Mary.

Table of Contents

Witness of God's Love
— *Bishop Earl Boyea* 25

From the Desk of Mother Assumpta Long, OP
....27

Foreword
— *Rev. William M. Watson, SJ* 29

Introduction
— *Sister Joseph Andrew Bogdanowicz, OP*
....31

Part 1: Foundations

Chapter 1
The Evangelizing Power of the Evangelical Counsels
— *Father Gerard Francisco P. Timoner III, OP*
....37

Chapter 2
Religious Vocations in the Third Millennium— Afresh!
— *Sister Joseph Andrew Bogdanowicz, OP*
....49

Chapter 3
Staking One's Life on the Reality of God:
Theology of Religious Life
— *Sister Albert Marie Surmanski, OP*
....81

Chapter 4
Happiness in Accord with Virtue:
Philosophy of Religious Life
— *Sister Catherine Thomas Brennan, OP*
....97

Chapter 5
Vocations Beget Vocations:
The Story Behind the Statistics of Religious Life
— *Sister Teresa Christi Balek, OP*
....113

Chapter 6
Two Suitcases and the Rest of One's Life:
Living the Charism of a Religious Order or Community
— *Sister Hyacinth Hayward, OP*
....129

Chapter 7
No "How–to" Manual:
Formation of Young Women in the Novitiate
— *Sister John Mary Corbett, OP*
....153

Part 2: Lived Experiences

Chapter 8
Merciful Love:
Personal Formation for the Apostolate
— *Sister Thomas Aquinas Betlewski, OP*
....171

Chapter 9
Ogniem i Mieczem:
Learning to Love God with an Undivided Heart
— *Sister Agnes Paulina Maciol, OP*
....185

Chapter 10
Blood of the Martyrs:
Everything is Grace
— *Sister Christiana Bui, OP*
....201

Chapter 11
The Beauty Seeker:
How I Left Boys, Beaches, and Ballet Flats for the Convent
— *Sister Gianna Marie Borchers, OP*
....211

Chapter 12
When the Good Life is Not Enough:
Baptism, Beekeeping, and Becoming the Woman God Created Me to Be
— *Sister Irenaeus Schluttenhofer, OP*
....225

Chapter 13
From South to North of the Border:
Known, Loved, and Awaited
— *Sister Maria Francisco Molina, OP*
....239

Chapter 14
Finding the Pearl of Great Price:
The World is Not Enough
— *Sister Mary Aquinas Cheng, OP*
....253

Chapter 15
Writing Straight with Crooked Lines:
How I Lost a Tooth (And My Way) But Found My Vocation
— *Sister Maria Benedicta Bete, OP*
....265

Chapter 16
God is Ever Faithful:
From Cajun Country to the Convent
— *Sister Mary Martha Becnel, OP*
....281

Chapter 17
Aim High:
From Combat Boots to…Well, Actually the Shoes Didn't Change That Much
— *Sister Peter Thomas Burson, OP*
....297

Chapter 18
God Loves Us All—Even the Pranksters:
Finding What Love Really Means
— *Sister Mary Perpetua Ha, OP*
....313

Chapter 19
An Invitation to Love:
Discovering the Double-Dominican-American Dream
— *Sister Mercedes Torres, OP*
....327

Part 3: From the Heart of the Church

Chapter 20
Put Out Into the Deep:
The Dominican Sisters of Mary, Mother of the Eucharist
— *Sister Joseph Andrew Bogdanowicz, OP*
....343

Chapter 21
And Mary Said "Fiat":
Growing in Your Spiritual Life & Prayers
....353

Glossary of Religious Terms
— *Sister Elizabeth John Wrigley, OP*
....375

Acknowledgments 387

WITNESS OF GOD'S LOVE

I'm delighted to recommend this second volume of a dynamic work of the Dominican Sisters of Mary, Mother of the Eucharist to women in discernment of religious life, as well as those who wish to better understand its theological roots through personal witness. This second volume, as did the first, portrays a healthy blend of theology along with personal testimonies of various Dominican Sisters in the community. It seems especially important for any woman discerning the Dominican charism to prayerfully read this book. It is unique among its kind and fitted with the real-life joys and challenges of recognizing and living the call to religious life.

Religious women bear witness to God's love for them and their love for Him in a world so desperate for love, desperate for God. They witness to Pope Francis's bidding to religious to "wake up the world" and evangelize by their lives of joy, lived for Christ! They also are living proof that God is real, and they are staking their lives on this truth.

In thanksgiving for you, women who are living the call to religious life, as well as those reading this second volume in discernment of God's will for your lives, I pray God's blessings accompany you.

Your brother in Christ and in consecration to Him and His service,

+ Earl Boyea

His Excellency, Bishop Earl Boyea
Bishop of the Diocese of Lansing, Michigan

From the Desk of Mother Assumpta Long, OP

It is with delight that I introduce this second volume of *And Mary's 'Yes' Continues*. In his 1996 Apostolic Exhortation *Vita Consecrata*, Saint John Paul II pointed with joy to the "constant attraction" that the "total gift of self to the Lord…continue[s] to exert, even on the present generation" (§12).

An age of uncertainties has a special need to rediscover what is constant and unchanging. The most important constant is, of course, God—His intra-Trinitarian unity and the love that spills over into creation. Another constant is the tremendous gift He gives the world in the vocation of consecrated life, an image of the Trinitarian communion and of Christ's faithful love for His

From the Desk of Mother Assumpta Long, OP

Bride, the Church. "The consecrated life," Saint John Paul II wrote earlier in *Vita Consecrata*, "has not only proved a help and support for the Church in the past, but is also a precious and necessary gift for the present and future of the People of God, since it is an intimate part of her life, her holiness and her mission" (§3).

This new volume contains updated essays from Parts 1 and 3 of the first volume, on the foundations and ecclesial nature of religious life and new stories of various Sisters' vocational paths. Our same beloved Pope John Paul assured us that religious life "continues to reassure the Christian people, for they know that they can draw from [it] powerful support on their journey towards the heavenly home." We hope that this book, too, provides you support on your journey towards Him.

Mother Assumpta Long, O.P.

Mother Assumpta Long, OP
Prioress General

Foreword

Looking back, I took for granted the Franciscan Sisters who taught me in grade school. It was a different time in history, but the influence of these intelligent, wise, humorous, and dedicated religious women changed my life. They may have even inspired my early reflections on whether I was called to be a priest.

One day when the school had a Solemn Mass, I had returned from receiving Holy Communion and was kneeling down for my reflection prayer. Little did I notice, but I was supporting my weight with my fanny against my pew as I knelt and folded my hands on the back of the pew in front of me. From behind, Sister Angelique gave a head tap to both me and Tim Williams, my classmate who was similarly posed. She quietly told us we were in a "three-point landing" position and Jesus deserved a two-point landing—no fanny on the pew, in other words!

The fact that I remember with warmth this small incident from nearly sixty years ago is a testament to the inspiration and faith of these great women. The Dominican Sisters of

Mary, Mother of the Eucharist are close to my memory of the intelligent, astute, and dedicated Sisters who taught me at Our Lady of Fatima. The Dominicans are responsible for this volume of reflections on the religious life in light of the challenges and opportunities our early third millennium culture presents to young women considering the consecrated life. It is savvy, grounded in real issues young women face today, and holds out the promise of guiding the discernment process of those women Christ and the Blessed Mother are calling.

In his book, *The Future is Faster than You Think*, Peter Diamandis speaks about five major migrations in global history, from the African slave trade to the displaced peoples from World War II that totaled 44.5 million people. He writes: "Yet today 321 million Americans already spend eleven hours a day online, and virtual reality's neurochemical cocktail will definitely increase that figure. It adds up to another great migration, an exodus of consciousness" (249).

The volume you hold will awaken you to consciousness—to your interior life—and enable you to hear the quiet voice of God. He is calling you to serve Him and His Blessed Mother. The question is what shape your service will take. If you thoughtfully read and pray with these chapters, you will likely reach some clear decision. Be not afraid!

Rev. William M. Watson, SJ
President and Founder, Sacred Story Institute
Author, *Sacred Story: An Ignatian Examen for the Third Millennium*

Introduction

Growing up in a beautiful Catholic family, this very inquisitive child was always asking questions! I wanted to know everything—and I wanted to know it immediately. My dear parents continued to claim me as their child even when my mind and mouth would never stop! I am blessed with a sister two years older who was the model child, and when I reached the tender age of five and a half and joined her at Saint Mary's Catholic School, the good Dominican Sisters quickly learned this child was not a replica of her sweet older sister.

Through what seemed endless corrections and punishments, I never lost my zeal to know truth. I often attempted to lead our family's dinnertime conversation, until my parents would quiet me with their question, "What did you learn in religion class today?" My sister and I would both get to explain the one subject we loved most. To push us further intellectually, my parents would then ask us questions about the Faith and, if we could not answer, they would prompt us to "ask Sister." Believe me, I did! Everything about Sister piqued my curiosity—her Dominican habit, her daily schedule, her prayer, her interior conversation with Jesus when she received Him in Holy Communion. How many Sisters were there in the world anyway? And, oh yes, how does a girl become a Sister?

Twelve years later, I stood with my Catholic high school class and joyfully accepted my signed diploma. Though it was most difficult for my mother in particular, her second and only other daughter would be following the first into the convent. The diploma was just a key; the real treasures I already had: my beautiful Catholic family and my acceptance letter to enter the Dominican Sisters in August! All my questions would finally be answered. If one Sister did not know an answer, some other of the hundred would—after all, Dominicans are teachers. But the most burning question in my heart at that time was how I could best live the rest of my life as a consecrated spouse of Christ. Though none of my friends accompanied me into the convent or went to a seminary, I knew even then that I would do everything possible to help others follow God's particular will for them to find their way to heaven. I wanted everyone to possess this union, this happiness.

Decades later, my heart is filled with immense gratitude for the many years I have been able to work as a vocation directress in my community. If it is true that we are born for a particular purpose, this has to be it for me! I thrill when anyone finds his or her vocation—be it religious life or priesthood, marriage or single life with a dedicated charitable purpose—but my heart leaps with particular joy when a young woman or man hears Christ's interior call to leave all and follow Him. The Church needs wise and loving dads and moms, both in good marriages and as spiritual fathers and mothers to the world!

Vocation work involves an abundance of both joys and sorrows. Joy wells up when I meet young people who are knowledgeable and open to the Holy Spirit's promptings. However, for decades now, young people have sadly known few, if any, religious Sisters. When a young woman expresses a passionate desire to give God "more", I ask if she is aware of consecrated life. Oftentimes, she had thought that such consecration ended with the death of Saint Thérèse of the Child Jesus! But upon meeting a joyful religious woman, hope rises instantly in her heart. If my time with such young women must be cut short, I hug them and encourage them to make one of our vocational discernment retreats, to pray openly to know and freely embrace God's beautiful will for them. I promise my prayers and continued support by e-mail!

Over the years it has become strikingly clear to me that I grew up in great times—not perfect, but promising times. I ask myself how many of today's families gather each evening for dinner, conversation, and the Rosary. Are children's questions being answered and, as they grow into maturity, are their innate spiritual desires being understood and nourished? Does anyone explain to teens their God-given challenge to become and give their best? And should a young person experience a deep desire to "love more", would anyone hear her and provide answers, whether by personal witness, prayer, wise counsel, recommended retreats or books?

This last thought reveals a serious problem. Where are contemporary books that show the beauty of religious life? For young women, I often suggest reading the lives of the Saints, the Church's documents on religious life, and other good Catholic writings. But books specifically treating the vocation to the evangelical counsels are sorely lacking. The responsibility to remedy this lies with seminaries and convents peopled with those who live the life of complete self-gift to God and have the grace to share with the world the splendor of that life.

To hold a book—the right book—in one's hands is to hold a world of answers to crucial questions; it begins the realization of dreams that the Holy Spirit wishes to bring to fruition in open hearts! To paraphrase the great Saint Augustine, whose Rule guides our Dominican life: "The Holy Scriptures are our letters from home" (Exposition of Psalm 90, Sermon 2). The book you hold in your hand is filled with letters from our home. May *And Mary's Yes Continues: Volumes 1 & 2* find yet another home in your heart.

Whether you be a priest, a parent, a candidate for religious life, or a young and inquisitive child, my Sisters and I pray that this book will open to you the exciting challenge of holiness to which God is inviting you! In the words of Pope Saint John Paul II, "Be not afraid to open your heart to Christ." Why would you not choose to live in Christ's freedom? It is the only way to fully embrace His Love!

Sister Joseph Andrew Bogdanowicz, OP
Vocation Directress

> How do we help build the Church, the Body of Christ? First, it is important to realize that we are only "helpers" or "assistants". The primary Builder is the Triune God, the model and source of communion. We know that the simplest yet deepest theology of communion is the prayer of Jesus for unity, which reveals his will and mission: "So that they may all be one, as you, Father, are in me and I in you, that they also may be in us, that the world may believe that you sent me." (Jn 17:21).

– Father Gerard Francisco P. Timoner III, OP
Master of the Dominican Order

The Evangelizing Power of the Evangelical Counsels

You have lost the love you had at first" (Rv 2:4). This is the complaint of the Spirit against the Church at Ephesus. Surely, the Ephesians worked hard, remained faithful, did not tolerate the wicked, even suffered for God's name; yet the Spirit has a complaint: they have forgotten the love they had at first!

The first space where consecrated people encounter Jesus in a profound way is their **vocation story**, a *religious experience* that prompted them to "leave everything" (see Mt 19:27) and dedicate their entire life to the love and service of God and the people of God, according to a particular charism. These little sacred stories of responding to God's irresistible call amount to the "love we had at first". We had a friar who was an official at a consulate in Hong Kong. He visited Rosaryhill during Vespers, and as he sat and listened to the chanting of the Psalms, he realized he was crying. He became a Dominican priest, and he was our Regent of Studies when I joined the Order. Another friar discovered his Dominican vocation through his girlfriend! He and his girlfriend took the national licensure examination for accountants and were praying hard for success. It was during this period of waiting for their examination results that his girlfriend brought him to Santo Domingo Church to pray a popular Marian novena. After the novena, he saw friars entering the choir, and was overwhelmed with a strong attraction to the religious life. He loved his girlfriend, but he could not shake off from his heart the desire to become a friar. His girlfriend understood his vocation, and he became a Dominican priest. When people ask him how he joined the Order, he would reply with a smile: "My girlfriend brought me to the Order!" Our vocation stories might be as plain as that of Peter, who was brought by Andrew to Jesus (see Jn 1:41), or as remarkable as that of Paul, who encountered Jesus on the road to Damascus (see Acts 9). But all vocation stories are sacred stories of our personal encounter with Jesus. Forgetfulness of this first love could lead to meaninglessness, emptiness and joylessness in religious life.

For that "love that we had at first" to flourish, we need to nurture it. The second space where consecrated people encounter and preach Jesus is the way they live the evangelical counsels. And these counsels, according to our brother, Thomas of Aquinas, are not ends in themselves but are instruments for the perfection of love. "The religious state is a school for the perfection of charity" (S. Th. II-IIae Q. 188, a. 1). As **evangelical counsels**, they have the power to *evangelize* not just those who embrace them but those who witness their concrete and varied manifestations. As instruments for the perfection of charity, the counsels help consecrated persons orient their lives towards the imitation of Christ, the one who is revealed as love (see 1 Jn 4:8).

Ekklesiastike Syneidesis: Conscience of the Church

ATTENTIVE OBEDIENCE

Everything about our Christian life—vocation, ministry, prayer and community—is brought together by obedience to God's will. As the Constitution tells us: "if a community is to remain true to its spirit and its mission, it needs that *unity* achieved through obedience" (LCO 17 § 1, emphasis added). The religious community or diocese or universal Church maintains communion because we are obedient to our superior, bishop, and Pope. In traditional theology, the grace or *res tantum* of the Eucharist is unity, communion. That is why in the Eucharistic Prayer, we name the Pope and the local bishop as a sign that the small congregation belongs to a larger communion. Obedience, *ob-audire*, is a virtue that enables us *to listen* to God's word and to one another, and strengthens our communion with the God who is in our midst. The Synod on the Word of God bears this out: "All this made us realize that we can deepen our relationship with the word of God only within the 'we' of the Church, in mutual listening and acceptance."[1]

We know that obedience, in its original sense, is a Christian virtue that enables us to let a brother or sister speak; and we listen to one another because we know that the Spirit of the Risen Christ is given to all the baptized, and therefore, truth is attainable within the context of the faith community. Of course, it presupposes that the one who speaks truly possesses *ekklesiastike syneidesis*, as Greek theology calls it, or *sensus fidelium* for the Latins.[2] All the baptized are called to be proclaimers of God's word[3], to speak, even on behalf of the Church. But one could only speak in the name of the Church if one first *listens* in attentive obedience to God's Word and what the Church teaches. For how could one speak rightly if one has not heard correctly? Here we see clearly why it is said that

Dominic was always either speaking *with* God or speaking *about* God. In fact, he spoke rightly of God because he first spoke with God.

The virtue of obedience fosters dialogue and discussion, which cannot go *ad infinitum*. Ideally, after everyone has been given fair hearing, the one in charge of the community (superior, bishop, or Pope), the one who possesses the grace of ecclesial office has the duty to articulate a decision based on what was heard. After listening to everyone, James, who was leader of the Jerusalem community, pronounced his judgment (Acts 15:19), a judgment that is rendered not as a personal one but as an outcome of a communal discernment under the guidance of the Holy Spirit: "It is the decision of the holy Spirit and of us not to place on you any burden beyond these necessities" (Acts 15:28).

Disobedience, the utter lack of capacity to listen attentively to voices other than that of the self or echoes that promote self-interest, is at the heart of conflict and division. Pope Francis accurately describes what disobedience looks like in a religious community:

> Factions fighting to impose the hegemony of their own viewpoint and preferences are fairly common in religious communities, both local and provincial. This occurs when charitable openness to neighbor is replaced by each individual's own ideas. It is no longer the religious family as a whole, which the religious defends, but only the part of it that concerns him. People no longer adhere to the unity that contributes to configuring the Body of Christ, but rather to the divisive, distorting, and debilitating conflict.

> "Only the chaste man and the chaste woman are capable of true love."
> -Pope Saint John Paul II

Yet obedience does not involve only consecrated persons listening to their superiors and vice versa. It also involves brothers listening to their confreres, sisters listening to their sisters, even listening, at times, to silent cries for help. This culture of listening among brothers and sisters is part of the evangelical counsel of obedience.[4]

CHASTE CELIBACY

The evangelical counsel of chastity should help us perfect our love for one another as brothers and sisters. Since the counsels are ordered towards the perfection of charity, then the first sin against chastity is the failure to love.[5] That is why it is not only those who violate the sixth commandment who are unchaste. Christians, especially consecrated persons who are grumpy and grouchy, cranky and crabby, who zap out your energy whenever they meet you—these persons are unchaste! How could they preach about the God who is revealed as love if they are unloving? To be sure, "Chastity is the successful integration of sexuality within the person and thus the inner unity of man in his bodily and spiritual being."[6] But chastity is more than just about sexuality, for it is a virtue that ought "to blossom in friendship"[7]. It is inclusive, "catholic" (not exclusive) love that makes our ministerial relationships healthy and holy.

Chastity is not a refuge from our "bodiliness" or corporeality. In fact, it involves witnessing to the importance of our bodies in the central mysteries of our faith: the Word becoming flesh, the sacrifice of the Body and Blood of Jesus in the Eucharist, and the resurrection of our bodies.[8] Our bodies are made holy in the Incarnation and Resurrection of Jesus.

> "For whoever wishes to save his life will lose it, but whoever loses his life for my sake will find it."
> Matthew 16:25

As preachers of the Word Made Flesh, we proclaim the holiness of our bodily existence. If we take this teaching seriously, then we need to ask ourselves these important questions: "Do we care for the bodies of our brothers and sisters, making sure that they have enough food, tend to them when they are sick, be tender to them when they are old?"[9] I often tell priests and religious during retreats that if their brother or sisters fail to visit them when they are sick, or give them at least some hot chicken soup, they could rightly go to their bishop or superior and report these companions as unchaste! Chastity is not just about sex or sexuality; it is about becoming loving and compassionate ministers in the name of the God who is revealed as love.

In a letter on common life, a former Master admonished us:

While the deepest sanctuary of our hearts is given to God—we have other needs. He has made us so that a large area of our life is accessible to others and is needed by others. Each one of us needs to experience the genuine interest of the other members of the community, their affection, esteem, and fellowship. Some may say that God is enough. But it has been well said, that God has made us so that we need more than prayer and renunciation. We need air, food, sleep, education...but above all love. At what point in our earthly pilgrimage do we cease to be human? Life together means breaking the bread of our minds and hearts with each other. *If religious do not find this in their communities—then they will seek it elsewhere.*[10]

EVANGELICAL POVERTY

"The community of believers was of one heart and mind... There was no needy person among them" (Acts 4:32, 34).

Does the huge number of poor people among us signify how distant we are from our aspiration to become an "authentic community of believers whose unity of heart and mind is manifested by a communion of goods"? Even in the Old Testament, an important part of God's covenant with His people is the assurance that "there shall be no one of you in need if you but listen to the voice of the LORD, your God, and carefully observe this entire commandment which I enjoin on you today." (Dt 15:4-5). Thus, the presence of so many poor people in our world is, from a Deuteronomic perspective, a sorry sign of infidelity to the covenant. Our heroic efforts at alleviating the plight of the poor indicate our desire to be faithful, to restore covenantal brotherhood/sisterhood.

In a world created by a provident God, there can only be poor people when the conditions for the sharing of the gifts of the Father are absent. It cannot be denied that the poverty of some people is of their own making. Their poverty is a result of wrong decisions or even sloth. But there are countless poor people who work so hard yet remain poor. Their impoverished condition is an unfortunate result of social and economic structures and self-serving policies by the few who have wealth and power. Pope Francis rightly said that "Poverty is a scandal in the human family."[11] It terribly offends a provident God. Riches in the midst of poverty further heighten this scandal. When people who have more live side by side with people who have less, hardly can we call them a community. Lack amidst plenty is a sign that something is sadly wrong in the way the members of society relate with each other.

How do we assure that no one among us is in need? The first community of believers *shared* so that everyone's need is served. Paradoxical as it may seem, evangelical poverty is the Christian solution to economic and spiritual poverty or destitution.

The meaning of *evangelical-poverty-as-sharing* serves as a corrective against the correlative evils of poverty (insufficiency) and excessive wealth (over-sufficiency). It truly becomes a virtue, for it stands midway between these two extremes. It puts into order a person's relationship with God and his or her neighbors. By sharing, a follower of Christ becomes acutely aware of his or her responsibility for the material well-being of the community. It also holds in check the divisive potentials of material goods. Like the early apostolic community, sharing of goods becomes a concrete sign of the kingdom of love. Consequently, it also orders one's relationship with God, who says: If you love me, feed my sheep (see Jn 21:17). To nurture the sheep of Jesus is to make sure that one's generous love leaves no one in need.

Evangelical poverty is not primarily about our relationship with material goods but with one another. If in one community discord arises because of the use of a new car, the offense against poverty is not that the community bought a new car but that there is lack of charity and understanding over the use of a material good. We ought to remember that that as an instrument for the perfection of charity, *the first sin against poverty is the failure to love*.

CONCLUSION

All the baptized, all followers of Christ are called to embrace the evangelical counsels of poverty, chastity and obedience according to their states of life.[12] These counsels have the power to evangelize both those who embrace them and those who witness how they are lived according to the different states of life in the Church. But in a special manner, consecrated people who strive towards the perfection of charity by means of the evangelical counsels become evangelizers by their fidelity to the vows they have professed. The instruction *The Pastoral Conversion of the Parish Community in the Service of the Evangelizing Mission of the Church* published recently by the Holy See affirms: "The contribution that consecrated men and women can bring to the *evangelizing mission* of the Parish [church] community *is derived firstly, from their "being", that is, from the witness of a radical following of Christ through the profession of the evangelical counsels*, and only secondly from their "doing", that is, from the works carried out in accordance with the charism of each Institute."[13] Thus, by our fidelity to our vocation, evangelization is not only *what* we do, it is *who* we are. For as we strive to live in perfect charity, we are able to preach the One who is revealed as love (see 1 John 4:8).

Father Gerard Francisco P. Timoner III, OP
Master of the Order

Fr. Gerard Francisco P. Timoner III, OP, became the 88th Master of the Dominican Order on July 13, 2019.

Notes

1. Pope Benedict VI, *Verbum Domini*, 4.
2. Joint International Commission for the Theological Dialogue Between the Roman Catholic Church and the Orthodox Church, *Ecclesiological and Canonical Consequences of the Sacramental Nature of the Church, Ecclesial Communion, Conciliarity and Authority*, (Ravenna: October 13, 2007), 7.
3. Pope Benedict VI, *Verbum Domini*, 94.
4. Pope Francis, *Umiltà, la strada verso Dio* (Bologna: EMI, 2013).
5. Timothy Radcliffe, OP, "Vowed to Mission" in *Sing a New Song: The Christian Vocation* (Dublin: Dominican Publications, 1999), 49.
6. *Catechism of the Catholic Church* (CCC), 2nd ed. (Vatican City: Vatican Press, 1997), 2337.
7. CCC, 2347.
8. Radcliffe, "The Promise of Life", 1998.
9. Radcliffe, "Vowed to Mission", 1994.
10. Damian Byrne, OP, Letter of the Master of the Order, "On Common Life", (November 1988). Emphasis added.
11. Pope Francis, *Evangelii Gaudium*, 191.
12. CCC, 915.
13. Congregation for the Clergy, Instruction, "The Pastoral Conversion of the Parish community in the Service of the Evangelising Mission of the Church" (June 29, 2020) no. 84. Emphasis added.

The Evangelizing Power of the Evangelical Counsels

" The world has need of a woman's touch, Our Lady's touch, a mother's touch. And who more embodies that spiritually than Sisters utterly open to God as was Our Lady? Filled with the Holy Spirit & grace as was Mary, Sisters radiate peace, joy, & healing to a tired & confused world, hungry for God, although it does not know it.

-Father Giles Dimock, OP
Saint Dominic Priory, Washington, D.C. "

*Inlaid into the hearts of all young people
is a desire for greatness*

RELIGIOUS VOCATIONS IN THE THIRD MILLENNIUM – AFRESH!

Updated for Second Volume

Sister Joseph Andrew Bogdanowicz, OP
Born in Oak Ridge, TN

Our world today is one of fast-paced change. All the change around us leads to change within us, and we are seeing new generations rise up quickly. The term *generation* today, as in the past, points to a group of persons distinguished from others by differences in upbringing and formational experiences; and yet, where earlier generations related to preceding generations as children to parents, recent generations—Millennials and iGens—relate to their elders more as younger siblings to older siblings.

This fast-paced change means that, within each group entering religious life today, there may be a variety of "typical" previous life experiences that will influence both how young women discern their vocations and what formation they will need once they enter a convent. What follows is an updated version of the introductory chapter of the 2017 volume of this book, seeking to describe afresh the generational situation in which we find ourselves in 2021.

THE DESIRE FOR GREATNESS OF THE YOUNG

Letters from the Heart

> "I've felt an inclination toward religious life since high school, but I did my best to try to bury that idea while I was away at college, hoping that it might just go away so I could proceed with the 'normal life' that my friends and family insisted should satisfy me. In an effort to find that satisfaction, I returned to school to study law... I don't think that I am suffering from any lack of courage, but I am lacking someplace to test that courage. I think my greatest fear is in saying 'no' to what may be an invitation from God to 'come and see'. I don't want to get down the road, into my forties or fifties and then begin to wonder 'what if'. What if I had accepted that invitation? Could spending my life for God, in the service of others, be that missing 'something' which I can't quite find now? I really need to find out."
>
> — A Hopeful Discerner

I smiled on that cold November morning when I opened my mail and read, in a rather long and detailed letter, the above words. Written by a twenty-seven-year-old lawyer who is practicing her profession in her father's law firm in upstate New York, this young woman is not that different from the young man

Religious Vocations in the Third Millennium-Afresh!

of the Gospel who approached Our Lord one fine day, almost two thousand years ago, and asked what more he could do for God. For inlaid into the hearts of all young people is a desire for greatness; and once a heart is turned toward God, no one can guess the height and depth and breadth of an individual's magnanimous spirit.

As I read this letter further, I began to hear my own irrepressible laughter. With obvious literary talent, this professional woman described her appearance one recent morning when she had approached her father to inform him she had found a relentless lover who had, indeed, been pursuing her for quite some time. "A heavy date last night, eh?'" questioned her solicitous but clever father as he studied his now obviously red-eyed daughter. Equal to the match, the young woman replied, "You can certainly say that, Dad, and he is not anyone you would suspect. But you need to know, Dad, that marrying him is going to necessitate for me a change of employment."[1]

The above reflections on this young lawyer's penned interest in a possible religious vocation were published in *Lay Witness* magazine in March 2001. I was Vocation Directress of our then only three-year-old community, and the many vocations we were receiving offered hope that the tide of disappearing religious women and decreasing priestly vocations was turning. Pope Saint John Paul II's call for the New Evangelization, his summons to "open wide the doors to Christ", and the electrified energy that sparked across the globe after each World Youth Day, resulted in many young people diving into an authentic search for their vocations with a burning desire to fulfill the Divine Will.

The 2001-published article continues:

> As the vocation directress for our three-year-old religious community, the Dominican Sisters of Mary, Mother of the Eucharist, located in the university city of Ann Arbor, Michigan, I can say that such messages are

ever-increasing in number and conviction. Young women across our country and beyond are valiant in their attempts to find God's will and to embrace it with all the love of their vibrant hearts. There seem to be no barriers that keep them from fulfilling their quest. Age, education, talents, family backgrounds, circles of friends and acquaintances, and their own religious history of fidelity or conversion, young people today are radiating the fire of the Spirit of Truth and blazing excellent trails that seem to be keeping all those who first forged the way in a steady run! My personal theory is that the ranks of religious life (and of the priesthood) were so depleted in the 60s, 70s, and 80s that many vacuums were left in vitally important areas of both the contemplative and the apostolic lives. It has been the new growth arising from the "springtime" predicted and, in large measure, planted and watered by the holiness of our Supreme Pontiff, Pope John Paul II, that is filling these gaps with an influx of priestly and religious vocations whose origins do not always fit the stereotypical vocation prospects of earlier years.

Twenty years later, much of this graced spirit remains, but it must now compete with radical societal and cultural changes. Vocation has always been a challenge: though some souls' road to sanctity is unusually clear to them—due to the richness of their graces and their ability to rise above the currents of society—generally speaking, most young people find it difficult to discover their unique personal dignity, talents, weaknesses, and ultimately, their God-given vocation. And this is especially true today. Self-knowledge is essential for authentic vocational discernment.

What are some of the differences between today's world and the world which crossed into the Third Millennium, and how might these differences affect authentic vocational discernment?

GENERATION GAP

Based on the year you were born, you may be written off as someone who is technologically inept, cynical, unmotivated, or entitled, along with a slew of other negative traits.[2] Meanwhile, you may view yourself as someone with a strong work ethic, as self-sufficient, a collaborator, or compassionate and determined.[3] While some may make sweeping generalizations, leaving you wanting to shout, "I'm not like that"—and perhaps you are not—nevertheless, the stereotypes persist, and the truth may lie somewhere in the middle. Your self-image as a Baby Boomer, Gen Xer, Millennial, or iGen (also called Gen Z) may greatly differ from the image wider society has of your generation. Generational perspective will influence both a young woman's vocational discernment process and the formational experiences she will need to embrace God's call fully.

Baby Boomer: Born between 1946-1964

Gen X: Born between 1965-1980

Millennial: Born between 1981-1996

iGen or Gen Z: Born between 1997-2021

Pew Research, "Defining generations: Where Millennials end and Generation Z begins", dated January 17, 2019

MILLENNIAL MUSINGS

Amanda just graduated *summa cum laude* from an Ivy League university. Laurie is a successful businesswoman living in a smart condominium in the city and working hard to pay off student debts. Maria is a nurse but has never felt fully satisfied with her work and cannot understand why. Caroline is a senior in high school, passionate about life and certain God has a plan for her future. What do they all have in common? Each young adult is planning to join a religious community and make vows of poverty, chastity, and obedience.

Who is this generation of Sisters? Where do they come from? What challenges do they face as they strive to give themselves more fully to God?

In 1965, religious life in the USA reached its peak, with the largest number of Sisters serving Christ and the nation. As of April 25, 2016, Millennials (born between 1980 and 1994) officially surpassed the previous largest generation of Americans, the Baby Boomers (born between 1946 and 1964). A comparison of these two generations and what they brought to their vocations proves fascinating.

The Baby Boomers filled their roles in society as loyal members of political parties, proud supporters of the military, defenders of traditional marriage, and active participants in religion. However, one glance at our world today reveals a marked contrast in young people. Today's Millennials are wary of authority; they distance themselves from established institutions, both religious and secular. Sixty-eight percent of Millennials have never been married, and those who do marry tend to wait until later in life. In the 1960s, for example, the average American woman married at age twenty-one and the average man at twenty-three. But in 2018, the average woman married at age twenty-seven and the average man at age twenty-nine.[4] Among the Baby Boomers, only seven percent of women completed their bachelor degrees as young adults, while today Millennial women with degrees actually outnumber their male counterparts. In the 60s, the majority of women were not in the labor force; now, the majority are, and among the women not working, twenty-two percent cite school as their main reason for not holding a job.[5] Baby Boomers had the difficult task of trying to understand developing technology; Millennials (as well as iGens) grew up with computers, iPads, and personal phones. Today, over three quarters of their generation has a profile on a social networking site.

Among the challenges, women seem to mature more slowly

today and fear making a life-long commitment. To many young adults, the options are limitless, and narrowing the possibilities to a single vocation can seem daunting. For example, when a Vocation Directress asks a young woman in her late twenties to describe her plans for the future, it is not uncommon for her to hear a vague, uncommitted "I have no idea. Maybe I will get another degree." The desire to settle down and to give one's heart fully to another simply is not a priority.

In the past, a Novice Mistress could assume her charges knew the faith and came from homes where religion was practiced. Today, the young women entering need a full course in the Catechism. Their love for the Church and knowledge of essential doctrines often develop mostly after they have entered a religious community.

Still another challenge is that many young women discern their vocation after pursuing numerous other options. By the time they open themselves to God's call, they are burdened with college debts and few resources to pay off student loans.

The number of women considering a religious vocation has dropped significantly. Those who do consider a vocation are seen as unusual by their peers. Women tend to face opposition from friends and family when they announce their plans to join a religious community.

ENTERING iGENS

While some of the women entering religious life today are Millennials, younger members are from the iGen or Gen Z generation, those born after 1994. What additional challenges and gifts does this new generation bring to their religious vocations?

Generational experts, professionals who claim to understand "the differences between [the generations] and how they can live, and most importantly, work together successfully,"[6] seem to agree that iGens or Gen Zers are somewhat overprotected and pampered by their parents. This atmosphere creates a culture of young adults who are able to do all the right things, usually out of fear of disappointing Mom and Dad: to check off the list of requirements needed to get into the college Mom and Dad expect them to attend, to strive to follow rules and to meet the expectations others have of them. At the same time, however, iGens view themselves, according to studies, as possessing "high levels of leadership skills", although they desire safety and are anxious about venturing out without Mom and Dad. According to Julie Lythcott-Haims, author of *How to Raise an Adult*, those born after 1994 are going to post-secondary schools with Mom and Dad in their pockets—that is, always only a text message away, ready to advise their child regarding the next step that should be taken.[7]

While Generation Z believes they are "independent, self-confident and autonomous,"[8] studies show that eighteen- and nineteen-year-olds act more like they are high school sophomores who still look to their parents for assistance.[9] iGens are less likely than preceding generations to have drivers' licenses, to obtain jobs, and to hang out with their friends away from Mom and Dad.[10] This may actually prevent them from attaining the individuality they perceive that they already possess. Driving a vehicle, holding a job, and being trusted by one's elders long enough to be without them demands that one make decisions—not simply follow rules—and develop the virtues necessary for true independence.

TODAY'S CHALLENGES ARE JUST THAT!

What does all this mean for the current generation of Sisters? For both Millennials and iGens entering religious life today, there are both challenges and reasons for hope. First off, let us tackle one of the strongest forces shaping young people today: technology.

Today's teens and even those in their twenties have never known a life without technology. It has been an integral part of their existence, and they have taken to it like ducks to water, assisting their parents in their struggles even to program a VCR. Teens can figure out manuals far more quickly than their parents, and they are fearless about experimenting with such gadgets. Personal free time often finds them on their mobile devices, which seem to them as extensions of their bodies and their lives, offering them a whole playground of endless excitement.

While this staying-plugged-in carries with it a host of problems, which can only be alluded to here, we might look at a few of the more serious effects regarding vocational discernment.

1) Acedia

In *The Seven Deadly Sins Today*, Henry Fairlie describes *acedia* as "a morbid inertia" that can totally shut down a person's life because he or she long ago stopped believing that life might involve something more, something better, something of such consummate goodness that it demands the utmost devotion![11] The extreme "busy-ness" to which mobile devices entice young people leads them from one titillating triviality to the next and numbs their interior moral sensibility. Because they are stimulated, active, and entertained, they do not recognize how empty and meaningless their lives have oftentimes become. Moreover, on the occasions that an inkling of such does break into their consciousness, they simply run out to buy the latest game or gadget to fill the interior void.

According to the Online Medical Dictionary, acedia results in "a mental syndrome, the chief features of which are listlessness, carelessness, apathy, and

> "Restore to me the gladness of your salvation; uphold me with a willing spirit."
> —Psalm 51:12

melancholia."[12] Kathleen Norris, poet and nonfiction author, in her book *Acedia & Me*, explains the difference between acedia and depression: "Depression is an illness treatable by counseling and medication; acedia is a vice that is best countered by spiritual practice and the discipline of prayer."[13] Carrisa Smith characterizes Norris' thought thus: "[T]he one sin of acedia is responsible for many of the ills of our high-tech, breakneck-paced, yet apathetic, contemporary world. ... In other words, the couch potato and the over-achiever may be suffering from the same problem, which ultimately boils down to the refusal to engage fully with life in the present moment."[14] How so? The over-achiever may also be compensating for interior emptiness but by the alternative means of frenzied, external activity.

2) Privacy issues

As one retreat priest phrased it for our Sisters, we all carry different baggage resulting from Original Sin. A young person with a healthy self-image, a good family life and thus a support system, and an accurate moral compass will know in whom to confide her insecurities and from whom to seek wise counsel in navigating friendships and the world today. However, one not so blessed or spiritually attentive may entrust such confidences to networking sites that can be hacked or may simply be open to public viewing. Later, if this individual seeks entrance into a novitiate or a seminary, these unguarded statements inevitably become part of the process of evaluation for admission.

3) Lack of social skills

Smartphones have carried Millennials and iGens into a mesmerizing world of instant interactions and information and thus a constant search for updates. A group of friends could be sitting together in silence because everyone is busy on a Twitter or Facebook page. Such communication is anything but social. Children do not know how to handle face-to-face conflict because so many of their interactions occur through technology.[15] Millennials and Gen-Zers, having been raised on technology, are manifesting yet another, newer symptom: the lack of rudimentary skills necessary for the real world. Can you imagine a vocational candidate using texting lingo on an application, or not knowing the basic social skills needed for healthy communication in an interview? Such problems are worrisome and yet common in today's young people.[16]

4) Lack of academic skills

Research from The Kaiser Family Foundation shows that students often juggle homework with entertainment. Over half of Millennial students from ages eight to eighteen were using the internet, watching TV, or using some other form of media either "most" (31 percent) or "some" (25 percent) of the time that they were doing homework.[17]

As early as 2000, the *New York Times* showed concern about digital distraction. In his article, "Growing Up Digital", Matt Richtel describes an intelligent young man entering his senior year of high school without having completed his summer reading. The student's explanation: "On YouTube, you can get a whole story in six minutes. ... A book takes so long. I prefer the immediate gratification."[18] Scientifically, this raises the concern of a generation of young people whose brains will be wired differently, resulting in an incapacity to stay on a thought more than a few seconds. Neuroscientists are presently studying what happens to the brains of young people who are constantly online.[19] Connected with these concerns are the questions raised by the increasing number of schools that rely on internet access and mobile devices inside the classroom. In the end, we might say that technology has created on campuses a new set of social types—not the thespian and the jock but the texter, the gamer, the Facebook addict, and the YouTube potato.

5) Lack of basic life skills and maturity

Generation Z has also been found to mature at a slower rate than previous generations. Jean Twenge, a generational expert teaching at San Diego State University, has found that, at the end of high school, [iGens] act more like 15-year-olds, who are not ready to be independent adults and feel they still need help from their parents. iGen are arriving at college with less experience with independence, so many are not ready to be on their own and thus rely on their parents.[20]

Universities and colleges are struggling to meet the needs of their freshman classes. Julie Lythcott-Haims, Harvard's former Dean of Freshmen, suggests that parents do not think their children can "be successful unless they are protecting and preventing at every turn."[21] Lythcott-Haims opines that parental fears of children being abducted, the tendency to give every child a trophy for showing up, and the emergence of the play-date have created a generation of young adults who lack basic life-skills.

Young people are showing up to college or entering the workforce with few of the necessary life skills. Since Mom and Dad have always been there, students do not know how to ask for help. Parents are accompanying their child to job interviews and calling their child's boss because they feel their child is working too hard. When their son or daughter is not achieving the results of which they think them capable, parents scold teachers, principals, and coaches. The result is a generation of young adults who are unable to live independently, make decisions, or stand up for themselves.[22] Lythcott-Haims notes that colleges and universities "nationwide [have noticed a] steady decline in the number of [iGen'ers] who seem capable of going out into the world as adults."[23] She proposes that parents, in trying to create a safe environment for their children to succeed, have actually done them a huge disservice.

AND AS FOR HOPE...

Today, despite increasing cyberspace dependency and the collapse of many traditions, some young people continue to base their whole lives on the love of God. Saint Bernard once wrote in his treatise *De amore Dei*, "The measure with which to love God is to love without measure." In the words of Pope Emeritus Benedict XVI, "To live no longer for ourselves but for Christ: this is what gives full meaning to the life of those who let themselves be conquered by Him."[24] Seminaries and convents remain God's citadels, strongholds where all people may find Him more easily, wherein the Heart of Jesus tenderly keeps watch. And yes, such truths are most appealing to young people who, by nature and by God's mercy, are idealistic and desirous of greatness. Witness the phenomenon of World Youth Days (WYDs), now with a history of over thirty years! Millions of youth have decided to brave monumental challenges, live through sacrificial pilgrimages, and sleep on wet, muddy ground surrounded by millions of other youths from around the world, all with the hope of catching a quick glimpse of the Holy Father and of hearing a message that expands their hearts to heroic dimensions! During his Mass at the 2016 WYD Poland, Pope Francis slipped in a warm greeting to the people of Brazil that seems to apply to all the estimated 3.6 million pilgrims in Krakow's Blonia Park: "I hope that this will be an opportunity to overcome difficult moments and commit … to working as a team to build a more just and safe country [world], betting all on a future full of hope and joy."[25] The effects of the Holy Father's presence and message will endure as WYDs stake claim to a permanent place in the hearts of the youth. Why? Because young people were

> "To live no longer for ourselves but for Christ: this is what gives full meaning to the life of those who let themselves be conquered by Him." -Pope Emeritus Benedict XVI

made to take risks, to display courage, to nurture the world to better things—and all this with the virtue that belongs foremost to youth: hope!

> "Be not afraid! Open wide the doors to Christ!"
> —Pope Saint John Paul II

Perhaps the best way to express this hope is by reversing the negatives outlined previously with possible positives.

1) Acedia

Saint Thomas Aquinas's teaching on acedia complements his prior teaching on charity's gifted "spiritual joy," to which acedia is directly opposed. As Aquinas says, "One opposite is known through the other, as darkness through light. Hence what evil is must be known from the nature of good" (*Summa Theologiae*, I, 48, 1).

After World War II, psychologists tried to explain how so many ordinary citizens acquiesced to fascism. The results of their research appear in the 1950 classic *The Authoritarian Personality* by T.W. Adorno.[26] In 1998, University of Pennsylvania psychologist Martin Seligman, in his presidential address to the American Psychological Association, urged psychology to "turn toward understanding and building [up] human strengths."[27] Seligman's teaching would earn him the title of the world's leading scholar on optimism. Labs changed their focus to study generosity, courage, creativity, and laughter. In 1999, the late Philip J. Stone, professor of psychology at Harvard, taught a positive psychology course to twenty undergraduates. Today there are more than two hundred such courses across the United States, with the University of Pennsylvania offering a master's degree in the field. Obviously, the answer to despair and acedia is found in a positive psychology. But this fact was elucidated many centuries earlier by the great Saint Thomas Aquinas.

Religious Vocations in the Third Millennium–Afresh!

The Angelic Doctor, in a superb text from the *Summa contra gentiles* on the fittingness of the Incarnation, opens up for us new perspectives on action "in Christ" (IV, ch. 54). Countering man's despair at the enormity of a vocation that he feels unable to achieve, the Incarnation of Christ offers a new principle of action that rescues man from the *taedium operandi* and allows him to open his heart once again to the gift of divine friendship. Christ, both true God and true man, achieves within himself in a singular way the union between Creator and creature that God desired, and the joy to which man is called if he will only open himself to the gift of divine friendship. Perhaps it is with this in mind that Pope Francis gave the world his 2013 Apostolic Exhortation entitled *Evangelii Gaudium* or "The Joy of the Gospel." In his writing, *joy* is used 109 times, second only to *love*, which claims first place at 154 times.

> "I could not stop staring in awe and wonder at the religious Sisters who truly took every step and action for Christ. Every action and smile that was given to those whom they were serving, came from giving themselves entirely as a bride of Christ."

Young people are seeking joy; they were made for it—we all are! Young women will notice religious Sisters who smile, whose laughter can be heard echoing through the halls of the schools or across the volleyball court in their students' competitions. As one young woman said about her own discernment, "I could not stop staring in awe and wonder at the religious Sisters who truly took every step and action for Christ. Every action and smile that was given to those whom they were serving, came from giving themselves entirely as a bride of Christ." Another young woman, after reading the 2017 edition of this book, said, "The joy of the Sisters shines through pages of this book just like it would in a personal encounter with one of them."

Might this joy be the antidote to the anxiety and lack of interior freedom that cause today's young people to hide from others behind their iPhones and videogames? Perhaps we have failed to engage youth in pleasurable and instructive experiences which will lift them out of themselves and open their hearts not only to enjoying others but to enjoying God! Such joy is essential before any young woman will ever begin serious consideration of a religious vocation.

2) Privacy issues

Aquinas explains that, under the direction of infused faith, all the moral virtues facilitate the infusion by God of grace's light into a person's will and sensible appetites. Aquinas grants a special role to the virtue of prudence, which acts as a monitor for the other virtues. Without this monitor, youth rush rashly into activities, impelled by a disordered desire for acceptance at any price.

> "Be shrewd as serpents and simple as doves."
> —Matthew 10:16

We look to the Angelic Doctor again for his explanation of this conundrum: "The truth of the practical intellect depends on conformity with a right appetite" (*Summa Theologiae*, Ia IIae, q.57, a.5 ad 3um). If youth lack moral training, they will never judge ill-advised actions as imprudent, including their sharing of private matters on the internet. These examples underscore the necessity of good moral training for young people. Parents more than ever must exemplify virtuous choices for their children. When this does not occur, religious Sisters may supply this necessary education with the joy, enthusiasm, and delightful freedom which rightfully accompany it.

It goes without saying that coupled with this education in virtue is a necessary education in self-control and inner discipline. If a young woman is serious about the sacramental life and personal prayer, she will find not only an inner ability to open herself to God's will but also a desire to know and follow it.

3) Lack of social skills

Our teaching Sisters know that the best thing we can do for our students is to equip them spiritually for their place in the world. Few schools concern themselves not only with the academic and physical aspects of education but also with the virtuous life by which students will reach their full potential as children of God. Under the leadership of Sister John Dominic Rasmussen, OP, our religious community hopes to fill this gap through the *Disciple of Christ, Education in Virtue*® curriculum, which is being used throughout the country today in many dioceses.[28]

> "Do to others as you would have them do to you."
> –Luke 6:31

By developing virtues such as magnanimity, courtesy, affability, docility, respect, sincerity, and loyalty, the young person learns the proper respect for the dignity of each human person, who reflects the image of the Creator.

As mentioned previously, a primary psychological motivation behind a person's hiding from others through the excessive use of technology is to escape the loneliness felt when faced with self. Pope Saint John Paul II addressed this topic at World Youth Day in Paris on August 23, 1997:

> Remember that you are never alone, Christ is with you on your journey every day of your lives! He has called you and chosen you to live in the freedom of the children of God. Turn to him in prayer and in love. Ask him to grant you the courage and strength to live in this freedom always. Walk with him who is "the Way, the Truth and the Life"!

Pope Benedict XVI re-echoed these sentiments in his Apostolic Exhortation on the Eucharist, *Sacramentum Caritatis*, writing that it is only natural for people who participate in the Eucharist to be concerned about the dignity of all. Along with the Eucharist, a healthy and honest daily examination of conscience, along with sacramental confession every two weeks, gains one the self-knowledge needed to discern and pursue one's vocation.

As loneliness drives an increasing number of young people toward the internet, the Dominican Sisters of Mary have given great effort in the creation of learning tools, interesting stories of saints lives, theological programs and stimulating interviews on podcasts which can be enjoyed (and some selections printed out) on *goledigital.org*.

4) Lack of academic skills

Reading what follows, you may detect the Dominican in me as I continue to stress the essential value of the sacraments, the virtues and a good moral life—yes, this is very Dominican—and in particular the virtue of studiousness. In his *Summa*, Saint Thomas Aquinas defines studiousness as "the virtue which disposes a person to apply his mind for the purpose of acquiring and extending knowledge" (II-II. Q. 166.a 1). Interestingly, he links this virtue to the virtue of temperance, which moderates one's appetite to prevent excess in the use of material goods (II-II. Q. 166.a 2). Most young people have to fight the temptation toward distraction during mental work. To labor at study is hard work! Even the great Aquinas himself referred to his study as a "crucifixion at the desk". Somewhat seriously, my Sisters often use the same phrase—and I certainly agree with them!

Honest efforts at study promote the acquisition of many necessary interior qualities. Study prepares us for prayer and can lead us into it. It readies the soul through the proper use of silence and develops the wisdom by which we draw forth deeper dimensions of truth needed for self-knowledge and a healthy sense of self-worth. It also results in a workable knowledge of the world whereby the young person can read, think, do business, and find freedom in the realms of creativity and art.

5) Lack of basic life skills and maturity

While there are many concerns regarding Generation Z's level of maturity and ability to function independently, there is also much good that they bring and from which Baby Boomers, Gen Xers, and Millennials alike can learn. So much of our religious life is about community: we pray, eat, work, and recreate together. It is difficult to work with people who are unwilling, or perhaps unable, to collaborate with others. It is a great joy to live with Sisters from Generation Z, because they bring enthusiasm to all that they do; they love to get as many people involved as possible in their projects, overlooking the shortcomings of others and finding ways to include everyone. They are quick to listen to new ideas and to incorporate what they can, striving to bring creative solutions to differences of opinion and thereby integrating as many ideas as possible in any venture.

A Sister ("Sister Director") wanted to do something to help the Sisters relax during the mad dash to the end of the school year. Knowing the musical talent of her Sisters and how much they all love to be entertained, she asked Sister Superior if it would be possible to stage a musical for the Sisters—no easy task, to be sure! Sister Director ascertained who would be interested in participating in such an undertaking and, with curiosities piqued, began to pull music together and recruit help to re-write the words to popular songs from Disney movies. With encouraging notes posted—"All are Welcome!", "Come and Join the Fun!", and "Be a Part of the Chorus!"—the cast began to grow.

Not wanting to leave anyone out, Sister Director asked the older Sisters, "Do you want to be a part of the musical, or are you more of an 'audience-person'?" One Gen Xer, not wanting to leave the young Sister in a lurch if she needed extra people, replied, "Well, I am more of the audience-type, but if you really need someone…"

"No, no: we actually would love to have someone in the audience, so that would be great!" Both Sisters were, no doubt, relieved, yet at the same time felt happy about being inclusive and included! iGens are masters at working together, using everyone's gifts, and helping people develop their talents.

> "I am not giving up everything and losing my freedom; rather I am choosing everything God is offering me and desiring a life of increased freedom to do whatever God is asking of me."

Not only gifted at collaboration and inclusion, this generation also excels at following rules and meeting expectations. In the weeks leading up to a big event, a Superior asked her iGen student-Sisters to be sure to complete all of their school work on campus during the day, so that their time in the evenings at home could be devoted to assisting with the preparations. The Sisters graciously accepted the challenge, even as they were taking an extraordinary number of classes, and were cheerfully available at home to make schedules, organize tours, make food, and so on. A desire to follow rules certainly helps a Sister in her vow of obedience. Of course, grace must build on this natural inclination.

While some may think that the life in monasteries and convents fosters dependence on others and stunts women's growth in maturity, there is nothing farther from the truth. Religious life in fact forces people to mature. As one young woman preparing to enter the convent explained, "I am not giving up everything and losing my freedom; rather I am choosing everything God is offering me and desiring a life of increased freedom to do whatever God is asking of me." The vow of obedience, properly lived, does not mean that Sister X does everything Sister Superior asks of her and must agree with her Superior's ideas and commands. Instead, it means that, even though she may disagree with the Superior's decision and reasoning, Sister X does as Sister Superior asks out of her love for God, having given her life wholly and completely to Christ for the salvation of souls, especially her own. That is, by conforming her will to God's through her acts of obedience to her superior, Sister X is able to discover and understand the rightly ordered relationship with figures of authority. I am reminded of Christ's words to Pontius Pilate, "You would have no power over me if it had not been given to you from above" (Jn 19:11). Jesus, the perfect Man, chose to be "obedient to death, even death on a cross" (Phil 2:8), out of love for His Father and love for all mankind. And love requires maturity.

As one of our Sisters explains, speaking of a realization during her own discernment prior to entering our community, "I was able to contemplate not what I would be 'giving up,' but how I would be freeing myself to love God and others more authentically." The religious life, in imitation of Christ, is indeed a school of love. As Saint Paul teaches us in his first letter to the Corinthians, "Love does not seek its own interests... [it] bears all things, believes all things, hopes all things, endures all things. ... When I was a child, I used to talk as a child, think as a child, reason as a child; when I became a man, I put aside childish things." (13:5, 7, 11). Another young woman stated as she prepared to enter religious life, "I am really not losing anything, but gaining *everything*; because, through the religious vows of poverty, chastity, and obedience, I am not only uniting myself to Him who is everything, but also living the life and mission God has always intended for me, and this brings so much fulfillment." It takes true maturity to see that a life of self-gift brings the fulfillment for which one's heart longs.

Letters from the Heart

Dear Sister,

Please pray before reading this…Ok, you can begin now…

I'm not sure why I'm writing; besides the fact that I have this nagging feeling inside of me that will not leave. I am a junior studying theology at a Catholic college. I took a year from college in '96-'97 to serve with NET (National Evangelization Team). I have a great love for the youth and really feel that God is leading me in that direction in regards to my career. Presently, I want to be a youth minister anywhere that God could use me.

I have always been against the possibility that the Lord may be calling me to religious life, and have been very adamant about that. So why am I writing you? The other day I went to confession and spent some time with Jesus in the chapel before heading home. As I was walking out of the chapel I did something I have never done before and walked over to the section holding brochures for religious orders. I didn't even really look at them except I saw yours with "Mother of the Eucharist" and grabbed it. I put it in my bag and didn't look at it again until the next day when this nagging feeling to write you began. The only logic I can see is that I have a great devotion to the Eucharist and am struggling to get my relationship with Mary back on track. So maybe I am just intrigued by the title of your order. It was Mary who brought me to the faith and led me to Christ. Unfortunately, I seemed to have put her on the back burner for the past couple of years, but she has been continuously pursuing me. The only other possibility that God has me writing you is to find out more information on your order. <u>That scares me.</u>

This is strange but I have this huge urge inside of me to mention that I would like to meet you, although I'm not sure I really do, but I felt like I had to write it down anyway. This is probably the craziest letter you have ever received and I feel really sheepish about it. So if you think I'm crazy please don't respond…with that said I'm not expecting to hear from you.

(continued)

(continued)

> If you are even reading this, I must have had a moment of great courage because this is just not like me. Okay, I'm going to stop this letter of insanity.
>
> Thank you for taking the time to read this. I'm sorry to have taken up so much of your time. It's good to see you Sisters wearing habits. It is so awesome to see Sisters in their habits; it is such a great sign of being wedded to God the Father.
>
> God bless you all! In Christ....

— *A Hopeful Discerner*

If the first email in this chapter left me smiling, the one just quoted left me in peals of laughter! Immediately I knew this had been sent by a young woman who quite possibly had a religious vocation, because she already possessed the necessary virtues of self-knowledge, honesty, an active sacramental life, a great sense of humor, gratitude in prayer, and even an eschatological understanding of the Church and of religious life. The theme of her "nagging feeling" is common among young women called to this vocation and living in the state of grace. Like the good "Hound of Heaven" He is, God gently yet relentlessly pursues!

How many young people today are frequenting chapels, confession, and Eucharistic Adoration, and struggling to get their relationship with Mary back on track? I have reason to hope that the answer is far more than we might realize! In our three yearly vocational discernment retreats, young women come from around the world, sleeping bag in hand—for we have no beds in the school which is the only place spacious enough to house the average 150 women that we receive. In those twenty-four hours, including all-night Eucharistic Adoration, young ladies lay their lives on the line for Christ. And His goodness does not leave them disappointed! Whatever their vocation, they begin to lean into it spiritually, and, should it be religious life, they prayerfully begin to discern a particular spirituality, charism, and thus religious community. This most important first step continues in the detailed application process of any particular community. For my community, that will include more one-on-one time with the Vocation Directress, the completion of psychological and physical examinations, obtaining reputable recommendations, submission of high school and college transcripts, and additional portions of the official application. Then there is a pre-postulancy week of living at the Motherhouse before a young woman is considered for official acceptance.

In her reference to NET ministry work, the author of the above letter also expresses that she has a heart for helping others know and live their Faith. Thus she already knows that it is in giving self away that one comes to find self. *Gaudium et Spes* expresses it thus: "Man, who is the only creature on earth which God willed for itself, cannot fully find himself except through a sincere gift of himself" (§24). And with that sincere self-gift, grace entices the young woman from her comfort zone into a moment of great courage, a vocational decision.

MARIAN DEVOTION

A woman who does not have, or wish to have, a personal devotion to the Mother of God would probably not begin to understand religious life. After all, a religious is married to Mary's Son, and thus she had best have an excellent relationship with her mother-in-law! A quote from a saintly nun and martyr in the concentration camp at Auschwitz, Saint Teresa Benedicta of the Cross (Edith Stein), elucidates woman's Marian likeness:

> The soul of a woman must therefore be expansive and open to all human beings; it must be quiet so that no small weak flame will be extinguished by stormy winds; warm so as not to benumb fragile buds; clear, so that no vermin will settle in dark corners and recesses; self-contained, so that no invasions from without can imperil the inner life; empty of itself, in order that extraneous life may have room in it; finally, mistress of itself and also of its body, so that the entire person is readily at the disposal of every call.[29]

A woman's soul must be expansive—thus possessing a universal motherhood that knows no bounds. It must be quiet and warm because it holds the lives of others within itself spiritually. Through her love and life, she provides security and peace for others' growth. Her soul must be self-contained and yet empty of self; it must be entrusted *to* God so that it may be entrusted *with* God. Then she will spiritually be another Mary—a woman fully alive with a maternal heart given to Christ and encompassing all His children. Indeed, the spiritual motherhood of religious Sisters serves as an example drawing others to this maternal self-gift. After having read the 2017 edition of *And Mary's 'Yes' Continues*, one young woman preparing to enter the convent said,

> I was also so encouraged reading the Sisters' experiences as spiritual mothers, especially to their students. I have

always wanted children (thirteen to be exact), and, though I knew I could be a spiritual mother instead, I have never witnessed that life. Once I read their stories, and how much the Sisters are there to pray with, teach, and just have fun with their students, it helped me to "Be not afraid!" as Pope Saint John Paul would say. And I'm looking forward to the day I can be a spiritual mother myself (God willing!).

SUMMARY

Young women who enter religious life are necessarily products of the age in which they live. In the 1950s and 60s when religious vocations were swelling in the United States, a young woman would have frequently been taught by Sisters, known a few Sisters on a closer personal level of friendship, experienced shared times both inside and outside the classroom, and felt her heart tugging her to knock on the convent door and express her interest in a possible vocation.

By the late 60s, young women had far fewer opportunities to see religious Sisters, let alone engage with them in common pursuits and prayer. Perhaps some of the Sisters they had known left their convents or changed their lives in ways unrecognizable to the young. Fewer girls knocked on convent doors, and this phenomenon continued until Saint John Paul II's brilliant WYDs began to bear fruit. Once again, young women began to consider religious life, even as newer religious communities were formed to attract their youthful joy and enthusiasm.

Today's situation is in flux once again. Societal pressures and cultural moral laxity are largely responsible for a new wave of distraction which filters through parents down to their Millennial and iGen children, now grown to their teens and twenties. Vocation Directresses and parents must acknowledge the challenges youth face today, while also giving them generous support in leading virtuous lives. God continues to call forth vocations, and those who work with young people need to be wise to encourage, bring forth, and nurture possible religious and priestly vocations.

In quick summary, young women today have:
- » Better educations and more experiences with the world;
- » Zeal to lead peers in their personal encounters with Christ;
- » A deep longing for community (in the Church and in their possible vocation);
- » Radical determination, since they often enter religious life in the face of great opposition from family and friends;
- » A natural ability to use media to evangelize;
- » Enthusiasm in all they do and in involving as many people as possible;
- » A natural desire to follow rules and meet expectations; and
- » Hearts on fire with a desire to live good lives and to leave the world a better place for their having lived here too.

In closing, allow me share two quotes which well express religious life and the manner in which the Church asks us to live it as witnesses to a world oftentimes gone astray but still retaining a deep longing for holiness:

[Where] there are consecrated people, seminarians, men and women religious, young people, there is joy, there is always joy! It is the joy of freshness, the joy of following Jesus; the joy that the Holy Spirit gives us, not the joy of the world. There is joy! But where is joy born? Joy is born from the gratuitousness of an encounter! It is hearing someone say, but not necessarily with words: 'You are important to me.' This is beautiful. ... And it is these very words that God makes us understand. In calling you God says to you: 'You are important to me, I love you, I am counting on you.' Jesus says this to each one of us! Joy is born from that! The joy of the moment in which Jesus looked at me. Understanding and hearing this is the secret of our joy.[30]

And finally one of our young Sisters provides great wisdom through her purity of heart: "I am so grateful to be here. Every day is a new adventure! But best of all, I am all His and He is mine. Nothing else could ever make me so completely happy!"

NOTES

1. Sister Joseph Andrew Bogdanowicz, OP, "Religious Vocations for a New Millennium", *Lay Witness*, Catholics United for the Faith, 2001, 36-37.
2. Lisa Walden, "3 Common Generational Stereotypes", Minnesota Society of Certified Public Accountants, accessed May 20, 2020, https://www.mncpa.org/publications/footnote/2014-04/3-common-generational-stereotypes.aspx.
3. C. Seemiller & M. Grace, "Meet Generation Z", December 12, 2016, https://sigep.org/sigepjournal/meet-generation-z/
4. Pew Research Center, "How Millennials today compare with their grandparents 50 years ago", March 19, 2015 (updated March 16, 2018), https://www.pewresearch.org/fact-tank/2018/03/16/how-millennials-compare-with-their-grandparents/
5. Ibid.
6. Dr. Alexis Abramson, "Generational Expert, Dr. Alexis Abramson", accessed November 11, 2020, www.alexisabramson.com/generational-expert-alexis-abramson/.
7. Julie Lythcott-Haims, *How to Raise an Adult: Break Free of the Overparenting Trap and Prepare Your Kid for Success*, (New York: Henry Holt and Co., 2015).
8. S. Robertson, "Generation Z Characteristics & Traits that Explain the Way they Learn", Julian Krinsky Camps & Programs, July 25, 2018, accessed May 11, 2020, https://info.jkcp.com/blog/generation-z-characteristics
9. J. A. Baumann, "What's Next", *ACUHO-I Talking Stick* 35(5), (2018, May + June), pp. 39-44, https://www.nxtbook.com/nxtbooks/acuho/talkingstick_20180506/
10. J. M. Twenge, "Have Smartphones Destroyed a Generation?", *The Atlantic*, September 2017, https://www.theatlantic.com/magazine/archive/2017/09/has-the-smartphone-destroyed-a-generation/534198/
11. Henry Fairlie, *The Seven Deadly Sins Today* (Notre Dame, IN: University of Notre Dame Press, 1978).
12. Farlex Partner Medical Dictionary, 2012, s.v. "acedia", accessed June 24, 2020, https://medical-dictionary.thefreedictionary.com/acedia

13 Kathleen Norris, cited in Lynell George, "Kathleen Norris battles 'the demon of acedia'", *Los Angeles Times*, August 11, 2016, https://www.latimes.com/entertainment/la-ca-kathleen-norris21-2008sep21-story.html.

14 Carrisa Smith, "Acedia: The Forgotten Sin", *Christ & Pop Culture*, October 8, 2008, https://christandpopculture.com/acedia-the-forgotten-sin/

15 Katie Bindley, "When Children Text All Day, What Happens To Their Social Skills?", *The Huffington Post*, Dec.10, 2011, https://www.huffpost.com/entry/children-texting-technology-social-skills_n_1137570.

16 Baylor University, "Cellphone Addition Harming Academic Performance Is 'An Increasingly Realistic Possibility'", *Science Daily*, August 18, 2014, https://www.sciencedaily.com/releases/2014/08/140828184733.htm

17 The Henry J. Kaiser Family Foundation, "Daily Media Use Among Children and Teens Up Dramatically From Five Years Ago", Jan. 20, 2010, https://www.kff.org/racial-equity-and-health-policy/press-release/daily-media-use-among-children-and-teens-up-dramatically-from-five-years-ago/

18 Matt Richtel, "Growing Up Digital, Wired for Distraction", *The New York Times*, November 21, 2000, https://www.nytimes.com/2010/11/21/technology/21brain.html

19 Ibid.

20 Twenge, "Have Smartphones Destroyed a Generation?"

21 Julie Lythcott-Haims, October 4, 2016, "How to raise successful kids - without over-parenting," TED, https://youtu.be/CyElHdaqkjo

22 Ibid.

23 Julie-Lythcott-Haims, "Be your authentic self", July 9, 2012, TEDxStanford, https://youtu.be/A_Y5DjSZUDE

24 Pope Benedict XVI, visit to Monte Cassino, May 24, 2009

25 CNA/EWTN News, "Pope on World Youth Day: Poland Reminds Us of Christian Vision and Message of Mercy," National Catholic Register, August 8, 2016, https://www.ncregister.com/news/pope-on-world-youth-day-poland-reminds-us-of-christian-vision-and-message-of-mercy.

26 T. W. Adorno, Else Frenkel-Brunswik, Daniel J. Levinson, R. Nevitt Sanford, *The Authoritarian Personality*, (New York: Harper & Brothers, 1950).

27   Shane Martin, *Your Precious Life: How to Live It Well*, (Dublin: Orpen Press, 2016).

28   See https://golepress.com/welcome/education-in-virtue/.

29   Edith Stein, *Woman*, 132f. Original emphasis.

30   Pope Francis, "Address for Meeting with Seminarians and Novices", July 6, 2013.

> People are hungering for Christ. The witness of the brides of Christ, consecrated women in love with Jesus and His Church bring the light and mercy of Christ to that hungry world today.
>
> —Fr. Meinrad Miller, OSB
> St Benedict's Abbey, Atchison, KS

Staking One's Life on the Reality of God

Theology of Religious Life

Sister Albert Marie Surmanski, OP
Born in Peterborough, Ontario, Canada

A religious vocation is rooted in the mystery of God made Man. When the Word of God took on human nature and died on the cross, He offered a sacrificial love able to captivate totally the human heart. The call to religious life flows out of this love.

WITHIN THE MYSTICAL BODY

Jesus offers His saving love to everyone. He died on the cross to save all of humanity. This does not mean, though, that He calls everyone to follow Him in exactly the same way. Even during His earthly life, Jesus interacted with different people according to the unique plans He had for each one of them. Jesus was born to Mary, the only woman ever chosen to be the Mother of God. Saint Joseph guarded Christ during His childhood as a foster-father, but disappears from the Gospels before the Crucifixion. Jesus preached the Kingdom of God to the multitudes. He healed many who came to Him. Out of those who responded to His preaching, He chose twelve men to be His Apostles and carry His message to the ends of the earth as the first bishops of the Church. He often visited the family home of Mary, Martha, and Lazarus, and was grateful for their hospitality. He told a rich and honest young man to sell all of his possessions and follow Him. In contrast, when the dishonest tax-collector Zacchaeus converted, Jesus was satisfied that he restored what he had stolen and gave half of his wealth to the poor (see Lk 19:8).

> "Jesus said to him, 'If you wish to be perfect, go, sell what you have and give to [the] poor, and you will have treasure in heaven. Then come, follow me.'"
> Matthew 19:21

Within the Church, the Mystical Body of Christ, there are many different but complementary roles, just as there are many different but compatible parts to the human body. All of the members of the Mystical Body share the same supernatural life. They are all united to Christ the Head, yet they live their friendship with Christ in different ways. In his First Letter to the Corinthians, Saint Paul says, "There are different kinds of spiritual gifts but the same Spirit; there are different forms of service but the same Lord. ... As a body is one though it has many parts, and all the parts of the body, though many, are one body, so also with Christ" (12:4-5, 12). To follow Christ as a religious Sister is one way of living out the Christian vocation as a member of the Church. It is a role vital to the health of the Mystical Body.

THE CALL

The desire to follow Jesus as a religious Sister is a response to Jesus's call. It is He who chooses us. Even though the decision to follow Him is a free, personal choice, He is the source of the strength to say "yes." The Church document *Essential Elements* describes this call as an invitation to enter into a life-giving relationship with God:

> God calls a person whom He sets apart for a particular dedication to Himself. At the same time, He offers the grace to respond so that consecration is expressed on the human side by a profound and free self-surrender. The resulting relationship is pure gift. It is a covenant of mutual love and fidelity, of communion and mission, established for God's glory, the joy of the person consecrated, and the salvation of the world.[1]

How is the call to religious life experienced? Some may literally hear Jesus speaking to them, but this is rare. Most often, Jesus begins to "speak to her heart" (Hos 2:14, Douay-Rheims) by quietly and gently drawing her to Himself. His call may be felt in the peace of silent prayer before the Blessed Sacrament. It can come through seeing the joy in the faces of those who have consecrated their lives to God. It can stir as a movement of compassion towards those in need and the desire to open a motherly heart to the suffering.

> "Therefore, I will allure her now; I will lead her into the wilderness and speak persuasively to her."
> Hosea 2:14

I think the first echo of a religious vocation came to me when attending a Catholic elementary school where the faith was taught poorly. I remember feeling sad that so many of my classmates did not seem to recognize Jesus in the Eucharist.

I first recognized the desire for religious life one day after Mass when I was fourteen years old. I was suddenly transfixed with the realization that the greatest joy in life was going to be found in knowing God. Whatever I did, He would be with me, giving light and meaning to my life. This was followed by a sense that Christ was inviting me to become a religious Sister. What was most important was not the intensity of this experience but the fact that the desire stayed in my heart. During the process of preparing to enter the convent and my formation as a Dominican, Jesus supported me and enabled me to take each step forward. This support of divine grace and the acceptance of my vocation by my community is what let me know that my call was genuine.

IN IMITATION OF CHRIST

Religious life is a way of drawing near to Christ through imitating His way of life. Christ lived a life of simplicity. He travelled from place to place with "nowhere to rest His head" (Lk 9:58). He never married, staying totally available for his work of proclaiming the Kingdom. During His life, Jesus would often "[depart] to the mountain to pray" and spend all night there (Lk 6:12). In this prayer, He found His refreshment in the overflowing Trinitarian love. His communion with the Father and the Holy Spirit sustained Him in His mission. Jesus also lived a life of obedience to the Father. He described His purpose on earth as the fulfillment of the Father's will. He said, "I came down from heaven not to do my own will but the will of the one who sent me" (Jn 6:38). A religious Sister shares in these three aspects of Christ's life through her vows of poverty, chastity, and obedience. By the vows she is consecrated to God and set apart for His service in a unique way.

THE EVANGELICAL COUNSELS

These three vows are known as the *evangelical counsels*.

They are "evangelical" because they come from the Gospel. They are "counsels" because the vows are not necessary to the Christian life. They are suggestions or advice lived by some but not by all. These counsels differ from the Commandments in that commandments are given to all. They either forbid absolute evils or enjoin necessary goods. For example, the first commandment tells us that we must worship the true God, not idols. Everyone must do this. In the same way, the fifth commandment forbids murder. To take human life unjustly is always wrong.

The evangelical counsels are not directly about avoiding evils. They are about setting aside lesser goods for the sake of focusing on the highest good of all: God. Their purpose is to foster virtue. They point the way down a particular path toward holiness. If the human race was not fallen, there would be no reason for the evangelical counsels. Every contact with anything God had created would lead us closer to Him. But our

> The Evangelical Counsels
> Poverty · Chastity · Obedience

hearts are easily distracted. Even good things can tempt us away from God. No one who looks at today's world with any degree of honesty can deny that it is all too easy to become enslaved by material things, pleasures, and power. When a religious makes her vows, she does not deny that material things, pleasures, and power are good when used rightly. By her life, however, she testifies that they are not the highest good. When a religious says "no" through the three vows, she is really saying "yes" to the highest good: God!

THE VOW OF POVERTY

By the vow of poverty, a religious Sister gives up the ownership of personal possessions. She will hold all things in common with the other members of her community. She will live simply, using the things of this world without owning them.

Foundations

> God Himself is a religious' greatest treasure.

In doing this, she expresses her trusting dependence on God to provide for her. She also enters a way of life in which she must live closely with the other members of her community, relying on them and having them rely on her. Having many possessions can be a distraction from God, either because the heart clings to them, wanting more and more, or simply because taking care of them can involve a lot of work. By setting aside personal possessions, the Sister's life is made simpler so she can focus on God more intensely. She testifies that God is her greatest treasure.

THE VOW OF CHASTITY

A religious Sister promises to abstain from marriage and sexual activity by her vow of chastity. She does not do this because marriage and children are a bad thing. Marriage is a holy sacrament, and children are one of the greatest blessings in this life. The consecrated religious gives up marriage and children in order to have a heart free to love God in an undivided way. Her vow makes her available to love in a sisterly or motherly way those whom God puts in her life. The life of celibate dedication to God began to emerge even in the early Church. In one of his letters, Saint Paul gives advice to the Christians of Corinth, reminding them that "an unmarried woman or a virgin is anxious about the things of the Lord, so that she may be holy in both body and spirit. A married woman, on the other hand, is anxious about the things of the world, how she may please her husband" (1 Cor 7:34). By their teaching, prayer, and witness, religious women should support families who take on the cares of raising children.

> Her union with Christ will help bring spiritual life to many.

When I was considering religious life, it was the vow of chastity that appealed to me the most. I came from a beautiful Christian home and liked the idea of marriage and children. But as I prayed about my direction in life, I felt that Christ was making such a strong claim on my heart that I could not give it to another man. Through the vow of chastity, a religious Sister is a bride. Her heart, her life, and her service belong exclusively to Christ. Given to Christ, then, she is poured out on those to whom He sends her. Although the Sister will not physically give birth to any children, this does not mean that her life will not be fruitful. Her union with Christ will help bring spiritual life to many. She is still a woman and will love with a woman's heart. As Dominicans, we experience this "spiritual motherhood" in a variety of ways—first and most importantly is through our life of prayer. We also experience it through our apostolate of teaching, in which we help our students receive and cherish the truth of Christ and so grow up into the men and women they are called to be.

THE VOW OF OBEDIENCE

By the vow of obedience, the religious woman gives her will into the hands of Christ, through the hands of her religious superiors. Of course, determining the path of one's own life is a good thing. But being totally available for God's mission is better. The vow of obedience is lived in accordance with a rule of life approved by the Church. Since its purpose is to enable the Sister to unite her will to God's will, it can never contradict the laws of God and of the Church. A Sister can never be asked under her vow to do anything evil. In such a case, she would not be bound to obey.

> The vow of obedience makes religious life an adventure.

The vow of obedience makes religious life an adventure. In our community, we receive our assignments yearly. A Sister may teach in the same place year after year or may be sent somewhere new. When I am given my assignment, I may not know why it was given to me. What I do know is that I will be where Christ wants me to be that year. I will encounter those whom He wants my life to touch. My responsibility is to seek His face where He wants me to meet Him.

I occasionally come across people who think that the vow of obedience means that religious give up thinking for themselves and become some sort of mindless robots who are no longer able to make decisions. This is not true. Yes, I have made a vow to choose to do the good that my superiors ask of me. But doing this requires all of my willpower, intelligence, and energy. For several years, my assignment was to teach at Ave Maria University in Florida. To fulfill this assignment, I had to prepare lectures, teach classes, translate Latin, meet with students, and take on all sorts of other activities. The vow of obedience stretches and shapes each Sister. It does not make her stagnate.

RELIGIOUS LIFE AS SIGN OF THE KINGDOM

While only some make vows to live by the evangelical counsels, all Christians are called to live by the *spirit* of the evangelical counsels. Jesus told His followers that the greatest commandment is, "You shall love the Lord, your God, with all your heart, with all your being, with all your strength, and with all your mind, and your neighbor as yourself" (Lk 10:27). All Christians must love God more than material things, must recognize that sexual love must be lived out in accordance with God's plan, and must seek the will of God in their lives. The laity (the baptized who are not priests or religious) seek the Kingdom of God by using the things of the world. They are responsible for transforming the world through their involvement in it. They might participate in politics, business, law enforcement, and so on. Religious, who live the counsels in the radical form of the vows, step back from certain earthly goods in order to be a reminder to all Christians that the things of God come first.

Unlike the vocations to the priesthood and married life, religious life does not have an additional sacrament connected to it. Religious consecration is a deepening of the baptismal consecration. At Baptism, the grace of the Holy Spirit enters the soul and dynamically directs the newly baptized onto the path of holiness. Religious consecration involves a free choice to live the baptismal call to holiness in a radical way. Saint Paul describes the Church as the "bride of Christ" as well as the "body of Christ". He tells the whole people of Corinth, "I betrothed you to one husband to present you as a chaste virgin to Christ" (2 Cor 11:2). The whole Church is the bride of Christ; all Christians partake in Christ's love for His people. Yet, as a consecrated bride of Christ, the woman religious lives within the reality of this love in a particularly intense way. She expresses the nature of the Church with her whole life. The Second Vatican Council underlined this by saying that religious life, "though it is not the hierarchical structure of the Church, nevertheless, undeniably belongs to its life and holiness".[2] If the religious life died out in the Church, something essential would be missing. A necessary message about the attractive power of Christ's love would be lost.

> The whole Church is the bride of Christ; all Christians partake in Christ's love for His people.

After the resurrection of the dead, at the time of Christ's second coming, there will be no more marriage. Christ said, "At the resurrection they neither marry nor are given in marriage" (Mt 22:30). The human community will no longer need to increase through children being born. The love of God will fulfill and overflow the hearts of all, and spiritual union with God will be the primary relationship for every man and women. Since religious now live an unmarried life, dedicated to God, they provide an image of the fulfilling union with God that all Christians will experience at the time of the resurrection. As a promise of this life to come, they are called an *eschatological sign*, a sign of Christ's future coming.

The Second Vatican Council expresses this theology:

> The profession of the evangelical counsels, then, appears as a sign which can and ought to attract all the members of the Church to an effective and prompt fulfillment of the duties of their Christian vocation. The people of God have no lasting city here below, but look forward to one that is to come. Since this is so, the religious state, whose purpose is to free its members from earthly cares, more fully manifests to all believers the presence of heavenly goods already possessed here below. Furthermore, it not only witnesses to the fact of a new and eternal life acquired by the redemption of Christ, but it foretells the future resurrection and the glory of the heavenly kingdom. Christ proposed to His disciples this form of life, which He, as the Son of God, accepted in entering this world to do the will of the Father. ... It clearly shows all men both the unsurpassed breadth of the strength of Christ the King and the infinite power of the Holy Spirit marvelously working in the Church.[3]

I remember speaking to a family friend the summer before I entered the convent. I had just graduated from college. She was in high school and seemed to be going through a crisis in faith. While our parents visited, we had a chat about my future plans. She listened attentively as I tried to explain what my life would be like in the Dominican novitiate the next year. Then, she suddenly broke into my explanation. In words I still remember, she asked, "But what if God doesn't exist?" She had grasped perfectly what I was saying. My life as a Sister would make no sense if God did not exist. Religious life is a supernatural way of life. The vows are only reasonable in the light of God's reality. This is precisely the message which the religious life is meant to convey to the world. Everyone who sees a religious Sister should realize that she has staked her life on the reality of God. What I am doing is meaningless if God does not exist. That I am able to do it with joy is evidence of God's sustaining help.

COMMUNITY

The communion with God fostered by the vows is expressed and lived within a religious community. As a Dominican Sister, I live in a convent with other Sisters. We share a common life, pray together, attend Mass together, work together, and relax together. The common life supports and sustains the vows. It is in turn enriched by the love that the vows generate. Within our Dominican family, we live according to the Rule of Saint Augustine and our Dominican Constitutions. This way of life, approved by the Church, gives a structure to my life where I can practice the vows and offer my life as a sacrifice to God. I am able to live out my vow of obedience by following our rule of life in accordance with the direction of my superiors. I am able to live out my vow of poverty by sharing both material goods and the daily rhythm of our simple life with my Sisters. The friendship of my Sisters supports my practice of the vow of chastity. Our religious habit

Monastic Rules

Most religious orders follow a monastic Rule, such as the Rule of Saint Benedict or the Rule of Saint Basil. Dominicans, while being founded by Saint Dominic, follow the Rule of Saint Augustine. The particulars of how a specific order lives (such as Dominicans) are called "Constitutions".

is a sign of our shared consecration to Christ and of our common religious family. I love it when I meet people who immediately recognize my community from my habit. It also reminds me who I am and how I have vowed to live. Enriched by divine charity, community life should reflect both the community of love within the Trinity and the nature of the Church.

APOSTOLATE

The foremost duty of a religious is "assiduous union with God in prayer."[4] We prayerfully offer the sacrifice of our lives in union with Christ's own sacrifice. A major component of the prayer life of a religious is the Divine Office, a rotation of Psalms, petitions, and readings by which we sanctify the hours of our day. We pray for God's mercy upon the Church and the world. At every hour of every day, religious and priests around the world raise their voices in prayer to God through the Divine Office. The laity are invited to join in this prayer but are not required to practice it.

The next way in which religious serve the Church is through our common apostolate. Each religious community has a mission within the Church. The Second Vatican Council describes the different religious families as fruit-bearing branches that grow on the tree of the Church: "Thus it has come about, that, as if on a tree which has grown in the field of the Lord, various forms of solidarity and community life, as well as various religious families have branched out in a marvelous and multiple way from this divinely given seed."[5] The apostolic mission of each community flows from the "charism" or spiritual gift that God gave to the founder of the community. This charism is confirmed through the approval of the hierarchy of the Church. The charism and apostolate of a religious community is the way in which that community carries on the work of Christ in the Church. Christ's life had an indescribable richness: He preached the Gospel, cared for the poor, healed the sick, welcomed children, called sinners to conversion, spent time in prayer, and agonized in the Garden of Gethsemane. Each religious community expresses one aspect of Christ's life. As Dominicans, we share in the work of Christ the teacher.

MARY

A final aspect of the life of a consecrated woman religious is that it is lived in union with Mary. Mary lived in total availability to Christ in all of the feminine richness of her mind and body. She gave her *fiat* to the overshadowing of the Holy Spirit, which consecrated her life to God in a unique way. She lived at Nazareth in humble simplicity. She was faithful to the end, standing beneath the cross of Christ, even when her heart was breaking. We look to Mary as the perfect example of a life of virginity and spiritual fruitfulness. She is our Mother and our model, the perfect disciple of Christ. Our prayer is that our lives will show her gentle love to the world.

NOTES

1. Sacred Congregation for Religious and for Secular Institutes, *Essential Elements in the Church's Teaching on Religious Life as Applied to Institutes Dedicated to Works of the Apostolate*, May 31, 1983, 5, http://www.vatican.va/roman_curia/congregations/ccscrlife/documents/rc_con_ccscrlife_doc_31051983_magisterium-on-religious-life_en.html.

2. Second Vatican Council, *Lumen Gentium: Light of the Nations*, November 21, 1964, 44, http://www.vatican.va/archive/hist_councils/ii_vatican_council/documents/vat-ii_const_19641121_lumen-gentium_en.html.

3. Ibid.

4. *Code of Canon Law,* c. 663.1, sec. II, III, http://www.vatican.va/archive/ENG1104/_INDEX.HTM.

5. *Lumen Gentium*, 43.

> "Women's religious vocations, when authentic, are deep reminders that spiritual fatherhood is learned from spiritual mothers throughout one's life. Both fatherhood and motherhood are ultimately self-giving, and therefore, require subjection to the providence and governance of God under grace. Without grace, self-giving becomes a sham of self-taking."
>
> – Fr. Basil Cole, OP, STD
> Professor of Moral and Spiritual Theology
> Pontifical Faculty of the Immaculate Conception, Washington, D.C.

Happiness in Accord with Virtue

Philosophy of Religious Life

Sister Catherine Thomas Brennan, OP
Born in St. Louis, Missouri

At first glance, religious life as a graced response to a divine call may seem to have little, if anything, to do with human philosophy. Religious life is supernatural in both its origin and its goal and is lived on the level of faith. Philosophy is the human investigation of reality and life's meaning, the pursuit of wisdom according to human reason. Did not Saint Paul indicate the futility of these exercises when he wrote to the Church at Corinth, "Has not God made the wisdom of the world foolish? ... [B]ut we proclaim Christ crucified, a stumbling block to Jews and foolishness to Gentiles, but to those who are called, Jews and Greeks alike, Christ the power of God and the wisdom of God" (1 Cor. 1:20, 23-24).

Saint Jerome, the fourth-century Doctor of the Church who is best known for his translation of the Scriptures into Latin, was famously rebuked in a dream by the Lord Jesus Christ for being more of a follower of human learning than a Christian. When he awoke, he dedicated himself to the study of the Scriptures.

However, it is also the case that for many saints of every age of the Church's life—Saint Justin Martyr, Saint Augustine of Hippo, Saint Thomas Aquinas, Saint Edith Stein—the pursuit of philosophy not only prepared the way for a life radically consecrated to God, but also supported the living out of their "yes" to God lived on the level of faith. Saint Thomas Aquinas, who seems to have been one of those saints who are holy from the cradle, went around as a child pestering those around him with the question, "What is God?"—a little philosopher from the start. Saint John Paul II extolled philosophy as "one of the noblest human tasks" and "the way to come to know fundamental truths about human life", an "indispensable help" for understanding and proclaiming the truth of the Gospel.[1] The very name philosophy, love of wisdom, points to the love of Him who is the very Word of the Father, "Christ the power of God and the wisdom of God" (1 Cor 1:24). For this reason philosophy is known as the "handmaid of theology". This chapter will investigate the ways in which insights culled from philosophy have informed the Church's teachings on consecrated life and continue to enrich the lived experience of consecration in today's world.

> "Born and nurtured when the human being first asked questions about the reason for things and their purpose, philosophy shows in different modes and forms that the desire for truth is part of human nature itself."
>
> -Pope Saint John Paul II

FIRST INSIGHT: AGERE SEQUITUR ESSE

One well-known philosophical dictum is *agere sequitur esse*—"doing follows being". In other words, what something does follows or flows out of what the thing is; how one acts is a function of who (or what) one is. What a squirrel does is not what a tomato plant does, because they are two different kinds of beings. Different kinds of beings have different capacities and potentials for different kinds of actions: tomato plants can produce tomatoes, cheetahs can run, and human beings can build cathedrals. To be sure, what one does affects what one is; what we do can either develop our potential or thwart it. But that brings us right back to being. Our actions can either develop or diminish our being, but without some being that exists in the first place, there is nothing to develop or diminish. Take the following obvious examples of health: One can eat well and exercise, and these actions help one to become healthy. One can fail to eat or move, and thus starve or atrophy. Thus, there are some actions that are necessary for a being to develop and flourish, and there are some actions that inhibit development or full flourishing. But unless some being exists in the first place, it would be nonsensical to speak about whether it is healthy or unhealthy.

> "Be who you are meant to be, and you will set the world on fire!"
> -Saint Catherine of Siena

The priority of being over doing is no idle philosophical speculation. This axiom has immediate and profound repercussions for daily life. We are meant to walk on our feet, not on our heads. If we reverse the priority to doing over being, attempting to walk with our feet in the air and our heads on the ground, the results will be painful. What would this look like in a culture that places high value upon success and possessions?

What does this philosophical distinction look like in a culture that values hard work and the self-made man or woman—that is, a culture very much like twenty-first century America? It becomes all too easy to define yourself in terms of where you went to school, your GPA, your salary, what clothes you wear, the car you drive, and the items in the pocket of your size-whatever skinny jeans. Doing and having become the measure of being and identity: the more I do/earn/have, the better and more valuable I am.

It would be nice if a fervent Christian life or a vocation to religious life made one immune to this line of self-deception. It does not. Francis Xavier Nguyễn Văn Thuận, the bishop of Saigon who was imprisoned for 13 years in a Vietnamese Communist prison camp, testifies that it was only there that he began to learn to "choose God and not the works of God":

> I could not sleep because I was so tormented by the thought of being forced to abandon my diocese, and of the many works that I had begun for God now going to ruin. ... One night, from the depth of my heart, a voice said to me, "You must distinguish between God and the works of God. Everything you have done and desire to continue doing...[t]hese are God's works, but they are not God! If God wants you to leave all of these works, do it right away and have faith in him! God can do things infinitely better than you can. He will entrust his works to others that are much more capable. You have chosen God alone, not his works!"[2]

The temptation to view one's identity in terms of work for the Kingdom of God, and to view work for the Kingdom of God in terms of measurable success, has a special edge for consecrated men and women. I am a good religious because I am on time for prayers and follow all the rubrics. I am reliable in my duties in community, and I work hard in the apostolate. All of these things are good; in fact, they are essential expressions of the total gift of self that religious consecration is. But they are not the most essential. The essential of essentials for the consecrated woman is that she is a bride of Christ. From being a bride she becomes a spiritual mother, and spiritual motherhood entails a great deal of doing. But that doing is a natural overflow of her intimacy with Jesus.[3]

Saint John Paul II exhorts consecrated men and women to recall the "superiority of being over having".[4] This remark, made in the context of the vow of poverty, fundamentally applies to the relationship between being and doing as well. The truths of creation and redemption are a beautiful reminder of the primacy of being over having and doing. God, who had no need of anything, created heaven and earth from nothing; the God who created us took on our own nature and saved us while we were dead in sin. We exist because we are loved; we are made God's beloved sons and daughters at our Baptism. We hear our fundamental identity proclaimed by Truth Himself: "This is my beloved Son, with whom I am well pleased" (Mt 3:17). At the farthest extreme of this Love, God pours out His life for us on the cross and remains hidden in our tabernacles to give us this life in the Eucharist. While He pours out His life and love for all, He calls some to a special intimacy with Himself, in the spousal relationship of religious consecration.

A Missionary of Charity Sister with whom I worked understood this truth well. We were selecting groceries, and a sticker reading "99 cents" somehow attached itself to her habit. I pulled it off, and her reaction was immediate and decisive: "99 cents? No! I am worth all of the infinite blood of the Son of God!" The immediacy of her reaction struck me as profoundly as her words did. Here was a woman who understood where her value lay: not in what she had or did but in the fact that Love loved her to the end.

SECOND INSIGHT: THE HAPPY LIFE IS CONTEMPLATIVE

Words of Wisdom

> But we must not follow those who advise us, being men, to think of human things, and, being mortal, of mortal things, but must, so far as we can, make ourselves immortal, and strain every nerve to live in accordance with the best thing in us; for even if it be small in bulk, much more does it in power and worth surpass everything.... [T]hat which is proper to each thing is by nature best and most pleasant for each thing; for man, therefore, the life according to reason is best and pleasantest, since reason more than anything else is man. This life therefore is also the happiest.[5]
>
> — Aristotle

In the last book of his *Nicomachean Ethics*, Aristotle makes an eloquent case for the joys of contemplation. For him, happiness is "activity in accord with virtue," where virtue is the excellence of our human capacities, our human powers honed for peak performance.[6] What kind of activity makes for authentic happiness? Aristotle distinguishes the different kinds of good things around which a person may center his life: pleasures of the body, active virtues such as contributing to civic life and providing for one's own needs and those of others, and the activity of contemplation, which he associates with "tak[ing] thought of things noble and divine".[7] For Aristotle, the power of reason "is man" and so the activity of reason is man living at the level of his truest self.

This may strike a twenty-first-century ear as impossibly removed from reality. Who would spend spring break or a paid vacation just thinking? But Aristotle's claim is precisely that the activity of contemplation is not only the "noblest" but also the "pleasantest", and that this is true not merely for some intellectual elite but for human beings as human beings.[8] The joy of contemplation is even more intense and more continuous than the pleasures of the senses (with whose traditional categories of food, sex, and entertainment we could include shopping, coffee and cocktail bars, and movies). Contemplation as the activity of reason par excellence is not simply an intellectual exercise like a logic puzzle. Contemplation is the gaze of the mind in fascination and wonder at beauty, truth, and goodness.

Anyone who has lost all track of time and felt stabs of joy and longing in the presence of some marvel of nature, or some masterpiece of human creativity, or in a fascinating conversation, or in a gaze of love on one's beloved, has had an experience of contemplation. Anyone who has had this contemplative experience wants more of it and can begin to see why he would "strain every nerve to live in accordance with the best thing in us; for even if it be small in bulk, much more does it in power and worth surpass everything".

The Christian life in general and religious life in particular draws upon the insight that contemplation is the most necessary and joyous activity in human life. According to the Second Vatican Council, the Church is "eager to act yet devoted to contemplation".[9] Saint Thomas Aquinas echoes many noble strands of ancient and medieval tradition when he proclaims that human life can be divided into action and contemplation, where action refers to the external activities of life and contemplation to the activity of the soul.[10] This distinction hearkens back to the Gospel episode of Mary sitting at the Lord's feet while leaving her sister Martha busy with serving the guests (cf. Lk 10:38-42). Christ draws the anxious gaze of Martha to Mary's choice of the "one thing necessary." Saint Thérèse of Lisieux understands this to mean that "souls thus on fire cannot stand still. Like Mary, they may sit at the feet of Jesus, listening to His sweet and exciting words. Jesus does not, of course, blame Martha's work, but only her worrying about it. For His Mother humbly did the same jobs when she got the meals ready for the Holy Family."[11]

> "You are anxious and worried about many things. There is need of only one thing. Mary has chosen the better part and it will not be taken from her."
> -Luke 10:41-42

Martha's activity is not rejected as such; the dinner party with Jesus would have become awkward if no one prepared the food or thought about bringing Jesus water. Martha's works were needed if His voice flagged while speaking at length with Mary, who represents contemplation. But activity is not the most important thing. If everyone at the dinner party was so taken up with "what needs to be done" that no one sat with Jesus and listened to Him, it would have been a very sad party indeed. Action and contemplation are both important, but contemplation is the wellspring and the goal of action.

Christian contemplation is Trinitarian and Christological: a child of God the Father turns the eyes of mind and heart to Christ in the Spirit. The activity of the Church, of the Christian, and of the consecrated man or woman will be supernaturally effective only to the degree that they are saturated with the presence of God, and we become saturated by God only in prayer. Work without prayer is social work—valuable, good, praiseworthy, but limited to the horizons of this world. Sometimes we hear, rightly so, "My work is my prayer." This is good! Our work not only can be but must be a continuation of our self-offering to God. The religious who leaves the chapel for the classroom or the kitchen or the hospital is going about her Father's business and is under His gaze. But she is fooling herself if work becomes a substitute for prayer, because this means that work has become a substitute for God, and she will only impoverish herself and others. Without contemplation, activity becomes a list of tasks to be checked off the to-do list, and persons become numbers on the list or interruptions to the list. Lists are well and good, but we were made for more than lists. The bride of Christ cannot give what she does not have. Work becomes work for the Kingdom (and hence prayer) when it is fed by an overflow of personal intimacy with Jesus.

> Our work not only can be but must be a continuation of our self-offering to God.

THIRD INSIGHT: FRIENDSHIP

The Second Vatican Council identified religious life with the "pursuit of perfect charity through the evangelical counsel".[12] As Saint Thomas Aquinas begins his treatment of the theological virtue of charity in his great *Summa Theologiae*, he consciously adopts Aristotle's account of friendship in the latter's *Nicomachean Ethics*. Simply put, for Saint Thomas, "charity is friendship", and he often draws upon Aristotle's insights into the nature of friendship to make the case that this is so.[13] Delving into these insights, then, will be of service to apprehending the nature of perfect charity to which the profession of the evangelical counsels of poverty, chastity, and obedience are directed. Aristotle's account of friendship can also illuminate our understanding of fraternal life in community.

What is friendship? Aristotle contends that "[t]o be friends, then, they must be mutually recognized as bearing goodwill and wishing well to each other."[14] It is not enough for one person to wish well to another; the other must also wish well to him, or this would not be friendship.

> "Without friends no one would choose to live, though he had all other goods."
> -Aristotle

The well-wishing must be not only mutual but known to be mutual; two people who admire each other from afar but have never met would not be called friends. Hence a certain sharing or communication is required for friendship.

Finally, the friends must desire what is good for the other for the other's sake rather than for his own. Aristotle delineates three main kinds of friendship based upon three different kinds of goods that the friends pursue: pleasure, utility, and virtue. In the case of friendships based upon pleasure and utility, the friend is not loved for himself but for whatever pleasure or usefulness one can get from him. In the case of friendship based upon virtue, what is loved is the virtue the two have in common; hence the friend is loved for his goodness. The friendship of the virtuous is also pleasant and useful to the friends, who delight in each other and seek each other's good as their own.

Interestingly, Aristotle actually denies that friendship is possible between man and God, since the two are too far removed to have sharing and communication.[15] Nevertheless it is precisely with friendship that Saint Thomas elects to describe the love of God for human beings and of human beings for God. Admittedly, in using Aristotle's terms to describe friendship, Saint Thomas radically elevates the definition. Saint Thomas explains what makes it possible for human beings to have this kind of communication with God:

[T]here is a communication between man and God, inasmuch as He communicates His happiness to us, some kind of friendship must needs be based on this same communication, of which it is written (1 Cor 1:9): "God is faithful: by Whom you are called unto the fellowship of His Son." The love which is based on this communication, is charity: wherefore it is evident that charity is the friendship of man for God.[16]

Thus, man's friendship with God is the fruit of the Incarnation: fellowship with God in His Son, who took on our human nature and who says, "I have called you friends" (Jn 15:15). God became man so that men might become sharers in the divine nature (see 2 Pt 1:4).

According to Saint Thomas, the soul loves God and others with the same love of friendship. This love is based upon fellowship in happiness, and so it extends to all who are capable of sharing in beatitude: one's self, the angels, and other human persons.[17] Thomas even includes one's own body[18] among the objects that we love with the love of charity, because he takes the resurrection of the body seriously. Our bodies are part of the "I" called to love God forever in heaven.

If fellowship in virtue is part and parcel of the human vocation, it is all the more so for the religious vocation. By their consecration, religious strive to pursue perfect charity, that is, the perfection of loving friendship with God in Christ and the extension to and inclusion of all others in that friendship. There is a great need for that friendship with God to be lived and experienced first by the individual religious; she cannot give to others what she does not have. Here we begin to see why community

> "Faithful friends are a sturdy shelter; whoever finds one finds a treasure."
> —Sirach 6:14

life is so essential to the pursuit of perfect charity. This point was repeatedly emphasized by the Second Vatican Council and in the Church's post-conciliar teachings on religious life.[19] Common life is the first witness that a religious gives to the reality of God's transforming love. Common life makes this love evidently real, and the first to receive this transforming love is the religious herself. This love turns total strangers into sisters and brothers. The new postulant may be startled to hear herself addressed as "Sister", but so she is. Community life, like the life of a family, is the first place for the giving and receiving of love, forgiveness, acceptance, support, and good example. Christ first called His apostles together around Himself to be with Him, and when He did send them out, He sent them two by two. Hence, the first apostolate of all religious is community life.

CONCLUSION

The Virgin Mary could rightly be called the first Christian philosopher. She was the first to live the truths cherished by the philosophers in the light of Christ. She, the faithful and humble one, asks questions when her reason is stretched by a mystery she does not comprehend: "How can this be, since I have no relations with a man?" "Son, why have you done this to us?" (Lk 1:34; 2:48). Ever ready to act in response to the needs of others, as at the Visitation or the Wedding Feast at Cana, she first puts the whole of her being in a posture of receptive readiness to her Lord's beck and call: "Behold, I am the handmaid of the Lord. May it be done to me according to your word" (Lk 1:38). She is the first and perfect Christian contemplative, turning the gaze of her eyes, and of her mind and heart, to Jesus, treasuring His words and pondering Him in her heart (see Lk 2:19, 2:51). The Mother of the Church and Queen of Apostles waits in prayer with the disciples for the coming of the Spirit of Truth, the Love of the Father and the Son, and this apostolic fellowship gathered in prayer with Mary and sent out afire is the icon of the Church and of religious life in every age.

NOTES

1. John Paul II, *Fides et Ratio*, 3, 5, *Vatican*, September 14, 1998, http://w2.vatican.va/content/john-paul-ii/en/encyclicals/documents/hf_jp-ii_enc_14091998_fides-et-ratio.html,

2. Francis Xavier Nguyễn Văn Thuận, *Testimony of Hope*, trans. Julia Mary Darrenkam and Anne Eileen Heffernan, (Boston: Daughters of St. Paul, 2000), 42.

3. "The purpose of the Religious Life is to help the members follow Christ and be united to God through the profession of the evangelical counsels. It should be constantly kept in mind, therefore, that even the best adjustments made in accordance with the needs of our age will be ineffectual unless they are animated by a renewal of spirit. This must take precedence over even the active ministry." Second Vatican Council, *Perfectae Caritatis*, 2. *Vatican*. http://www.vatican.va/archive/hist_councils/ii_vatican_council/documents/vat-ii_decree_19651028_perfectae-caritatis_en.html.

4. John Paul II, *Redemptionis Donum*, 4, *Vatican*, March 25, 1984, http://w2.vatican.va/content/john-paul-ii/en/apost_exhortations/documents/hf_jp-ii_exh_25031984_redemptionis-donum.html

5. Aristotle, *Nicomachean Ethics*, sec. X.7, trans. W.D. Ross, *MIT Classics Department*, http://classics.mit.edu/Aristotle/nicomachaen.10.x.html.

6. Ibid.

7. Ibid.

8. On the other hand, it is also the case that virtue or its absence shapes our desires. For the vicious or non-virtuous person, the true good can appear undesirable, and lesser goods can appear more satisfying than they really are, much as how a sick person may not be able to eat anything but pudding and saltines. The cure for this, of course, is not settling for lesser goods but striving for virtue, which makes us capable of living on the level of our greatest desires. Also, Aristotle does limit the number of persons who can, in practice, live the most-happy contemplative life. Even for the virtuous person, contemplation requires leisure and the possession of health, long life, and enough of this world's material goods to meet life's necessities (see *Nicomachean Ethics* X.8).

9. Second Vatican Council, *Sacrosanctum Concilium*, 1, *Vatican*, December 4, 1963, http://www.vatican.va/archive/hist_councils/ii_vatican_council/documents/vat-ii_const_19631204_sacrosanctum-concilium_en.html.

10. Thomas Aquinas, *Summa Theologiae*, II-II q. 179.1.

11 Thérèse of Lisieux, *The Story of a Soul*, trans. John Beevers, (New York, NY: Random House, 2001).

12 Second Vatican Council, *Perfectae Caritatis*, October 28, 1965, 1, http://www.vatican.va/archive/hist_councils/ii_vatican_council/documents/vat-ii_decree_19651028_perfectae-caritatis_en.html

13 Saint Thomas quotes Aristotle four separate times in a single brief article Thomas Aquinas, *Summa Theologiae*, II-II q. 23 art. 1. http://dhspriory.org/thomas/summa/SS/SS023.html#SSQ23OUTP1.

14 Aristotle, *Nicomachean Ethics*, VIII.2.

15 "If there is a great interval in respect of virtue or vice or wealth or anything else between the parties; for then they are no longer friends, and do not even expect to be so. And this is most manifest in the case of the gods; for they surpass us most decisively in all good things. But it is clear also in the case of kings; for with them, too, men who are much their inferiors do not expect to be friends; nor do men of no account expect to be friends with the best or wisest men. In such cases it is not possible to define exactly up to what point friends can remain friends; for much can be taken away and friendship remain, but when one party is removed to a great distance, as God is, the possibility of friendship ceases" (Aristotle, *Nicomachean Ethics*, VIII.7).

16 Aquinas, *Summa Theologiae*, II-II q. 23 art. 1.

17 Aquinas, *Summa Theologiae*, II-II q. 23 art. 1; q. 24.

18 Aquinas, *Summa Theologiae*, II-II q. 24 art. 5.

19 See: *Perfectae Caritatis*, 15; *Evangelica Testificatio*, 47; *Essential Elements*, 19; *Christus Dominis*, 15; *Redemptionis Donum*, 15; *Vita Consecrata*, 41, 61; "Fraternal Life in Community," 2, 3, 8, 26, 68; "Directives on Formation in Religious Institutes," 26; *Ecclesiae Sanctae*, II 25-29.

Philosophy of Religious Life

> Religious Sisters are the spiritual mothers of our Church—nourishing the Church and caring for us. They gently guide us to Our Lord. Just as a family would be a hollow shell without a mother, the Church would be lacking in those vital needs without our Sisters.
>
> – Fr. Patrick Baikauskas, OP
> Catholic Center at Washington University, Clayton, MO

Vocations Beget Vocations

The Story behind the Statistics on Religious Life

Updated for Second Edition

Sister Teresa Christi Balek, OP
Born in St. Louis, Missouri

At the intersection of Rhode Island and Connecticut Avenues in Washington, D.C., stands a monument dedicated to the over 600 religious Sisters from 12 communities who served in field hospitals during the American Civil War. The monument's bronze relief depicts these "Angels of the Battlefield", and the etched granite stone describes how "[t]hey comforted the dying, nursed the wounded, carried hope to the imprisoned, [and] gave in His name a drink of water to the thirsty." This monument hails the dedication of these valiant consecrated women who served the wounded on both sides of America's bloodiest war. While many Americans were generally suspicious of the Catholic Church in the nineteenth century, the Sisters' brave service helped their fellow citizens see that a good

Catholic could also be a good American.[1] In her recollections from the war, Mary Livermore—a prominent American journalist, abolitionist, and women's rights advocate—noted similar sentiments regarding the nursing Sisters she encountered:

> Never did I meet these Catholic Sisters in hospitals, on transports, or hospital steamers, without observing their devotion, faithfulness, and unobtrusiveness. They gave themselves no airs of superiority or holiness, shirked no duty, sought no easy place, bred no mischief. Sick and wounded men watched for their entrance into the wards at morning, and looked a regretful farewell when they departed at night... Every patient gave hearty testimony to the skill and kindness of the Sisters. If I have ever felt prejudiced against these Sisters as nurses, my experience with them during the war would have dissipated it entirely.[2]

During my formation, I was sent to study American history at The Catholic University of America and was blessed to visit this monument just months before I renewed my temporary vows. Located at the corner of a busy intersection and towered over by the Cathedral of Saint Matthew, it is easy to miss this monument, as "unobtrusive" as the Sisters' humble work that Livermore describes. After dodging cars, I safely arrived on the monument's platform and paused with deep reverence and gratitude for the Sisters who had gone before me. These Sisters had heroically built America's educational and health care systems with their bare hands, amid privations and persecutions, and on their knees. Much like how their monument stands in the middle of a busy intersection, the Sisters prayed, worked, and had daring vision alongside the noise and turmoil of their times. Looking toward the future of religious life in America I am aware of the spiritual giants on whose shoulders my vocation stands. Their ongoing prayers before the Triune God continue to breathe life and prayerful responsiveness into religious life in America today, despite how different our times are now. Monuments do not merely reflect a by-gone past, but remind the present to be their student and the future to be one of trustful hope.

SISTERS IN AMERICA: THE GROWTH

In the decades following the Civil War, Catholic immigrants came to America in astonishing numbers, just as they had done in the few decades preceding the war. The Catholic population in America increased from just over 6 million in 1880 to almost 16.5 million in 1910. Catholic immigrants constituted half of the American population increase during these decades when the total population rose from 75 million to 95 million.[3] As the American Catholic population increased, so did the number of religious Sisters, both immigrants and native born. There were 22,000 religious Sisters in 1880 and 90,000 in 1920.[4] While prejudice against Catholics remained strong during these decades, the Sisters played a vital role in teaching children and providing health care to the poor and rich, Catholic and non-Catholic alike. Their practice of the spiritual and corporal works of mercy pointed many to the hope that is Jesus Christ and His Church and helped ease anti-Catholic tensions.

By the post-World War II era, Catholicism had gained acceptance in America and Catholic Americans experienced an economic, social, and political upturn. The shift from being socially outcast to accepted can largely be attributed to the Church's successful educational and social institutions, staffed mainly by religious Sisters, which supported and taught adults and children how to be both good Catholics and good citizens. A quick examination of popular culture demonstrates this conclusion: anti-Catholic (and more specifically, anti-religious life) novels were best-sellers in the 1830s, while motion pictures such as *Going My Way* and *The Bells of St. Mary's* (which lauded

Catholicism and religious life) earned a total of 17 Academy Award nominations in the 1940s.[5] Thus, in the span of a mere one hundred years, Catholicism took root in America, largely thanks to the humble work of thousands of religious Sisters.

By 1966, the Catholic Church in America boasted 181,421 Sisters; almost no Catholic hospital or school was without them.[6] Raised in that era, my mother fondly recalls the Sisters who taught her in the 1950s on the South Side of Chicago in the packed classrooms of large parish schools. My mother was one of the over five million children taught in Catholic elementary and secondary schools in the 1950s and 1960s, where the large majority of the teachers were Sisters.[7] The Sisters' impact on millions of American Catholics, especially at an early age, was evident in the strength of the faith among Catholics in the pews and Catholic families.

God only knows the number of souls that Sisters touched by their apostolic work and prayer. Undoubtedly, they influenced scores of priestly vocations at this time, particularly among the children they taught. An older Franciscan priest once told me of how enchanted he was by his seventh-grade teaching Sister as she baton-twirled for the class after they earned so many good marks. He said that the Sisters who taught him encouraged his priestly vocation by their own example. Many priests of his generation speak of how a Sister in the school they attended encouraged their vocation to the priesthood. This also extends to the scores of young women who entered novitiates after high school; vocations, faithfully and joyfully lived, beget vocations.

In addition to their encouragement of other religious and priestly vocations, Sisters influenced those who have served in the civil and secular realm. In his autobiography, *My Grandfather's Son: A Memoir*, Supreme Court Justice Clarence Thomas recalls his Catholic elementary and high school education and praises the Sisters who taught him "that God made all men equal."[8] The Sisters clearly taught him why he existed: "We learned that

God made us to know, love, and serve Him in this world and to be happy with Him in the next."⁹ The Sisters gave Justice Thomas not only a good education but a clear understanding of his human dignity, which undoubtedly laid the foundation for his future years of civil service to our country.

SISTERS IN AMERICA: THE DECLINE

In the twenty-first century, the landscape appears to be quite different. Many people, even practicing Catholics, have never seen a Sister. Just recently I was stopped on the street by a mother and her young daughter. Despite her daughter's attendance at a Catholic school, the mother felt the need to make sure that her daughter met me since no such other example was in her life. I have had countless people approach me and ask, "Are you actually a nun? I didn't think anyone did that anymore!" The statistics speak to this reality: in 2017, there were 45,605 Sisters in the United States, which is about half the number of Sisters in 1995.¹⁰ Even more startling is that today only 1.6 percent of teachers in Catholic schools are Sisters, whereas they were the overwhelming majority fifty years ago.¹¹

The question of why there has been such a drastic decline in religious life membership is multi-faceted, but not as complex as some make it out to be. Some say that young women are simply not interested in religious life because they now have other career options. While it is true that women have more options now than they did in the 1950s, the truth of the matter is that the religious life is not one option among many, like choosing a university or career. *A vocation to religious life is not the same as a career.* It is a calling from God to which a young woman is invited to respond in love, no matter her other options. Indeed, God is still calling young women to the religious life and, thankfully, His invitation is not constrained by its apparent lack of popularity in our modern age.

But this fails to address the question of the decline in numbers. The modern age has brought with it some significant complexities for women discerning religious life, and these have reached into some religious communities as well. The Second Vatican Council called for the renewal of religious life to make it more fruitful in the modern age. The Council encouraged communities to make necessary reforms, yet some communities mingled these reforms with the social and political ideas of the 1960s, which had secularism as their end.[12] As a result, many communities thought that addressing the needs of the modern age meant moving out of the traditional apostolates of teaching and health care, altering their practices of prayer and community life, and putting off identifiable religious dress.

As Sisters disappeared from the classrooms, many young women were left without a concrete witness to the beauty of religious life. They began to move through their formative years not knowing what to do with the aching in their heart for the eternal "more" that so characterizes an authentic religious vocation. It is easy for a young woman to become distracted by both the good and not-so-good options presented to her by the modern world, leaving her unable to cultivate a quiet heart that listens to God. Thus, she fails to understand that her vocation is the most important thing in her life, something she needs to discover and whole-heartedly embrace. She may have an inkling of the call, but without the witness of Sisters in her life, she may not find much support or anyone who can adequately direct her. Additionally, she lives in a world that prizes material and professional success—which can make the vows of poverty, chastity, and obedience seem ridiculous and even cruel without a living example. For these reasons, and many others, the number of young women consecrating their lives to God for the good of the Church and the salvation of souls has drastically declined in the past fifty years.

SISTERS IN AMERICA: TODAY?

In present times, very few young women have frequent contact with Sisters during their early school years. This makes the way they discern a call and meet a religious community different than it was years ago. Certainly more Sisters teaching in schools would make a world of a difference for women answering the call, but at present, that is simply not the case. It is something we must build again and, in the meantime, we must be creative in helping a new generation hear God's call under different circumstances. God's grace is always active in every age. The fact that young women have answered the call in a noisy, distracting, and downright vice-filled modern age is indicative of the Holy Spirit's action in the present Church. It also points to the essential and enduring aspects of a growing religious community.

BREAKING IT DOWN

Examining what women who have recently entered religious life have reported about their upbringing and discernment is vital for understanding the current landscape of vocational discernment. According to a 2019 report by the Center for Applied Research in the Apostolate (CARA) at Georgetown University, young women entering religious life in 2018 were on average 19 years old when they first started considering a vocation. This is well past the school-age years

The Ages of Women Discerning a Vocation in 2018

Average age when starting to consider a vocation: Age 19

Average age of entering a religious order: Age 28

52% were under the age of 25

31% were between the ages of 26 and 36

when many older Sisters say they first experienced a call. Of young women who entered communities in 2018, their average age was 28 years old: 52 percent were under the age of 25, and 31 percent were between 26 and 36 years old. The report also considered where these young women were born and their racial and ethnic background, all of which is indicative of a growing shift in the Catholic cultural diversity in America: 75 percent were born in the United States, 9 percent were born in Asia, and 8 percent were born in Mexico or Latin America; 75 percent reported being of European/Caucasian background, 12 percent as Hispanic or Latino, and 10 percent as Asian. They have a variety of experiences related to their upbringing, yet the following statistics are notable: 7 percent were converts to Catholicism; 83 percent said both their parents were Catholic; and 75 percent said they had three or more siblings.[13] In general, these young women came from families where the Faith was given to them as a living example.

As for education, 41 percent of young women entering religious life received a Catholic education in at least elementary school, which is similar to other American Catholics. 20 percent were home-schooled for an average of four years. Since much of this essay has discussed the role of

Cultural Diversity

European/Caucasian: 75%

Hispanic/Latino: 12%

Asian: 10%

Upbringing

Catholic Parents: 83%

Converts to the Faith: 7%

3+ Siblings: 75%

Education

Catholic Education: 41%

Homeschool: 20%

Graduated with Undergraduate Degree: 50%

education, it is good to pause here. The CARA report notes that there is a correlation between the years of Catholic education received and the likelihood of entering religious life, noting that going to a Catholic high school and college on top of a Catholic elementary education made it more likely that a young person would enter religious life compared to other American Catholics who did not receive the same Catholic education. Yet a full Catholic education is sadly not available to all young American Catholics. Surprisingly, the majority of those entering religious life in 2018 did *not* attend a Catholic elementary school or high school.[14] Clearly God's grace is at work in the current situation, but imagine the impact on vocational discernment if young people received twelve or sixteen years of Catholic education *with* the presence of Sisters in their schools!

Given that young women report first discerning religious life at the age of 19, and that 50 percent had completed undergraduate degrees when they entered, it is important to note the role of faith formation programs in the years leading up to and during their time in college: 80 percent participated in retreats for young people, 40 percent participated in the March for Life in Washington, D.C., and 18 percent attended a World Youth Day (an international gathering of Catholic youths started by Pope Saint John Paul II in 1985). About half also participated in parish youth groups in high school, as well as in liturgical and catechetical ministry as parish volunteers.[15] Clearly the young women entering religious life sought to be formed by the teachings of the Church, experienced communal support in their spiritual life, and gave of their time and talents as laywomen prior to entering. They are a generation that sought to live an authentically Catholic life as they neared adulthood despite the increasingly secularized culture.

The role of the family in vocational discernment has new dimensions as well since religious life may not be held in as high esteem as it was in previous generations. Despite their mostly Catholic upbringing, just less than half of young women who entered religious life said that telling their family was easy and only 39 percent of young women were encouraged to consider a religious vocation when they were younger by family members. More likely, they received encouragement from members from a religious community, with 94 percent reporting such encounters that led to initial discernment. Likely from those encounters, they were put into contact with the community's vocation director with 91 percent saying that a vocation director greatly aided their discernment. Then, 67 percent attended a "come and see" retreat offered by the community, which is an opportunity for interested women to experience firsthand the community and their way of life. Others outside of the religious community encouraged vocations as well, with 90 percent of those who entered saying they were encouraged by a spiritual director, 83 percent by friends or people at their parish, 77 percent by priests, and 69 percent by a campus minister. Within their families, 66 percent were encouraged by their parents.[16] Compared to years past, encouragement to discern religious life has come from a variety of people within the Church, which is a reminder that

> **Events Attended**
>
> March for Life: 40%
>
> World Youth Day: 18%
>
> Parish youth groups, catechetical ministries, parish volunteers: ~50%

> **Sparks of Interest in a Vocation**
>
> Encouraged by family: 39%
>
> Encouraged by a Religious Community: 94%
>
> Assisted by a Vocation Director: 91%
>
> Attended a "Come and See" Retreat: 67%

people in all vocational and ministerial roles have the responsibility to encourage young people to consider the call. Yet, above all, this must be something discussed in families and encouraged at a young age by parents.

The way a young woman first met the community she entered highlights a variety of avenues for encounter, but there are some consistent factors as well. In our age of technology, it is not surprising that 31 percent first encountered their future community through an internet search, and 23 percent said that their community's social media posts or other media were influential in their discernment. Yet, 36 percent said they met the community through a recommendation from a friend or advisor.[17] These numbers accounts for one's initial contact with a community; the statistics show that personal contact with the community and its members through visits and conversation were what ultimately helped one discern an authentic call to religious life. Technology is a tool for discernment, especially when used as an initial introduction, but cannot replace the significance of personal contact. Young women discerning religious life know the seriousness of a call and seek out relationships to help them in their discernment, despite the cultural emphasis on social media.

After the initial introduction and contact with a religious community, a clear

Encouragement Along the Way

By a Spiritual Director: 90%

By Friends or Parish Community: 83%

By Priest(s): 77%

By Campus Minister: 69%

By Parents: 66%

Encountering the Community

Through Internet Search: 31%

Social Media & Other: 23%

Personal Recommendation: 36%

institutional identity and mission, dedication to communal prayer, and life in community are what over 90 percent of young women find attractive in a religious community. For example, 94 percent state that the community's fidelity to the Church's teachings is important to them. Of the 98 percent who said they desired communal prayer, 98 percent of those said they desired daily Mass and 86 percent the Liturgy of the Hours; 88 percent said that Eucharistic adoration is an important practice of prayer. Other devotional prayers, such as the Rosary, are favored by 82 percent of young women discerning religious life. Of the communities young women entered, 85 percent wear identifiable religious dress at all or at certain times. The sharing of a communal life with other members, which includes living, praying, recreating, working, and sharing meals together, is desired by over 90 percent of young women.[18] Thus, the essential elements of a religious community, in continuity with the Church's vision of consecrated life, is ultimately what is attractive to young women.

CONCLUSION: A FUTURE WITH HOPE

Despite the daunting statistics, the future of religious life in America is bright, because the young women entering are walking on firm ground. While they are significantly fewer in number than in the past, these young women understand and seek the authentic forms of prayer, community, and apostolic life that the Church holds as essential to the consecrated life. Many of them discerned their call in a much different way than in the past and with many personal and cultural obstacles. Vocation directors, "come and see" retreats, college campus ministry, websites, and social media are now prominent aids in discernment and to posing the initial question: "Have you ever thought about religious life?" Yet, ultimately, nothing replaces relationships that encourage spiritual growth and openness to a religious vocation. Above all, the Holy Spirit is active despite the downfalls and wrong turns of the past and despite the present secularized culture.

These statistics—and more importantly, the story behind them—show us that the Church needs more Sisters, not just to support its institutions, but to be a prayerful light in this very dark world. The presence of women religious and the power of their consecration can indeed transform hearts. God is still calling young women to this way of life, and there is no need to think that the drop in numbers is irreversible. Rather, it is a matter of helping young women listen for that call and respond to it with courage. Encouraging religious vocations is the responsibility of the entire Church, but no one does it more authentically than a religious Sister herself. A vocation lived in love necessarily encourages more young people to follow give—to Jesus Christ

> ### What's Attractive?
> Communal Life: over 90%
>
> Fidelity to Church's Teaching: 94%
>
> Daily Mass: 98%
>
> Liturgy of the Hours: 86%
>
> Eucharistic Adoration: 88%
>
> Other Devotionals (such as the Rosary): 82%
>
> Identifiable Religious Dress: 85%

and to the world—in a total way. This will always be attractive, in every time and place, to those who truly seek. As in years past, may a plentiful harvest of generous women respond to the call to be living monuments of the joy of the Gospel and lights in the world.

NOTES

1. For a general history of the Catholic Church in America, see Dolan, J.P., *The American Catholic Experience: A History from Colonial Times to the Present*, (Garden City, NY: Doubleday, 1985).

2. Livermore, M. *What Shall We Tell Our Daughters: Superfluous Women and Other Lectures,* (Boston: Lee and Shepard, 1883), 117-178.

3. Hennesey, J., *American Catholics: A History of the Roman Catholic Community in the United States*, (Oxford: Oxford University Press, 1981), 173.

4. Stewart, G.C., *Marvels of Charity: History of American Sisters and Nuns*, (Huntington, IN: Our Sunday Visitor, 1994), 565.

5. The Academy of Motion Picture Arts and Sciences, The 17th Academy Awards: 1945, *Oscars Ceremonies*, 2015, http://www.oscars.org/oscars/ceremonies/1945. The 18th Academy Awards: 1946, http://www.oscars.org/oscars/ceremonies/1946. For more on Catholic culture at this time, see Massa, M.S., *Catholics and American Culture: Fulton Sheen, Dorothy Day, and the Notre Dame Football Team,* (New York: Crossroad, 1999).

6. National Catholic Educational Association, "Catholic School Data: Enrollment and Staffing", 2019, https://www.ncea.org/NCEA/Proclaim/Catholic_School_Data/Enrollment_and_Staffing/NCEA/Proclaim/Catholic_School_Data/Enrollment_and_Staffing.aspx

7. Ibid.

8. Thomas, Clarence, *My Grandfather's Son: A Memoir*, (New York: HarperCollins, 2007), 14-15, 29.

9. Ibid., 15.

10. Center for Applied Research in the Apostolate, "Clergy, Religious, and Lay Leaders", *Frequently Requested Church Statistics*, 2020, http://cara.georgetown.edu/frequently-requested-church-statistics/

11. NCEA, "Catholic School Data: Enrollment and Staffing".

12. For more discussion on the history of religious life post-Vatican II, see Carey, A., *Sisters in Crisis Revisited: From Unraveling to Reform and Renewal*, (San Francisco: Ignatius Press, 2013). Also, see *Perfectae Caritatis: The Decree on the Adaptation and Renewal of Religious Life* issued by the Second Vatican Council in 1965.

13. Gautier, M. L., Bandiho, H.A. & Do, T.T., "Women and Men Entering Religious Life: The Entrance Class of 2018", *Center for Applied*

Research in the Apostolate, 9-13, 20, https://cara.georgetown.edu/EntranceClass2018.pdf. This report represents 70 percent of those who entered religious life in 2018.

14   Ibid., 14-15.
15   Ibid., 14, 18-19.
16   Ibid., 16-17, 20, 30.
17   Ibid., 27.
18   Ibid., 25, 38.

> "Most of our parishes today are single parent homes! In many places across the United States we have a number of wonderful priests who are great spiritual fathers. Many young men are answering the call to this noble vocation. However, there is something these great and faithful priests cannot give: the gift of motherhood that only the Sisters can give!
>
> – Fr. James Junipero Moore, OP
> Oakland, CA"

Two Suitcases and the Rest of One's Life

Living the Charism of a Religious Order or Community

Sister Hyacinth Hayward, OP
Born in Ottawa, Ontario, Canada

What makes a young woman pack her life into two suitcases and leave her city, her state, or even her country, to enter a convent? People wonder: "Why don't you just enter the Sisters who have a convent close by? Why move so far away? Isn't it all pretty similar?"

For a little perspective, let's look at this from a different, more familiar lens: marriage. If you are going to get married, you want to find the right man, even if that means that you have to move across the country to do so. If people were to tell you that you should marry the closest available man, as they are all fairly similar, you would probably think they were a little crazy. "It's not just about his being available," you would say. "We have to be right for each other. There is only one man I am meant to spend my life with and I have to find him—husbands are not interchangeable!"

Yes, husbands are not interchangeable—and neither are

religious communities. Each religious order, each individual religious congregation, is unique, and the Lord calls a young woman not to a generic religious vocation, but to be a religious within a specific community. While communities share some common aspects, what makes each one distinct is its charism, which is a special grace given by God for the building up of the Church. To see how this affects the way a woman lives out her religious life, we will divide this chapter into two major sections. First, we will look at religious life and charism through the lens of discernment. Second, we will examine in detail the way a charism influences the elements of religious life, using the case study of the Dominican charism.

> "Charisms are graces of the Holy Spirit which directly or indirectly benefit the Church, ordered as they are to her building up, to the good of men, and to the needs of the world."
>
> Catechism of the Catholic Church, 799

PART I: RELIGIOUS LIFE AND CHARISM
COMMON ASPECTS OF RELIGIOUS LIFE: AM I CALLED TO BE A RELIGIOUS?

For most of us, the first aspect of vocation that we discern is a general one: am I called to be a religious? In my own journey to religious life, this was certainly the first stage. As I grew in my faith and in my life of prayer and intimacy with the Lord, I felt a pull on my heart—one that was essentially saying: "I want you for Myself." There were no actual words, no Saint Paul-like moment of revelation and conversion, but a slow, growing tugging at my heart. I came to know that the Lord was calling me to be a religious, but I didn't know where. I just knew that I was being called.

Called to what, you might ask? What are the basic elements of religious Life? Perhaps they could be listed as follows: consecration, prayer, apostolate, and community. We will consider each of these elements.

CONSECRATION

Religious women are consecrated to God through the public profession of vows. Our vows of poverty, chastity and obedience set us apart for God and for service to the Church. This act of profession roots each Sister in her identity as a bride of Christ. This is the common bond which unites all religious—we are set apart for God.

PRAYER

Canon Law tells us that "The first and foremost duty of all religious is the contemplation of divine things and assiduous union with God in prayer."[1] Every community has a life of prayer, both communal and individual, liturgical and private. Prayer and the sacraments, particularly the Mass, are the central focus of our day. While each religious congregation has different expressions and methods of prayer, time set aside for contemplation of God is an essential element for all religious.

APOSTOLATE

In addition to a life of prayer, religious live a life of service to the Church. This service is called an apostolate and may take various forms. It is here, much more visibly than in the life of prayer, that young women who are discerning begin to distinguish between the charisms of the various religious orders and congregations. Sisters carry out many apostolates within the Church: teaching, nursing, working with the poor, and numerous others.

COMMUNITY

All religious institutes live some form of community life. Part of the witness of religious is given through the way we live, work, and pray together. Religious are called to be a sign of the Kingdom of Heaven, which is not a collection of individual people doing their own thing, but a communion of saints united in adoration and worship of God.

NOT "ONE SIZE FITS ALL": RELIGIOUS ORDERS AND SPIRITUALITIES

After recognizing that one is being called to religious life, the next step is to look more closely at the specific religious family to which one may be called. Within the Catholic Church there are many different religious orders and families, comprising priests and Brothers, nuns and active Sisters, and lay people, who are united in a common spirituality and charism given to their founders. This vast array can be rather daunting to consider, as each religious order or congregation has a unique charism at the service of the Church.

Perhaps the best way to think about the great variety of religious is to consider it in the same way Saint Thomas Aquinas does in speaking of the multiplicity of creation:

Because [God's] goodness could not be adequately represented by one creature alone, He produced many and diverse creatures, that what was wanting to one in the representation of the divine goodness might be supplied by another. For goodness, which in God is simple and uniform, in creatures is manifold and divided and hence the whole universe together participates the divine goodness more perfectly, and represents it better, than any single creature whatever.[2]

If we simply substitute "religious charism" for "creature" in this passage we see the reason for the great variety among religious orders: they represent God's infinite goodness. Once we recognize the purpose of having diverse charisms and Communities, we then have to ask: "Where do I fit?" While the Church's history has been blessed by countless orders and congregations, we will briefly discuss a few main orders and their charisms.

BENEDICTINES

While not specifically an order, the Benedictine tradition traces its history to the founder of Western monasticism, Saint Benedict of Nursia. The Benedictine tradition of *ora et labora* (prayer and work) has attracted people for more than a thousand years.

Others who follow the Rule of Saint Benedict include the Cistercians and the Trappists, both of which began as a reform of the monastic life intended by Saint Benedict. Saints such

as Saint Gregory the Great, Saint Bernard of Clairvaux, Saint Scholastica, and Saint Gertrude all found their way to holiness through this spirituality.

CARMELITES

Tracing their spiritual heritage to Elijah and the hermits of Mount Carmel, the Carmelite Order is perhaps best understood through the lives and work of some of its many saints: Saint Teresa of Avila, Saint John of the Cross, Saint Thérèse of Lisieux, Saint Elizabeth of the Trinity, and Saint Teresa Benedicta of the Cross (Edith Stein). The Carmelite spirituality centers on a direct experience of God in prayer. In works such as *The Way of Perfection* and *The Dark Night of the Soul*, Carmelite saints highlight that each individual comes to know God more deeply through progressive purification.

FRANCISCANS

The Franciscans, who were founded by Saint Francis of Assisi in the early thirteenth century, are one of the great mendicant orders, along with the Dominicans and the Carmelites. This

means that they supported themselves by begging. The hallmark of the Franciscan life is poverty—Saint Francis would often speak fondly of "Lady Poverty". While Franciscans may be found teaching and nursing, they are best known for their work with the poor. The Franciscan order is home to many great saints, including Saint Anthony of Padua, Saint Bonaventure, Saint Clare, and Saint Agnes of Prague.

DOMINICANS

The Order of Preachers (Dominicans) was founded by Saint Dominic in 1216. For eight hundred years Dominicans have been living the charism of the order—to preach and teach the truth—in many different ways. As study is an essential part of the charism, they are often involved in education at some level. The saints of the Dominican order give witness to a great variety of gifts: scholars, such as Saint Thomas Aquinas and Saint Albert the Great; artists, such as Blessed Fra Angelico; and preachers, such as Saint Vincent Ferrer and Saint Hyacinth. The women saints of the Order of Preachers are no less illustrious, and include Saint Catherine of Siena, Saint Rose of Lima, Blessed Imelda, and Saint Catherine de Ricci.

FINDING THE RIGHT FAMILY: RELIGIOUS CONGREGATIONS

When I was discerning religious life, I had a good friend at the university who was also discerning. We both decided to attend a retreat held by the Dominican Sisters of Mary, Mother of the Eucharist in Ann Arbor, Michigan. We arrived with two different frames of mind: she was pretty sure this was the Community she was going to enter, while I did not really know where God wanted me and was not overly interested in teaching. God had other plans for both of us. I left the retreat with application papers, and she left knowing that she was called to religious life, but not in this specific community. She is now a Sister of Life.

While my friend and I each discerned religious life in communities who have very different charisms, the same scenario can occur when we discern congregations that share a basic charism or spirituality. Each Dominican, Franciscan, or other congregation is unique. While they share the basic charism of their order, it is manifested in each congregation in varied ways; rather like families, no two congregations are exactly alike.

I had the opportunity to study this past summer with Dominican Sisters from two other congregations. While there is great joy when we meet to study or pray together, at the same time these gatherings highlight the differences that make our congregations unique. Some of our Sisters, as well as those from other Dominican communities, have said that when they first visited a Dominican congregation, they knew they were called to be a Dominican, but knew that it was not in that specific community.

What does this all mean for a young woman discerning religious life? First, remember that no two communities are exactly alike. If you are attracted to the basic charism and spirituality of an order, don't be worried if the first community you visit doesn't seem to be the perfect fit. If it seems close, perhaps you should continue looking at other communities which are tied to the same order, whether Dominican, Franciscan, Carmelite, Benedictine, or something else. If you find that it is not so much a question of the right "family spirit," but more a question of the larger way that order lives religious life, perhaps you should take some time to look at other communities outside of that specific order.

> No two Communities are exactly alike.

Second, remember that you are not in charge. God has a way of surprising us and inviting us to a life that we might not have thought about or preferred on a natural level. The amazing thing is that as we say "yes" to the call to religious life in the congregation to which God has called us, we grow ever more deeply in love with Him through living and assimilating the charism of our specific congregation.

PART II: LIVING THE CHARISM
THE ROAD TO HEAVEN

In this second part of the chapter, we discuss what happens once a young woman crosses the threshold of the convent to begin her religious life. By entering religious life, she is saying, in effect, that she believes this is the way God is calling her to get to heaven. When she makes her Final Profession of Vows, she knows this definitively. Her whole religious life is shaped and lived according to the specific charism of her religious community. A Sister's whole life, whether she is in initial formation or under final vows, is spent learning and deepening her understanding of the specific charism of her community. The basic building blocks of religious life, which we mentioned in the first part of this chapter, now resolve into greater clarity as they are refined in the practice of a specific charism.

One of the most poignant ways this occurs is through the observance of the vows. The three vows of poverty, chastity, and obedience are joined in some congregations by a fourth vow, usually related to the community's charism. For example, the Religious Sisters of Mercy of Alma, Michigan, vow "to serve the poor, sick, and ignorant"[3], while the Sisters of Life make a fourth vow "to protect and enhance the sacredness of human life"[4], and the Missionaries of Charity profess "wholehearted and free service to the poorest of the poor"[5]. Conversely, the Dominican nuns, following the tradition of the Dominican order, profess only obedience, because poverty and chastity are both considered to be contained within the vow of obedience.

GETTING TO HEAVEN THE DOMINICAN WAY: THE DOMINICAN LIFE AND CHARISM IN DETAIL

To demonstrate how the charism of a religious community shapes the foundational elements of religious life in more depth, I will use the example of the Dominican charism as it is lived by the Dominican Sisters of Mary, Mother of the Eucharist, since this is the charism with which I am most familiar. Although our practice may differ slightly from other Dominican congregations, the main aspects of the Dominican charism will be the same.

CONSECRATION

While the Dominican nuns and friars profess only the vow of obedience, active religious Sisters profess the three vows of poverty, chastity and obedience. As Dominicans, we are called to preach and teach the truth of Christ to all, and so the way we live out our vows is consonant with that end. Here is a brief look at a Dominican understanding of the three vows.

POVERTY

- Dominican poverty is modeled on the poverty of Christ and the apostles who were itinerant preachers. Our lack of material goods makes it easier for us to "get up and go" wherever we may be sent. It is a reminder to others and to ourselves that Christ is our greatest treasure. Dominican poverty is poverty for mission. Material things are not bad, but our renouncing them frees us to be available to bring

> "Christ proposes the evangelical counsels, in their great variety, to every disciple."
> -Catechism of the Catholic Church, 915

God's message of truth to the world without being caught up in the world.

CHASTITY

- Dominican chastity is founded in the essential goodness of the human being as body and soul. Saint Dominic founded the Order of Preachers while combating the Albigensian heresy, which was rampant in the Languedoc region of France at the beginning of the thirteenth century. One of the major tenets of the Albigensians was the belief that all matter was evil. Thus, they held that even the human body and marriage were evil. Saint Dominic challenged the beliefs of the Albigensians by proclaiming that the body is good. Saint Dominic is still known for his nine ways of prayer, which are ways of praying using both body and soul.

- The vow of chastity is an essential aid to Dominican study and contemplation. Chastity frees us to love God with our whole heart and to love others with His love. Chastity helps us to guard our purity of heart, which, according to Saint Thomas, assists us in our contemplation of God as the practice of the virtues render us more like Him.[6]

OBEDIENCE

- Obedience is the hallmark of Dominican life. As previously mentioned, the Dominican nuns and friars only profess the vow of obedience, since the vows of poverty and chastity and all they entail fall under obedience.

- Obedience gives us the assurance of using our talents for the salvation of souls. In living a life of obedience, we are configured ever more closely to Christ, who became "obedient to death, even death on a cross" (Phil 2:8). At no moment of His life was Christ the Preacher more eloquent than in the few words He spoke from the cross. It is through our conformity to Christ on the cross by our vow of obedience that our preaching and teaching are made effective. Through this conformity to Christ we are truly able to recognize that our lives are not about us or what we are able to do on our own. Rather, the Order's work for the salvation of souls is really about allowing the Lord to use us as He knows best, through the mediation of our superiors.

- Dominicans, in love with truth, place great emphasis on the fact that obedience must be intelligent. We are not automatons, and we recognize that our intellect and will are gifts which render us capable of knowing God through grace. The early desert fathers' tests of obedience—which often featured ridiculous or futile tasks like planting things upside down, just to see if the subject would obey—do not find a home in a modern Dominican community. I have never yet met any Dominican who was asked to plant cabbages upside down!

PRAYER: PREACHING TO THE PREACHERS

Prayer, both communal and private, is essential to the Dominican life. Before founding the Order of Preachers, Saint Dominic was a canon—a priest dedicated to the celebration of the liturgy—in the cathedral church of Osma, Spain. Because of his deep formation in and devotion to the liturgy, he bequeathed to the whole Order a great love for the Mass and the Liturgy of the Hours. As a Community, we gather daily in the chapel to pray the hours of Lauds, Daytime Prayer, Vespers, and Compline together.

Perhaps the best summation of the role of the Divine Office in the life of a Dominican Community comes from Father Bruno Cadoré, former Master of the Order of Preachers:

> "Prayer is the raising of one's mind and heart to God or the requesting of good things from God."
> —Saint John Damascene

> The liturgical celebration of the Hours, repeated several times a day in community, must be a time when the Word of God, and not ourselves, comes to be our center. It is when we allow the Word to seize us, to take hold of our desire to give our life and enable this desire to do far more that we could ever do ourselves. This celebration repeated each day and in each liturgical Hour gives us the courage to expose ourselves to the Word; to listen to the words of Scripture and the prayers of the tradition; to become accustomed to the familiarity that the Word wants to have with us; to discern through the words of Scripture the face of the Son that is revealed and who is the very source of obedience. We need constantly to regain our strength, to take heart. It is in this mystery of the liturgy that we learn how to do this, or better, in the liturgy we can implore the Lord to do it in us.[7]

The rhythm of prayer for a Dominican is an essential part of the interplay between our life of contemplation and our active life in the apostolate. As Father Cadoré continues, "The liturgical celebration of the Hours is the place par excellence where our communities bring into the presence of God our aspirations for the world to which we are sent as Preachers."[8] The work of the apostolate fuels our prayer, yet at the same time our life of prayer and contemplation of God fuel our apostolic desire to go out and make God's love known to others.

The Dominican method of praying the Office is itself designed to lead us to contemplation and to foster zeal for souls. The community chants the psalms in two choirs facing each other. During the psalms, the two sides of the choir alternate sitting and standing, which symbolizes the proclamation of the Word to each other. During the "Glory be to the Father" at the end of each psalm, we bow profoundly, as did Saint Dominic, humbling ourselves before the majesty of God. In the very gestures of our prayers we preach to ourselves, and to those who may join us for prayer, of the great goodness of God and of the respect that we owe Him.

Within the setting of the hours of the Divine Office, the jewel of the Eucharist shines out. As a community, we have an hour of Eucharistic Adoration daily, allowing us time face to face with our Spouse. The community Mass is the high point of our day. It is from here that we derive the strength for our apostolate. It is only fitting that immediately after receiving the Lord in Holy Communion we go out to our work for the day. It reminds us that we are to bring, not ourselves, but Christ to souls.

Another aspect of our community prayer that is deeply rooted in the Dominican tradition is devotion to Mary. This occurs *par excellence* in the daily communal renewal of each Sister's Marian consecration. The recitation of the Rosary is also given an important place, prayed as a community immediately after Vespers. Tradition holds that the Rosary was given to Saint Dominic by the Blessed Mother as a weapon in the fight against heresy. Throughout history, Dominicans have been at the forefront of preaching about the Rosary. This devotion provides an avenue for contemplating the mysteries of Christ's

> Within the setting of the hours of the Divine Office, the jewel of the Eucharist shines out.

life with His mother, helping us to grow deeper in our love and knowledge of God.

APOSTOLATE: PREACHING THE WORD

The year 2016 marked the 800th Jubilee of the Order of Preachers. Dominicans today are still following the charism and apostolate that Saint Dominic first laid out in 1216. Over time, some religious orders either cease to exist or, like the military orders of the Middle Ages, have had to change their apostolate, since their original apostolate is no longer necessary. Preaching the truth, however, is always in season, and so there is always work for Dominicans to do!

The Dominican apostolate can be summed up in the various mottos of the Order: *Veritas* (Truth), *Contemplare et contemplata aliis tradere* (To contemplate and to give to others the fruit of one's contemplation), and *Laudare, Benedicere, Praedicare* (To praise, to bless, to preach). At first glance, these may seem rather broad ideas from which to distill a concrete apostolate, but they all point to the same reality of preaching and teaching truth.

The apostolate of holy preaching takes on a different hue in each Dominican congregation. As women religious, we do not preach in the strict sense of preaching during Mass, but in the broader sense of proclaiming truth. The main manifestation of the preaching charism in our community is through Christian education. As teachers, we bring our love of truth to our students, helping them to encounter Christ in their studies. Dominicans recognize that all truth is a participation in the first Truth, who is God. Thus the study of any discipline, when approached with humility and openness, can lead us to a deeper knowledge of God. Seeing the order of creation through the sciences leads us to contemplate God's wisdom; the beauty of art and music help us to know God's beauty. In math, graphing limits, which approach infinity but never reach it, can lead us to ponder what it means to say God is infinite. Building on this implicit preaching within mainstream academic disciplines, Dominicans explicitly preach the faith. We aim to teach our students both the doctrines of the faith and also how to live them by cultivating a life of virtue.

> In order to preach the truth, Dominicans must first come to know it.

Outside of the classroom, we preach the truth by giving retreats and talks, writing, singing, and many other activities. Preaching occurs within everyday encounters; sometimes it is explicit, and sometimes we preach through the example of our lives. Whether it is answering someone's questions on a plane or interacting with fellow students while studying at a university, we are always seeking to bring people to an encounter with Jesus Christ, who is Truth.

In order to preach the truth, Dominicans must first come to know it. Thus, study is an essential part of the Dominican charism. This first means the study of theology, but it extends to other subjects as well, particularly those needed for our work of teaching. Dominican study is not simply an intellectual exercise but rather an avenue to contemplation. It is not as though a chasm separates the choir and the classroom; they are multiple expressions of one reality.

As was mentioned in the discussion of prayer, contemplation of divine truth and the active work of preaching are intimately linked. We sometimes speak of balancing these two aspects as though they were two sides of a coin, where only one side is visible at a time. While making the point that contemplation and action are equally part of the Dominican life, this analogy falls flat in that it introduces a false dichotomy, as though one can be contemplative or active but not both at once.

I would like to propose as an alternative the image of the ocean tides. The ebb and flow of the tide is very much like the Dominican life. We are always to be centered on God and in the contemplation of truth, but we are often pulled out into the world to meet the needs of our fellow man. Similarly, when the tide comes in it does not lose its connection to the rest of the ocean, but brings the ocean to the dry land. The tidal ebb can be seen as our return from the world to the cloister at the end of the day. What I find attractive in this analogy is the fact that if we see our contemplation of truth as the essential aspect of our life, then we see can see the ocean as our Dominican life. What changes with the tides is not the ocean itself, but the location of the water—being pulled out of itself towards the land and then returning to the depths. What changes in Dominican life is, in like measure, the location and expression of our contemplation of truth.

COMMUNITY LIFE

Community life is an essential part of the Dominican life. Saint Dominic sent his first friars out two by two, in the tradition of Jesus sending out the seventy-two disciples two by two, to preach the Gospel. Living in community strengthens us in our vocation and intensifies the witness of our lives.

No one can live in isolation, and this is an essential truth in religious life as well. We need the other members of our community—just as those in the world need the members of their family—to call us out of ourselves to a life of self-giving love. Community life strengthens each Sister in her own vocation through the faithful witness of her fellow Sisters. We find support when times are challenging, and we give that support to others as well. Community calls us on to holiness.

Spending time with our Sisters also strengthens us by giving us time for leisure. Each evening we spend an hour of recreation together. This can involve anything from playing board games to working on crafts, to simply sitting and talking. How we spend the time is less important than the fact that we are able to be together and to rest from the work of the day.

While community life is essential to the living of our vocation within the convent, it is also an important part of our apostolate as well. We have a corporate apostolate—not in the sense of a corporation, but in the sense of a body: we share an apostolate as a community. Normally we have at least two, and in some cases as many as five or six Sisters in a school in which we teach. When we work together at a school, we give witness not only to the fact that God exists, but also to the reality that the following of Christ is a deeply fulfilling and joyful way of life.

> "The vocation of humanity is to show forth the image of God and to be transformed into the image of the Father's only Son. This vocation takes a personal form since each of us is called to enter into the divine beatitude; it also concerns the human community as a whole."
>
> -Catechism of the Catholic Church, 1877

MONASTIC LIFE WITHIN AN ACTIVE COMMUNITY

In addition to the elements shared by all religious congregations, Dominicans also have an additional wellspring of tradition that provides an important dimension of living our charism as preachers of truth. From the beginning, Saint

Dominic included certain monastic observances in the life of the order. These all contribute to building and sustaining within the convent an atmosphere conducive to contemplation and sacred study, so that in the classroom and elsewhere, we can be effective preachers and teachers. Saint Dominic gave to these monastic practices, already well established in religious orders in his time, a specific orientation toward the salvation of souls.

SILENCE IS GOLDEN

The order's saying, *Silentium pater praedicatorum,* means "Silence is the father of preachers." In observing times and places of silence, we are given the physical and mental space necessary to pray, study, and live in God's presence without external distractions. It is this climate that fosters the contemplation necessary to the life of a Dominican; our prayer fuels our apostolic work, and we share with others that which we have first spent time contemplating in silence. As Dominican Sisters of Mary, Mother of the Eucharist, we observe silence daily in the morning before leaving the convent for the apostolate, as well as after Compline in the evenings. Our meals are normally taken in silence while a Sister reads aloud from a spiritual book. This spiritual reading allows us to feed our minds upon truth even as we feed our bodies. On special feast days and holidays, dispensation from the usual silence allows us to live the liturgical year with greater intensity. Even on feast days, however, we maintain silence in certain places in the convent, including the chapel, sacristy, and cells. This designates these locations as very special places set aside for encounter with and contemplation of God, regardless of the time or day.

> "Silence is God's first language."
> —Saint John of the Cross

CLOISTER

The word cloister usually conjures up images of nuns who never leave their monastery. Certainly, the most well-known kind of cloister is that lived by contemplatives who neither leave the convent nor invite others to come into the enclosure. As an active religious community, we are not cloistered in this sense, because we must leave the convent during the day in order to teach and study. However, there are still parts of our convent designated "cloister", meaning that they are reserved for the exclusive use of the Sisters. While we go out to the world to preach and teach, we do not allow the world full access to our life. This separation provides a protected space, away from the bustle of the world, for us to be alone with God and with our Sisters. Without this space for our prayer and religious life, we simply could not serve the souls entrusted to us.

PENANCE

No life, whether religious or lay, is complete without some form of sacrifice. We see this vividly in family life: for example, parents waking up in the middle of the night to care for a sick child, or spouses making compromises for each other's good. In the Dominican charism, penance, like every other aspect of our life, is at the service of the salvation of souls. Saint Dominic prayed and sacrificed nightly in reparation for his own sins and those of others. Unfortunately, today penance is often viewed with distaste or mistrust. But recall for a moment the aforementioned sacrifices of parents. Would they say that they would rather dispose of their child and be comfortable? No. Usually the answer is, "It's worth it. It may be hard, but it's worth it."

> No life, whether religious or lay, is complete without some form of sacrifice.

Penance in religious life ought to follow a similar pattern. It is not about great acts of mortification but about living each aspect of our life faithfully and embracing the small and big sacrifices that flow naturally each day from that fidelity. These sacrifices open our hearts to love God and souls with a purer love. We also should be able to say, "It's worth it."

IT IS WORTH IT!

Yes, it is worth it! Religious life, lived with fidelity to the founding charism, brings all sorts of challenges, adventures, and surprises. But when we are living the life to which we are called and for which we are made, we will experience the joy Christ wishes to share with us. The Lord reminded the apostles that in His Father's house there are many mansions (see Jn 14:2), just as in our mother the Church, there are many religious orders and charisms. The Lord's promise to prepare a place for the apostles applies equally to each young woman called to religious life. If He calls you to religious life, He will prepare a place for you—not a one-size-fits-all answer but a place in a specific congregation, following a specific charism and path to holiness.

NOTES

1. *Code of Canon Law*, Latin-English Edition (Washington, D.C.: Canon Law Society of America, 1995), 663, §1.

2. Thomas Aquinas, *Summa Theologica*, trans. Fathers of the English Dominican Province, (Benzinger Brothers, 1947), I Q.47 a. 1. http://dhspriory.org/thomas/summa/FP/FP047.html#FPQ47OUTP1.

3. "Vows," *Religious Sisters of Mercy, Alma, Michigan*, http://rsmofalma.org/vows/vows.html.

4. "About Us," *Sisters of Life*, http://www.sistersoflife.org/about-the-sisters-of-life.

5. "Missionaries of Charity—Region of the Immaculate Conception—East Coast/USA & Canada," *Council of Major Superiors of Women Religious*, http://cmswr.org/member-communities/member-communities/74-missionaries-of-charity-region-of-the-immaculate-conception-east-coast-usa-canada.

6. Thomas Aquinas, *Super Evangelium* S. Matthaei lectura, trans. R.F. Larcher, O.P., 5-2, http://dhspriory.org/thomas/SSMatthew.htm#5.

7. Bruno Cadoré, OP, "*Laudare, Praedicare, Benedicere*: Letter on the Liturgical Celebrations of the Hours," 4, (Rome, 2012), http://www.op.org/sites/www.op.org/files/public/documents/fichier/cadore_letter_hours-en.pdf. Emphasis in the original.

8. Ibid, 2.

Living the Charism of a Religious Order or Community

> "To see a religious Sister is to catch a glimpse of the Blessed Mother. In schools, sisters reveal Our Lady raising our Lord at home in Nazareth. With the poor, sick, and dying, sisters show us Mary on Calvary. In their chapels, one hears the echo of Mary's earthly Magnificat and heavenly intercession. I am so very thankful to our Sisters because this world is less whole when it lacks their Marian presence. I pray this book would help any young woman called by God to religious life say, "Fiat.""

— Fr. Christopher Sullivan
Saint Rose of Lima Parish
Massapequa, NY

No How-To Manual

Formation of Young Women in the Novitiate

Sister John Mary Corbett, OP
Born in Yonkers, NY

Peter said to him in reply, "Lord, if it is you, command me to come to you on the water." He said, "Come." Peter got out of the boat and began to walk on the water toward Jesus. But when he saw how [strong] the wind was he became frightened; and, beginning to sink, he cried out, "Lord, save me!" Immediately, Jesus stretched out his hand and caught him, and said to him, "O you of little faith, why did you doubt?" (Mt 14:28-31).

What did Peter see in the eyes of Jesus as he met His approaching gaze while walking toward Him on the sea? The Scriptures do not reveal an answer to this question. What we do know is that Peter trusted Jesus enough to come at His bidding and follow Him out onto the water. As Peter fixed his gaze on the Lord, he stepped out into the unknown, and walked on the water toward Jesus, something impossible by his own power. When Peter diverted his attention from Jesus and noticed the wind, his faith wavered, and he began to slip. But not a moment passed before his cry was heard, and the strong hand of Jesus raised him up and drew him to Himself, back into the safety of the boat.

> Who cannot recall a time in her following of Christ when her faith was shaken by the experience of her own weakness...and when she was subsequently buoyed up by the saving hand of Christ?

Many fruitful insights can and have been gleaned from this poignant account in Saint Matthew's Gospel. Who cannot recall a time in her following of Christ when her faith was shaken by the experience of her own weakness or perhaps painful suffering or circumstances in the family, and when she was subsequently buoyed up by the saving hand of Christ, either through prayer, the grace of the sacraments, or the advice and support of a friend? This Gospel passage may also serve as a valuable point of departure for observations about another area at the heart of the Church's life, which necessitates no less courage or faith: the formation of young women entering religious communities today as postulants and novices.

STEPPING INTO AND OUT OF THE BOAT

The young woman accepted into a religious community makes an initial, radical choice for Christ in response to a supernatural call of grace. Likewise, when we meet Peter in this narrative, he has already been called by Christ; he is already in

Formation of Young Women in the Novitiate

the boat. It is as if he is a few months into his postulancy. He is evidently one of Christ's followers, but we know that he is not yet ready to lay down his life for Christ. His faith has to be tested, and he has much more to learn from living closely with Christ as His disciple. The time of formation as a postulant and novice in religious life may be likened to the time of preparation and instruction that Peter and the apostles spent with Christ during the three years of His public ministry. This time affords the Sister the precious opportunity to test her vocation and to discern, under the guidance of her superiors, if indeed He is calling her to a particular community. After responding to the initial call by entering a community, or "getting into the boat", she must then step out in faith onto the water and live out her vocation in community by fully engaging in the formation process. She will not be alone and will have others to assist her in keeping her eyes fixed on Christ as she moves forward in the adventure that is religious life.

A GIFT FROM ABOVE

There is something observable about one who is deeply in love: she has a one-track mind, or rather, a one-*person* mind. She is preoccupied with her beloved. He is the center of her thoughts and desires. She wishes only to please him and is happiest when she is with him. The same may be said of the bride of Christ who has found happiness in her vocation. The vocation to belong to Christ as His bride in religious life is a response to a divine call for a more radical union with Christ patterned after His own way of loving. This vocation is a gift from God and invites an ongoing response in freedom.

> The religious life makes no sense if we lose sight of its supernatural dimension.

One of my favorite musicals as a child was *Annie*,

especially the song "It's a Hard-Knock Life". This song has come back to me frequently, and I have often thought that one song a religious could appropriately sing in her heart would be: "It's a supernatural life for us!" As long as the religious is humbly aware of her calling's unique origin, she will seek Him above all else, and be able to live her vocation with great joy and freedom, relating all things in this life to Him as He desires. The religious life makes no sense if we lose sight of its supernatural dimension. During my years serving as a postulant mistress and novice mistress, I sought to draw the Sisters' attention as frequently as possible to this fundamental reality.

The papal apostolic exhortation *Vita Consecrata* states beautifully, "Formation should therefore have a profound effect on individuals, so that their every attitude and action, at important moments as well as in the ordinary events of life, will show that they belong completely and joyfully to God."[1] The postulant and novice became daughters of God at their Baptism. As religious, they are called to a deepening of their baptismal promises through the profession of religious vows, by which they will belong to Christ even more intimately.

The young woman accepted into the religious community is responding to this divine call from God, Whom she believes is inviting her to love Him more perfectly in this life unto the next. She enters into religious life knowing that He is inviting her to sacrifice the great goods of an earthly marriage and children, free use of material possessions, and self-determination, for the sake of higher, supernatural goods. These sacrifices are only possible by God's grace and in response to His call, with humble awareness that He will sustain her.

THE GIFT OF TIME

Jesus does not mince words when He tells His disciples, "And everyone who has given up houses or brothers or sisters or father or mother or children or lands for the sake of my name will receive a hundred times more, and will inherit eternal life" (Mt 19:29). The young women do, indeed, leave behind what is familiar to begin

> "Teach us to give and not count the cost."
> -Saint Ignatius of Loyola

a new life out of love for Christ on their entrance day, and they learn quickly that this radical surrender is not a "once and for all" experience. The Lord will call her to a lifetime of *fiats*, and each day will bring new opportunities to renew her "yes" as she comes to understand more intimately Who it is that has called her and the life He has called her to embrace. Emboldened by his budding faith, Saint Peter left his father and his fishing nets to follow Jesus, but he still had much to learn about discipleship and what it meant to take up the cross. Jesus bid him to come towards Him, but Peter was distracted and saw the wind and began to sink. He was not yet ready for his ultimate vocation that would culminate in leading the Church as the first Pope and to his martyrdom. He needed to be formed.

All this points to the treasured time and gift of the novitiate in the religious life. While some religious communities require both a postulancy and two years as novices for their Sisters, the Church at minimum requires a canonical novitiate of one year for all religious. This is precious time safeguarded by the Church. Each stage of formation has its specific end or purpose, and the Sister is called to throw herself one hundred percent into the life, cooperating generously with the means of formation offered to her. The great Dominican Biblical scholar Père Marie-Joseph Lagrange, OP, reflected back on the time of his novitiate as follows: "The novitiate is a time of hidden life. And I did indeed spend this year seeking God. Why then speak of it to others? Because I am convinced that the graces I then received provided me with such light that the faith was more firmly rooted in my spirit."[2]

It is notable that Jesus did not hand the disciples a how-to manual on discipleship. He did not sit them down for an all-nighter on day one and spell out for them what the next several years would hold. There were few explicit details that would dispel their fears or the concerns of family members. Just as Jesus expected His first followers to come and remain with Him, without knowing entirely what the future held, so too is the religious in formation called to trust the community and cooperate in the formation process. This involves a gradual unfolding of the religious life to the candidate who over time more completely participates in the life of the institute. Formation is gradual for a reason. As eager as the young Sister may be to learn everything all at once, and regardless of how seemingly ready or ill-equipped she may feel (or truly be) at the time of entrance, in time she will be given the guidance and grace to meet the demands that religious life inevitably brings. The *Directives on Formation* states, "It certainly is not required that a candidate for the religious life be able to assume all of the obligations of the religious life immediately, but he or she should be found capable of doing so progressively."[3] The Church is a wise Mother and knows from experience that a firm foundation laid over time will bear fruit in a strong religious life that can weather any storm.

A GOD OF SURPRISES AND VARIETY

Members of the Dominican family often remark that they cannot be pigeonholed in terms of personality or talents. Meet one Dominican and you have met only one Dominican! At the same time, it is our hope that after spending some time among our Sisters, one will perceive a shared spirit that flows from our charism as well as common ideals and fidelity to common observances. As a formator, it was a joy to witness a young Sister growing in her religious identity and to see her unique personality start shining through as she lives her Dominican vocation! This was a gift to be welcomed, not stifled.

Each group that has entered our community has been characterized by a variety of ages, educational backgrounds and experiences. Within one postulant group, there might be a few 18-year-olds, a handful of young women who have come in the middle of their college studies, and some who have entered after working for a few years after college. Some grew up in intact families; others have divorced parents. A few Sisters may be converts to the faith. The personal experiences of each new Sister will be as vastly different as their family and education backgrounds. Once the postulants don their "blues" on entrance day, they all become part of the same group and start on equal footing. What binds them together from henceforth will be the pursuit of God's will in this religious community.

The Church has increasingly emphasized the personal dimension of religious formation, recognizing the uniqueness of each person God calls, in the context of the formation that so necessarily takes place in community. The role of the postulant or novice mistress is a vital one, and she above all seeks God's will for the young women under her care, ever mindful that the Holy Spirit is the primary agent of formation.[4] One of my favorite intercessors, Saint Thérèse of Lisieux, related the following from her time in the Lisieux Carmel working with the novices: "From the beginning I realized that all souls have more or less the same battles to fight, but on the other hand I saw that since no two souls were exactly alike, each one must be dealt with differently."[5]

My experiences working with the young women who enter our community resonated with this insight from Saint Thérèse. The Postulant and Novice Mistress should have a great reverence for the unique working of God in the individual souls of her Sisters. Recognizing the precious gift of a religious vocation, she will pray and sacrifice for her Sisters and get to know each individually. The formator seeks to channel the Sister along the path the Lord is calling her. The Sister in formation is "invited unceasingly to give an attentive, new, and responsible reply."[6] In other words, the Sister has a vital role in her own formation, and only she can say "yes" to God and live out her vocation each day. The formator cannot say "yes" for her!

Returning to the above narrative of Peter's attempt to walk on the water, the role of the formator could be likened to that of one who is constantly pointing out the way to keep one's eyes fixed on Jesus, the goal of all our striving. She points out the pitfalls, gives advice about how to withstand the wind, and provides timely encouragement on how to keep moving forward despite, at times, feeling one's unworthiness, or perhaps not even seeing Jesus ahead or hearing His voice.

THE BLUES ARE BACK!

"It's so good to have the blues back!" This phrase is often heard around our Motherhouse during the first few weeks after our postulants' entrance each year at the end of August. The "blues" refer to the postulants, or more explicitly, to the nav blue polyester outfits that distinguish them from the rest of the community. Each Sister in the community who no longer wears blue, and now wears white, can recall her own days of wearing the "blues" and especially all that they learned in the joyful blur of their first few weeks as postulants. While there is only a four-week window each year in our community when we are without postulants (the period after the previous years' postulants receive the habit and became novices at the end of July, and the entrance of a new postulant group in late August), there is something about the presence of postulants in the community that seems to make life at the Motherhouse joyfully complete. Everything is new for the postulants. When we witness their delight and awe at our family customs as they experience them for the first

Formation of Young Women in the Novitiate

time, we are reminded of our own first Christmas as postulants, for example, or when we first fumbled at tablewaiting, and the encouraging smiles that the other Sisters gave us, which heartened us to keep trying. We have all been in their shoes, and as we get to know them and pray with them and for them, they truly become our Sisters in Christ.

GETTING TO KNOW THE COMMUNITY: POSTULANCY

> "Religious orders are not formed for the purpose of gathering together perfect people but those who have the courage to aim at perfection."
> -Saint Francis de Sales

Pope Emeritus Benedict XVI is attributed as saying to the youth of the Church, "The world offers you comfort. But you were not made for comfort. You were made for greatness."[7] Pope Benedict recognized in young people—as did his predecessor, Saint John Paul II—a capacity for greatness, and frequently called upon them to move beyond the lies of relativism that dominate our culture. He challenged them to seek the fullness of Truth in the Person of Jesus Christ.

As Postulant Mistress and Novice Mistress, I have encountered young women who have heeded the calls of these great pontiffs. They are not strangers to the culture and have come to encounter the Person of Jesus Christ in a variety of ways. They have not come to the convent seeking a life of comfort but with a profound desire to give themselves unreservedly to Christ in the service of the Church. I have been humbled over and over again by the generosity of these young women when they first enter the convent. They have so much joy and willingly hand over all the material things that were once of value to them in the world. They leave cell phones behind, turn in their credit cards, and are eager to make every preliminary sacrifice in order to begin learning the ins and outs of convent life.

The main purpose of postulancy, the stage of formation preceding the novice years, is to assist the Sister in transitioning from lay life in the world to the religious life, which officially begins when she becomes a novice. As Postulant Mistress, it was my primary role to introduce the postulants to the essentials of the religious life.

> "The world offers you comfort. But you were not made for comfort. You were made for greatness."
> —Pope Emeritus Benedict XVI

This combined practical matters like learning the rubrics of the Divine Office (how we chant our prayers, when we bow, etc.) with a variety of classes in theological and catechetical subjects. Initially, the postulant's focus is upon learning what she needs to do and where she needs to be day in and day out. As she gradually becomes more at ease with the schedule and the rhythm of the life, she becomes freer to see and understand the purpose behind the various practices of our daily life, all of which are potential means to glorify the Lord and deepen her relationship with Him. For example: the invitation to unite her own prayers to those of the whole Church five times a day in community prayer will likely become more meaningful when the postulant is more confident finding her place in the breviary.

The postulancy is also a very important time for human formation. All aspects of formation are ongoing, and human formation should continue for all religious well beyond her initial years of formation. However, her postulancy is a time when she begins to take on her identity as a religious Sister, and so is a particularly crucial time for human formation. The Church teaches that formators, in union with the Father and the Holy Spirit, are called to shape "the attitude of the Son in the hearts of young men and women".[8] Hence, the whole of formation and the principle task of formators is to create a firm grounding in a Sister's identity as a religious.

The Church recognizes that sound human formation within religious life is of great urgency today, perhaps more so than in years past. The breakdown of many families and a pervasive secular culture often leave young people with deep wounds, of which they may or may not be aware. It is not unusual that young women with religious vocations enter the convent, only to discover over time that they lack the necessary freedoms in certain areas of their lives to give themselves fully and peacefully to God and their neighbor, or to make the lifetime commitment that the vocation requires. These wounds need to be healed before they are able to surrender themselves fully to their vocation.

> "Yet, LORD, you are our father; we are the clay and you our potter: we are all the work of your hand."
> -Isaiah 64:7

There is also a crisis of maturity among some young people entering religious life today. These young women are emerging from secular culture that perpetuates indecision and a kind of arrested development among an age demographic who, a generation earlier, were settling down, having children, and making other important and permanent commitments. I often reminded the postulants and novices that they were adult Catholic Christian women. This may sound obvious, but it is a mindset that is often lacking, even among young women in their late twenties.

We would do well to consider what it means to be an adult

Catholic Christian woman today. What is their prior experience of being a Catholic woman in the world? I encouraged them to reflect upon the reality that they should think of themselves this way, and that they would be treated as adult women in our community, and expected to relate to one another in the same regard. We could discuss personally any difficulties or challenges. Even if perhaps their family members or friends did not view them or treat them as adults, the Sisters could still respond in an adult manner. Religious life must be embraced as adult Catholic Christian women.

We would then go further into the essence of Catholic womanhood and the gift of femininity. Formation in this area is ongoing in the life of every religious woman. This is essential for living with other women in community and laying the foundation for how we relate to one another. We seek to communicate with each other and those outside the community as mature women. A healthy identity as religious depends upon this fundamental truth. Also, when the Sisters study the vows as novices, they come to understand how each vow specifically must be lived with an adult maturity. We seek to be childlike as Jesus called us—not to be childish.

BRIDES-TO-BE: NOVICE YEARS

Some time ago, I had the unique experience of being mistaken for a bride at a photo shoot while at a state park with the postulants for a picnic. A woman caught sight of me in my white habit from a distance (perhaps she did not notice the black veil?) and inquired of the postulants as they approached if they were the bridesmaids for my wedding. The postulants kindly explained that they were Sisters, and pointed out my religious habit. They further clarified that they did not have the habit yet (but God willing, soon!) and that we were there for a picnic.

Afterwards, the Sisters and I had a laugh about that, and suspected that the woman in the park had likely never encountered religious Sisters in habit before. We also wondered what she thought about the postulants' "blues" as potential bridesmaids' dresses! Finally, we acknowledged the bit of truth in the woman's observations. While not the type of bride she thought me to be, I was, indeed, wearing my wedding garment, the religious habit I received on my reception day as a novice. The start of the novitiate in most communities is marked by a ceremony in which the Sister receives the habit of the community, and a new religious name. Postulants long for this day to come, and in many communities, great speculation (and suggestions) abound, regarding the potential names the new novices will receive.

> We seek to be childlike as Jesus called us—not to be childish.

The new religious habit, the white veil of the novice, and the new religious name distinguish the Sister as a member of the specific religious community. In consequence, the new novice represents no longer herself, but the Church, and her specific community, in a whole new way. The dramatic change of the habit and the new name reflects the beginning of a new level of responsibility as she begins to prepare for religious profession. She is a public witness to the primacy of Christ by the habit she wears and a reminder of God and life eternal to all those who see her.

The canonical year of the novitiate that the Church requires is of particular importance and is dedicated to deepening the novices' prayer life and study of the vows. While community living begins as postulants, the novices grow in self-knowledge and have concrete opportunities to practice the virtues as they live and work closely with their fellow novices, day in and day out. Along these lines, *Fraternal Life in Community* states the following: "Religious community is the place where the daily and patient passage from 'me' to 'us' takes place, from my commitment to a commitment entrusted to the community, from seeking 'my things' to seeking 'the things of Christ'."[9]

The novice years may be likened to a courtship in a relationship, in which the Sister is given precious time to get to know her Spouse-to-be very intimately. As the novice takes on more duties and comes to a deeper understanding of the vows and the community's particular charism, she should above all be seeking the Lord's will. Is the Lord calling me to love Him in this way as a religious? Am I willing to make the sacrifices this life requires? Do I have the necessary freedom to make a complete gift of myself to God and to others for the love of God? Learning to be comfortable in silence is also essential for the novices, and they need to be taught in this area. This becomes even a more urgent necessity in our age inundated by social media and noise.

On the level of community, the novice is being guided and formed. The Church emphasizes the importance of ongoing dialogue with formators who assist the young Sisters in discerning God's will. In addition to prayer, study of the vows, and silence, most communities limit the novices' contacts with relatives and friends to a greater extent during the years as a novice. During my years working in formation, the Sisters struggled at times with missing family and the human element of this separation. That was certainly normal and understandable. However, these same Sisters most often also welcomed and saw the importance of having a time that freed them to focus more on their relationship with Christ and understood why the Church safeguarded the novitiate in this way.

On the other hand, while many families do support their daughters and sisters and respect the regulations of the religious life, I have seen just as many offer vocal resistance to the way of life that these young women have chosen. Some express ongoing displeasure and accuse their daughter or sister of hurting her family by her choice to enter religious life. While I do not wish to underestimate the sacrifice that a family makes in supporting the religious vocation of a loved one, I can attest that these young women are keenly aware of how their families feel and the pain they may be causing them by their choice.

I encourage family members who may struggle with their daughter's decision to enter religious life to prayerfully consider that her choice is an adult choice made freely. As families often struggle with this, I also encourage openness to understanding that choice over time. My own family, as well as the families of many other Sisters, can verify that they slowly found out that they did not lose a daughter when she entered the convent. Rather, they gained more daughters than they could ever have imagined—over a hundred and fifty more! Each Sister's family becomes part of a larger family when she enters religious life, and the Lord will bless parents and siblings for the sacrifice they make in supporting their loved one's religious vocation. It takes time, trust, and sacrifice. And they will receive many, many prayers!

A final note about the novice years is that many communities have a second year in addition to the canonical year. In my own community, we call this year the *apostolic* year. This year, when provided, calls for the novice to experience the apostolate of the community. She is to be given a taste of what she will eventually experience on a larger scale as a professed religious. At the same time, the time of the novices' prayer is safeguarded, and she is not given the full responsibility of a professed Sister. Our community is a teaching order, so our apostolic novices spend one day a week at our schools, observing in the classrooms, assisting the teachers, working with the children, and at times teaching lessons. Additionally, the novices have opportunities to go on apostolic trips with professed Sisters throughout the year for vocations and bear witness to Christ in a variety of settings.

All the while, they are being guided by the Novice Mistress at the Motherhouse, and seeking to interiorize all that they are learning both inside and outside the classroom. After two years as a novice, if she believes herself ready, and is accepted by the community, the novice professes her First Vows of poverty, chastity, and obedience, and becomes officially a bride of Christ!

MARY, STAR OF THE SEA

> We respond only with the help of His grace, and move forward not by our own power, but by keeping our eyes firmly fixed on Him.

Returning to the scene of the Gospels in which Peter moved forward toward Jesus on the water, it is true to note that Peter *did* walk on water, however briefly. While I am not seeking to give an exact equivalence of formation or religious life to walking on the water, the words of Pope Benedict bear repeating: God calls us to greatness! The Lord chooses whom He wills. We respond only with the help of His grace, and move forward not by our own power, but by keeping our eyes firmly fixed on Him. If He calls you or someone you love to the religious life, please encourage them to seek His will, which will undoubtedly bring the greatest happiness and everlasting joy. As we all move forward toward Christ on our paths to holiness, may we be strengthened by Mary, Star of the Sea, who illuminates our path to her Son and never ceases to pray for us!

Notes

1. Francis. "Address to the Sick and Disabled Children Assisted at the Seraphic Institute," Vatican, October 4, 2013, https://w2.vatican.va/content/francesco/en/speeches/2013/october/documents/papa-francesco_20131004_bambini-assisi.html.

2. During his pontificate, Saint John Paul II repeatedly called for this New Evangelization, which aimed to proclaim the faith to "entire groups of the baptized (who) have lost a living sense of the faith, or even no longer consider themselves members of the Church, and live a life far removed from Christ and his Gospel" (*Redemptoris Missio*, 33). That is, he intended the New Evangelization to reach those who live in historically Christian countries, such as the United States. John Paul II, "Address to the CELAM Assembly," trans. Dominican Sisters of Mary. Vatican, 1983, http://w2.vatican.va/content/john-paul-ii/es/speeches/1983/march/documents/hf_jp-ii_spe_19830309_assemblea-celam.html.

"The Church is like a ship. But what kind of ship? A nuclear-powered aircraft carrier. And who is the reactor core? Women religious. With them, the Church's life is powered until the end of time. Without them, the Church is dead in the water. May God bless us with Dominican sisters with hearts like fusion-powered neutron stars of divine joy."

– Dr. Donald Bungum
Assistant Professor of Philosophy and Catholic Studies, University of Mary

Merciful Love

Personal Formation for the Apostolate

Sister Thomas Aquinas Betlewski, OP
Born in Houston, Texas

Those who are well do not need a physician, but the sick do. Go and learn the meaning of the words, 'I desire mercy, not sacrifice.' I did not come to call the righteous but sinners. (Mt 9:12-13)

At the heart of every religious vocation is a definitive acceptance of God's infinite mercy. A Sister cannot "call herself" to religious life; such a self-willed project would be a chimera. A vocation is a demonstration of Divine Mercy in that it is a free gift, given in spite of the lowliness, sinfulness, and poverty that is at the core of all human existence. A religious woman is called to accept the mercy that is her vocation, a vocation to an exclusive intimacy with Christ and a participation in His mission for the salvation of souls. She is called *by name*, that is, uniquely and irrevocably, in the context of her own subjectivity, despite any resistance she experiences within herself, or any external pressure from the society from which she comes.

Through my religious life, I see myself in this dynamic of Divine Mercy. As I don my religious habit each morning and make my way to the chapel for morning Holy Hour, I am reminded of the mercy that is at the heart of my vocation. I do not deserve to number myself among those chosen by Christ for His purpose. As I kneel before the Eucharist in those first moments of the day, I know a deep joy, despite the fatigue or distractions, a joy that springs from the mercy that pours into me. Other religious—within my own and other communities—also speak of this joy, which is a gift from the Bridegroom and a fulfillment even now of the spousal intimacy with Jesus to which we are called.

This experience of Divine Mercy is at the heart of my vocation, and it is also a call to share with others the message, meaning, and power of God's mercy. All religious women are called to proclaim to others the beautiful line from Our Lady's *Magnificat*: "The Mighty One has done great things for me, and holy is his name. His mercy is from age to age, to those who fear him" (Lk 1:50). Among Dominicans, this proclamation takes on the unique form of teaching and, for me specifically, teaching at the high school level.

Giving a living witness to mercy is at the heart of a Sister's teaching. The message of mercy is more necessary than ever for the young people entrusted to our care. In a world of fierce competition, high expectations for an almost unattainable perfection, and frequent incidence of family breakdown and teenage depression, anxiety, and suicide, the reality of God's loving mercy is desperately needed. The living witness of one whose entire existence and work attests to the loving mercy of God—the religious woman—provides an ideal answer and image for our young people today. In sum, this is the essential meaning of the religious woman at the high school level: to proclaim the infinite mercy of God in a world that is hurting.

This is not to say that a Sister is the same as a campus minister, or that she ought to assume the role of a therapist for her students. She is first and foremost a teacher, and her daily task is to educate the minds and hearts of future generations. Nevertheless, the dynamic of her religious vocation enables her to give a profound witness to mercy; in the midst of her daily teaching, whether in geometry, world literature, physics, Spanish, or United States history, her being speaks to her students of God's mercy. She teaches not merely a subject but a way of life, showing how the acceptance of God's mercy sets the human personality on the path toward holiness. When she lives in joyful surrender to grace, she becomes a model of the pursuit of virtue. The sole motivator for a Sister's effort in the apostolate is to fulfill the will of God lovingly and thus strive to be of one mind and heart with Jesus Christ.

THE FEMININE GENIUS AND SPIRITUAL MOTHERHOOD

A woman's innate vocation is to motherhood, whether physical or spiritual; the very design of her body and her manner of love show her the truth of her vocation to motherhood. This feminine vocation brings a particular *genius* to the classroom that is both different from and complementary to her male counterparts. Pope John Paul II describes the beautiful link between motherhood and education:

> I would like to call to mind woman as teacher. It is a well-founded hope, if one considers the deep meaning of education, which cannot be reduced to the dry imparting of concepts but must aim at the full growth of man in all his dimensions. In this respect, how can we fail to understand the importance of the feminine genius? She has a unique capacity to see the person as an individual, to understand his aspirations and needs with special insight, and she is able to face up to problems with deep involvement. The universal values themselves, which any sound education must always present, are offered by feminine sensitivity. Wherever the work of education is called for, we can note that women are ever ready and willing to give themselves generously to others, especially in serving the weakest and most defenseless. In this work they exhibit a kind of affective, cultural, and spiritual motherhood which has inestimable value for the development of individuals and the future of society.[1]

This remarkable passage is a charter for all women, but especially for religious women who have devoted their lives to the classroom. By living out her call to spiritual motherhood, in service of her witness to mercy, a religious woman becomes more than just a teacher. Of course, like any teacher, a Sister relies on professional and human development, years of experience in the classroom, and advanced degrees in her subject area. Yet a Sister also combines feminine genius and spiritual motherhood with her experience of God's mercy and her intimacy with Jesus. This unique and powerful synthesis is the extraordinary gift that a Sister gives her students and the school community she serves.

I think of the countless times in my own life of giving a mother's heart to students through my prayer. I remember in particular a young man who was talented on the soccer field and very popular among his peers. He did not ask directly for prayers, probably because he did not want to appear weak or vulnerable. Yet he knew that no matter how he made the request, I would come through with my support. He came into my classroom, took a piece of paper and wrote down the name of his father, and slid this piece of paper across my desk to my hand. Although I didn't know exactly why he was giving me the paper, I just knew this young man needed my spiritual motherhood through loving prayer. A few weeks later I received word that his father had died of an aggressive stomach cancer. When I saw him at the funeral Mass, he gave me a hug and said simply, "Thank you."

A religious woman gives witness to mercy wherever she goes, but for our community, one of the principal ways this is done is in her classroom and broader school community. By means of her spiritual motherhood, a Sister becomes a channel of grace for her students and fellow teachers.

COMMUNION

Perhaps the most noticeable gift a religious woman brings to her teaching is the witness she gives of mercy received and lived *in community*. I was recently at a store with the three Sisters on my mission, and we passed a young dad holding his little daughter by the hand. When she saw the four of us in our habits, she exclaimed, "Look! They are all one!" We laughed at this delightful moment, but later reflection, revealed the profundity of this little girl's exclamation. While she meant, "They are all wearing the same thing!" she touched on the deeper unity signified externally by the wearing of the habit.

So often our students comment on the amount of time we must spend together, and they ask why we do not ever seem to argue or fight. How do we get along? Due to the frequency with which this question is asked, I believe that our witness of healthy community life does more than support our own religious life; it also helps our students to see that unity of life and friendship is both possible and rewarding. Our community life is a blessing and requires effort and sacrifice to nurture its growth. We are not always able to come to every basketball game or to chaperone the homecoming dance. Our time in community is a priority which often leads us to sacrifice involvement in the active extracurricular and athletic world of our students for the sake of community activities and prayer. We make time for community because we desire to be "all one", in the words of the little girl at the store. We have the conviction that community life is the habitat in which authentic communion lives and grows, and it is authentic communion among the Sisters that in turn supports and nourishes our consecration to God.

The witness we give of knowing and loving one another is tangible to the students and communicates to them the possibility of finding and maintaining human friendship and love throughout one's life. Throughout their high school years, young people are forging new bonds of friendship with one another and exploring the dimensions and complexities of relationships with the opposite sex. They find that relating to one another authentically requires effort and involves making mistakes. Oftentimes, students approach the Sisters for advice in the area of human relations, because they instinctively see the Sisters as experts at communion. The questions they ask involve how to interact with others and to secure their own identity in the process, and a Sister provides ideal accompaniment in this delicate development.

INTELLECTUAL VIRTUES

Integrated into the Sister's fundamental desire to do God's will is her love for truth, which I have found powerfully expressed in my own community's Dominican charism. I have lived and taught with Sisters who served in mathematics and science departments, in the humanities, and in my own

> "Modern man listens more willingly to witnesses than to teachers, and if he does listen to teachers, it is because they are witnesses."
> —Pope Saint Paul VI

department of theology. These Sisters continuously inspire me by their efforts to advance human knowledge and to introduce their students to the nobility of the intellectual life. They take their academic subjects seriously and teach with thoroughness and passion. Their students learn the disciplines while being trained in the intellectual virtues. A life of the mind requires diligence, perseverance, and industry, and these virtues are modeled by the Sisters on a daily basis. Like our Holy Father, Saint Dominic, we strive to be preachers and teachers of truth and grace, and it is our joy to see high school students discover their interests and passions.

Furthermore, in a world where objective and subjective truth are often confused and absolute moral norms are clouded by relativistic ideas, the necessity of teaching philosophical principles has become essential.

THE VOWS

Perhaps the preeminent witness of mercy that a religious woman gives is her living of the evangelical counsels of poverty, chastity, and obedience. As markers of her consecrated existence, these vows are the distinguishing signs of her total belonging to

> "Nothing conquers except truth, and the victory of truth is love."
> —Saint Augustine

God and her surrender to His infinite and loving mercy. They also serve as powerful signs of contradiction for her students.

In our world today, the message is clear: the more you have, the happier you will be. We are constantly bombarded by empty promises of happiness arising from material possessions. This lifestyle is costly, not only in a material sense, but also on the human and spiritual levels. I have observed in the lives of my students and their families the deep spiritual and emotional poverty that often accompanies the amassing of possessions and money. In this culture, the vow of poverty starts profound conversations. My students are shocked that I do not own a smartphone, and that I only use a tablet or laptop insofar as teaching requires them. My vow of poverty exudes the simplicity that has become my home, so to speak. The students recognize—often in spite of themselves—that possessions only increase feelings of isolation and, when used without purpose and moderation, may dehumanize. The fact that religious women live without these distractions causes our students to stop and consider embracing moderation in the use of material goods. They recognize this desire to *give up* possessions as a way to *have more* spiritually; thus is fostered a dynamic maturity and independence which even the youth find refreshing. Further, I have found that students from lower-income families have a special identification with the Sisters, as we see beyond possessions, style, and popularity to our students as persons.

The vow of chastity is likewise a powerful witness of God's mercy to young people today. Even if her subject area does not include Catholic sexual morality, a religious woman teaches the value of chastity by her very presence. Chastity is not simply about abstinence; the joy and calm that radiate from an integrated chastity demonstrate that chastity embraces interpersonal relations and our respect for self and others. I have often explained to my students that I see my vow of chastity not as a "no" to sex and marriage but as a "yes" to a full life of love consecrated to Jesus Christ. Chastity is personal, not impersonal. It is dynamic, not static. Sexual behavior among teenagers today remains on the rise, and what better way to introduce high school students to the beauty and fulfillment of a chaste life than through the witness of a religious woman? In my own classes, students have asked me frankly if real love is possible. Because of the witness of my consecrated life, I believe the answers I give are especially credible.

Self-assertion and actualization are the prized end-result of democratic education—more than ever before, students are encouraged to "define themselves." Even community service is meant to assist students to "feel good" about themselves as participants in "making the world a better place." Planning one's future is the principal task of today's high school graduate, and self-determination is seen as the ultimate goal of adulthood. What a challenge the vow of obedience provides to these standards of self-aggrandizement! My students are amazed that the Sisters can be happy while surrendering their wills, their futures, and their plans to the will of another human being! The peaceful manner in which a Sister embraces her assignment each year shows students the inestimable value of emptying oneself for God and for His work. When moving from one school to another, with His grace, and with our daily "yes" to the Divine plan, we trust that we will meet these young people once again, and pray that we will be with them for all eternity. The vow of obedience frees me to love the students I teach each year as chosen gifts from Christ for me.

> "It is not hard to obey when we love the one whom we obey."
> —Saint Ignatius of Loyola

PRAYER

The life of a religious is above all a life dedicated to prayer. Whether a religious lives a cloistered life or teaches in a classroom, her primary work is to lift her heart and mind daily to God in prayer. The Divine Office, mental prayer, spiritual reading, and *lectio divina*—all of these punctuate her day to remind her of her duty to praise and adore her God. These periods of prayer are the expressions of her spousal bond with Christ and cannot be set aside as extra or secondary to her work as a teacher. Perhaps one of the most rewarding aspects of teaching remains the dedicated task of praying for my students. As we take this seriously, students know that in a unique way we belong to them, and one way we honor this bond is through prayer. I love when a student entrusts me with a special intention, whether for a family member, an upcoming final exam, or some kind of personal difficulty. As a religious, I am entirely free to dedicate my time of prayer to students who I think are struggling or who suffer from some unarticulated burden. Our prayer reaches where we cannot go, and one of the chief means of expressing our spiritual motherhood is prayer and sacrifice.

By living my religious life, as embraced and articulated by my particular community, I give witness to the infinite mercy and goodness of God. I show forth the value of a life given to God, and, by wearing the religious habit, I witness to my students how important my religious life is to me and to the world today. Despite my imperfections, God has called me to religious life. He had mercy on me. Through His merciful love, I witness to this Divine Mercy in the very weaknesses of my humanity, and tell forth, like Our Lady, the great things God has done for me.

CONCLUSION

As Sisters in a high school classroom, we enter the youthful fray each morning, reinforced by the prayers we have already offered to the Lord on behalf of each of our students. Although we bring our own human hopes, desires, and frailties, we do not come alone; we come with Christ. The Sister's role is to represent her Spouse, Jesus Christ; through the work of the apostolate and spiritual motherhood, she seeks to bring as many of His young people to Him as possible in her lifetime. Sisters in the classroom educate for heaven, because we believe that our students are offered and can accept the same gift we have received: the inestimable gift of the gracious Mercy of God.

> Although we bring our own human hopes, desires, and frailties, we do not come alone; we come with Christ.

NOTES

1 John Paul II, *Pope John Paul II on the Genius of Women*, (Washington, D.C.: USCCB Publishing, 1997), 29.

Personal Formation for the Apostolate

> Thanks be to God for the gift of consecrated religious women! Like Our Lady, they embody the mystery of the Church and the call of every disciple: to receive Jesus Christ in the heart and to bear forth his saving presence in the world.
>
> —Father Bryan Y. Norton, SJ
> Professor of Latin, St. Louis University, St. Louis, MO

Ogniem i Mieczem

Learning to Love God with an Undivided Heart

Sister Agnes Paulina Maciol, OP
Born in Rabka, Poland

Maintaining the Polish tradition, pronouns referring to
the Mother of God in this essay are capitalized.

Each of us is a masterpiece in progress. Like the potter's jar (see Jer 18:1-4), God makes and remakes us into "a people specially His own" (Dt 26:18). The response to this slow sculpting process in the gentle but "jealous" palm of Our Lord should be our trust in Him, though it is not always so. He wants us to be entirely given over to Him and longs for us to love Him completely. The amazing part is that, whether we acknowledge it or not, we are made for and want that too: "Our hearts are restless until they rest in Thee, Lord," wrote Saint Augustine. On this earth, each vocation story begins with the first tug on the heart and ends with the last heartbeat given to our Lord. This call to give God absolutely everything—heart, mind, body, and soul—is the simple yet difficult vocation of every consecrated religious. Saint Augustine describes it magnificently in these words: "To seek God is the greatest adventure, to love Him the greatest of romances, and to find Him, the greatest human achievement."

The story of my vocation is divided here into three main parts. The first pertains to my upbringing in Poland, the second focuses on my pursuit of the American Dream while searching for the truth, and the third describes how I found my new home among the Dominican Sisters of Mary, Mother of the Eucharist.

"I AM THE LORD YOUR GOD"
CHILDHOOD AND THE TRANSATLANTIC MOVE TO THE PROMISED LAND

"I am the Lord your God, who brought you out of the land of Egypt, out of the house of slavery. You shall not have other gods beside me. ... Hear, O Israel! The LORD is our God, the LORD alone! Therefore, you shall love the LORD, your God, with your whole heart, and with your whole being, and with your whole strength" (Dt 5:6-7, 6:4-5). Memorizing the Our Father and the Hail Mary, and finally being able to recite these verses to my parents at a very young age, is one of my earliest memories of learning how to pray. My parents' goal was to teach me how to live out these words in post-

> **What is a Litany?**
>
> A litany is a repetition of prayers, asking Our Lord, Our Lady, or a saint to pray for us. Examples include:
>
> **Litany of the Sacred Heart**
> **Litany of the Blessed Virgin Mary**
> (also known as the Litany of Loreto)
> **Litany of Saint Joseph**
> **Litany of the Precious Blood**
> **Litany of the Saints**

communist Poland where I was born and raised. However, faith was easy to assimilate when it was woven into every Pole's memory of the war. Hard labor and the constant need to rely on divine providence was a reality that put the fear of God into all hearts. In fact, whenever a regime tried to systematically stamp out religion, the Polish people would respond by clinging to God all the more. From Corpus Christi processions and the singing of the Litany of Loreto in May and the Litany to the Sacred Heart in June, to praying the rosary especially in October and attending the Stations of the Cross and the Easter Triduum services, our lives seemed to revolve around the liturgical calendar. My elementary school and gymnasium (middle school) friends shared the same sentiments, and under the careful watch of the Salesian priests and Sisters, our devotion grew steadily. At school, we were all mesmerized and deeply inspired by the valor and the virtue of knights and heroes in the old Polish classics like *Pan Tadeusz* (Mr. Thaddeus) and *Ogniem i Mieczem* (By Sword and By Fire). We had no desire to question the Faith. The Faith instead questioned us: "Would you, too, give your life for Christ, like your forefathers did at Oświęcim, Grunwald, Katyn, Gdańsk, or the Warsaw uprising?"

Our belief was enflamed by remembering the sacrifice of the men and women who gave their lives in the fight against various forms of aggression which always attempted to strike at Poland's Catholic

Our Lady of Częstochowa

The image of our Lady of Czestochowa is a painted icon that has been venerated in Poland for centuries. It is traditionally thought to have been painted by Saint Luke.

heart. This heart has always been carefully protected in the hands of Our Blessed Mother. Marian devotion thrives throughout Poland and did so especially under the great leadership of Pope John Paul II. Hence, like many other Poles, every August my parents and I would make the pilgrimage to the shrine of Our Lady of Częstochowa, the walls of which are covered in various ex-votos for graces and healings obtained there. After an early morning's journey, I would open my eyes to the unveiling of the miraculous image, a symbol of Mary's reign over the whole country from a hill outside of Kraków throughout a thousand-year bloody history. This was the beginning of my lifelong lesson on the power of Mary's intercession. I remember asking my mom what the two lines on Mary's cheek signify. She explained how the image, barbarously stolen during war, was struck twice by a sword wielded by a cruel foreign soldier. In the end, the war was won and the country freed from religious persecution. This image became for me a symbol of Mary's unconditional love. I longed to console this Sorrowful Mother in my heart. Saint Faustina teaches us that love is measured by the degree of suffering; our Blessed Mother did not back away from the Cross. She always understands, protects, and guides Her children.

She also never abandons Her children, regardless of how far they go. Therefore, when my family immigrated to the United States in the early 2000s and I came upon the same beautiful icon of Her in our Polish church on the outskirts of Los Angeles, my heart exclaimed: "She is here too; all will be well then!" That is not to say that, all of a sudden, beginning tenth grade in the melting-pot of California would be easy. Learning how to navigate family life in a foreign country meant that sacrifices had to be made often, but never in terms of the Faith. My new large Polish-immigrant family, and the priests and Sisters who ran our Polish parish, became a firm witness to the Faith throughout the years of weekly Masses, retreats, other spiritual-cultural events, and festivities. During the week, on the other hand, I attended a large California public school and encountered a robust mix of beliefs and colorful and captivating cultures: Mexican, Chinese, Vietnamese, Japanese, Swedish, and German. My Catholic faith, like never before, had to become an anchor in a world of divergence and contrast.

Putting all differences aside, I rolled up my sleeves and got to work, taking great pains to master the English language and high school studies in hopes of going to college and living out the "American dream." Adolescence brought with it questions about the meaning of human life and love. I knew that, ultimately, the answer to all my questions was God, but I wanted to know how. I wondered how His providence fit into the world at large and my own "pursuit of happiness." What was my calling? Up to that point, I had seen plenty of religious Brothers and Sisters, but if the rare thought of ever becoming one came to mind, I dismissed it almost immediately, though I did admire missionary life very much. I remember meeting an order of such Sisters on one occasion as they were fundraising for the marginalized population they served in Eastern Europe. Their supernatural joy and the sacrifice they had made at so young an age really struck me, but I thought, "Surely, this kind of happiness is only for holy people," and went back to my college plans.

"YOU SHALL NOT HAVE OTHER GODS"
THE PURSUIT OF THE AMERICAN DREAM

For as long as I can remember, I always enjoyed studying. That included most anything in grade school and high school, but developed into a particular interest in the physical and natural sciences during college. This love of learning gave me a natural curiosity as to how the origins of the world and the physical laws that govern it fit into the Catholic tradition. I decided to set out on a long and arduous journey of investigation. Biology and chemistry were my two main areas of study, and it was fascinating to work through the processes that nurture and uphold life during long hours in a biochemistry lab. However, a question would always impose itself: "What caused this process in the first place?" Ultimately, I was looking for what the Greek thinkers, and later Saint Thomas Aquinas, referred to as "the first cause." Although I did not know it at the time, I was searching for the Who or What that made the world appear according to our scientific understanding. Meanwhile, by the workings of some mysterious grace (and probably my parents' prayers), I never let go of the conviction that God was behind it all. I knew that He is all truthful and cannot deceive us; therefore, I will never forget how heartbroken I was after our professor presented the nitty gritty nuances of life's beginnings during a physical chemistry lecture. I do not know whether the professor intended the heartbreak, but he ultimately left us with the following open-ended question: "Did human life begin in a clump of molecules that happened to come together in just the right—although highly unlikely—set of circumstances?" Statistically speaking that chance was possible, but in my heart of hearts, I just knew it could not be so. My infatuation with science ended. I knew that God had created the world and cared deeply about it and that He had sent His only Son so that we may know and love Him. Pope John Paul II wrote about these realities:

> Faith and reason are like two wings on which the human spirit rises to the contemplation of truth; and God has placed in the human heart a desire to know the truth—in a word, to know himself—so that, by knowing and loving God, men and women may also come to the fullness of truth about themselves. (*Fides et Ratio*)

No one can fly with only one wing, and as disappointing as it was, the purely scientific explanation of my professor helped me understand that there is more to life than knowledge.

The potential of science to improve life still attracted me strongly—so much so that by my junior year in college, I had decided to serve others through clinical drug discovery research as a pharmacist. Unknowingly, I was climbing up the ladder of the four levels of happiness described by the great Jesuit theologian and author, Father Robert Spitzer, SJ, to the point of "service". I thought this would finally be it, so I started yet another long and laborious five-year journey of becoming a pharmacist.

Though studies were hard, the clinical opportunities were boundless, and I will always cherish the encounters with human suffering in the patients we met. As fascinating as it was, yet another questioning voice appeared in my soul during this time: "Why are these people, including children, suffering from cancer, permanent injuries, and non-curable chronic diseases? Why are they left to die alone or without receiving the Last Rites? Where is God in this? Is it ethical to help end someone's life? What are my treatment regimens and drug knowledge really worth here in the face of death? What can I personally do for these people, and am I doing everything I can? What about their souls?" I found my only consolation in praying the Divine Mercy Chaplet at the bedside of the sick and the dying. I had to bow my head low to the redemptive mystery of human suffering which even science cannot conquer.

The Divine Mercy Chaplet

In 1935, Saint Faustina Kowalska had a vision of Jesus Christ, in which He gave her instructions to pray the Chaplet of Divine Mercy and spread this devotion throughout the world. He also encouraged the chaplet to be prayed at the bedside of the dying, saying, "When they say this Chaplet in the presence of the dying, I will stand between My Father and the dying not as the just judge but as the Merciful Savior."

One day a fellow classmate invited me to go to daily Mass with her during Lent. I was drawing closer to the idea that I needed to give the spiritual life more time, but I did not do much about it. A long-term relationship was my only form of discernment at the time. I progressed in this limbo state through the rest of pharmacy school and then through a very intense year of pharmacy residency at a large California hospital. With the world at my feet, I still did not feel completely happy or fulfilled. I asked God to show me the way as my eyes caught a glimpse of a picture of John Paul II at home one day. I knew instinctively that he had given his life for something that was true, or rather, Someone who was Truth. At that instant, and to my own surprise, I asked John Paul II to help me find that something for which I could lay down my life. Little did I know he would take me up on my request literally!

After finishing residency, the hectic merry-go-round routine of the previous years ended, and I decided to visit my roots in Poland. I re-discovered the loving family atmosphere and the warmth of a people who always clung to and trusted God with their whole hearts. They were deeply happy without any huge external achievements other than their loving and thriving families. I could not understand why the transcendental ache in my heart would not go away and why I seemed to be on a round-about journey through life that was not *it*! Had I missed the sign for "the land of happiness" somewhere along the way? Like the Israelites, I seemed to have been circling in the desert after crossing the Red Sea. Had God forgotten about me? However, looking at my family, I reasoned, "Maybe He is not as distant as I think

> "The secret of happiness is to live moment by moment and to thank God for all that He, in His goodness, sends to us day after day."
>
> -Saint Gianna Beretta Molla

He is", and admitted that I had not learned how to give God full reign in me. Waking up one morning, I felt a conviction that Mary wanted to do something in this regard, and I agreed to do whatever She would tell me (see Jn 2:5), as I instinctively knew I could trust Her.

"YOU SHALL LOVE THE LORD, YOUR GOD" THE DOWNPOUR OF GRACE & THE WAY HOME

My return to the United States found me bouncing between various job searches and all the fitness activities I could pay for through Groupon. One day, some mysterious force brought me to Mass on a random weekday. I had just let go of a relationship and, in accordance with the long-standing Catholic tradition, thought it clever to put Saint Joseph in charge of making sure that a real Prince Charming made it safely to my doorstep. I even promised to do whatever God wanted—for a time—in exchange. I subconsciously knew this was a form of idolatry called "treat God like an ATM machine", but I had reached a point of desperation.

"Do you want to learn how to pray? Do you want to grow in your relationship with God?" The words seemed to be jumping out at me from a flyer I randomly found in the back pew of the church. Since then, I have come to see that there are no random events when it comes to Divine Providence, because that purple flyer changed my life forever. I filled out the return portion of the paper and mailed it in. I almost forgot about it until a notification came asking me to come to the first class. I had apparently signed up for a ten-week course on the Spiritual Exercises of Saint Ignatius at a thriving local Catholic parish. During the classes, we dug deeply into the spiritual life thanks to the Oblates of the Virgin Mary who ran the program. This became the hardest non-working ten weeks of my life. In my stubbornness, I decided I was going to persevere in those daily holy hours, in the footsteps of Fulton Sheen, and I was attending daily Mass no matter what.

Never before had I realized what was lurking in the secret recesses of my heart—secret gods of wanting to control my own life at all costs, and other vices that ate away at my joy through the years. I see now that God led me through a spiritual battle over the course of that year, and I am grateful for all the guidance I received from His representatives on earth. After my general confession, I again felt as light and as free as a bird. The brilliant thing about the Exercises of Saint Ignatius is that they end not only in a contemplation "to receive divine love" but also in a meditation on the "Call of the King". Saint Ignatius proposes: "Imagine two Kings: one is Christ and one is Satan. Which one would you rather serve?" You must choose the One or the other. There simply is no other option on this earth. While I hope all of us would gladly and immediately say, "I will serve you, Lord Jesus!" we can sometimes get stuck in this vacuum of mediocrity, not wanting to commit, because we fear what service to Our Lord will cost us. How unsatisfactory this is to the human heart and soul!

Therefore, when in the quiet of Adoration, the Lord gently asked, "Will you give Me your *whole* heart?" I started getting nervous and felt guilty for not exactly jumping out of the pew in excitement. It became apparent that I had never really taken religious life seriously. In fact, almost every time vocational discernment in any shape

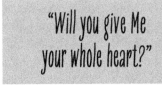
"Will you give Me your whole heart?"

or form was mentioned around me, I felt uneasy. As much as I enjoyed learning about an array of saints, I wanted to take things into my own hands again and invent my own way to sanctity. This did not exactly include the convent. When my spiritual director said I would make a good Dominican, my first reaction was shock, then anger, then sadness at still not being open to God's voice in my life. It seemed like my heart was not entirely His. "All for the greater glory of God"—so long as it did not include wearing a habit!

Since there was practically nothing that attracted me to religious life on the natural plane, the decision became even harder. I mustered countless reasons in my head for not looking into consecrated life. I was terrified at the thought of wearing a habit. I felt I had to take care of my family and "repay" what they had made possible for me—even though that would be impossible and not at all anything my family would ever ask. From a practical standpoint also, after all this time spent in school and working to pay back all the loans, it seemed quite irresponsible to "throw away" an incredible in-patient hospital job that had finally landed right in my lap. An amazing group of God-loving and God-fearing friends now also surrounded me. Young, upright, Catholic men seemed to spring up from the ground like never before! However, over the next several weeks of daily Mass and Holy Hours, of praying, searching and asking about retreats, through spiritual direction and simple everyday conversations, it became more and more clear that God meant to have my *whole* heart for Himself alone. I came to a point of really wanting to know and do God's will, though I still needed help with this tough decision. I knew Mother Mary would help me obtain all the graces necessary, since She has never failed me before, so I decided to pray to Her daily.

A week or two after the initial suggestion, I remembered again the theme of Dominican Sisters. "Are Dominican Sisters even alive? Where would I even find them? Are they back in Poland?" I skeptically initiated an internet search for "Dominican Sisters". The website of the Dominican Sisters of Mary, Mother of the Eucharist, was the only one I saw that day. I looked at the horarium and to my delight found it included daily Mass, Holy Hour, and the Rosary in common. In the website's video footage, I saw to my surprise that the Sisters were not at all slowed down while playing sports in their habits! I was partly drawn to this, and partly incredulous, but decided to "come and see" this marvelous place during the April 2014 weekend discernment retreat.

> "Do not be afraid, open wide the doors to Christ!"
> -Pope Saint John Paul II

The retreat happened to be over the Sunday when John Paul II was being canonized, and during the retreat's all-night Eucharistic Adoration, we all listened to the Mass being broadcast from Rome. Hearing the Pontiff's famous: "Do not be afraid, open wide the doors to Christ!" wrenched my heart. Furthermore, during the next morning's Sunday Mass in the Sisters' Motherhouse chapel, the Sisters sang an old familiar Polish tune of my childhood called *Abba Ojcze* ("Abba Father") during Holy Communion. A coincidence? I am not so sure anymore! In that one instant of Eucharistic thanksgiving, I came to know that this was my new home, the one for which I had been searching and in which Jesus in the Eucharist is loved dearly. I asked to be admitted to the community that day, because I knew I had to give this great adventure called the religious life a try. The rest is a beautiful history!

"LOVE WITH YOUR WHOLE HEART"
WHY RELIGIOUS LIFE AND WHY THIS COMMUNITY

You see, not everything in life can be reasoned through. Listening to the heart and taking a great leap of faith are both essential. In fact, the words "mind" and "heart" are often used in the Bible interchangeably because of their close relationship. At one point during the discernment process, I recognized that God finds ways to bless and sanctify us in any vocation. However, in my heart of hearts, I finally reached a point of feeling a great need and urgency to give Him absolutely everything and to keep nothing for myself. Saint André Bessette explained it beautifully when he said, "It is not necessary to have been well-educated, to have spent many years in college, to love the good God. It is sufficient to want to do so generously."

This task of loving God completely, though not easy, continues here for all of us Sisters each day with the help of the Sacraments. The Dominican motto Laudare, benedicere, praedicare (meaning "to praise, to bless, to preach") calls us to "share with others the fruits of contemplation" in Catholic schools around the country and to balance the active and contemplative dimensions of our life. The four pillars of the Dominican life—prayer, community life, study, and the apostolate (teaching and the New Evangelization)—provide endless opportunities to pursue a virtue-driven "freedom for excellence." In fact, according to Father Spitzer our life can reach the highest form of happiness called worship, when our complete trust and love of God inundates it with His presence. Only then can our hearts truly become a place of giving God praise and thanks (1 Thess 5:16-18)! Did I know that I was going to enjoy religious life? No, but I knew that God is always good!

> "It is not necessary to have been well-educated, to have spent many years in college, to love the good God. It is sufficient to want to do so generously."
>
> -Saint André Bessette

I have also come to understand the beautiful meaning of our religious habits and to appreciate the 800-year-old heritage of the Dominican spirituality they symbolize as an outward sign of consecration to Christ. God dissipated the apprehension of leaving my family behind and has taken care of them far beyond what I could have done for them on my own. He cannot be outdone in generosity if we only follow His will wholeheartedly. God's invitation does not go away even when our human nature questions the possibility of a religious vocation. Such questions might include our appreciation for material possession, our important business opportunities and public status, even our desire always to be in control. In the end, none of this will bring us the only thing we ultimately desire. If one can surrender to the divine embrace, the answers are all filled in, and the soul is set free to love with abandonment.

> "Rejoice always, pray without ceasing. In all circumstances give thanks, for this is the will of God for you in Christ Jesus."
>
> -1 Thessalonians 5:16-18

The daily example of my Sisters challenges me to follow God's will more ardently and to trust He will catch me when I fall in doing so. Jesus never fails to supply opportunities and graces for our sanctification. Will you trust that He wants holiness for you too? Let us all pray to *Matka Boska*, our Mother Mary, to help us listen attentively to the voice of God in our lives and to give Him our complete and undivided hearts!

> Without the witness of consecrated virginity, the Church would lose a tangible proof of the grace she now transmits and a powerful sign of the heavenly future in which she hopes.
>
> – Father Aaron Pidel, SJ
> Assistant Professor of Theology at Marquette University

Blood of the Martyrs

Everything is Grace

Sister Christiana Bui, OP
Born in Bao Loc in the Lam Dong Province of Vietnam

In mid-nineteenth-century Vietnam, Minh Mạng issued an edict ordering all Christians to renounce their faith or be killed. My maternal great-great grandmother, walking home from the market one day, was stopped by the authorities and commanded to renounce her belief in Christ and trample a cross. She flatly refused and was pushed into the nearby river, where both she and the child she was carrying in her womb died. Weeks later, her husband, my mother's great-grandfather, was taking a stroll in the park with his brother one day, when they were stopped by the authorities for questioning. Brought to prison for further interrogations because of their faith, but refusing to renounce their Lord Jesus Christ, they were buried alive. Their two children were left orphans to be raised by relatives.

It is incredible to think about the martyrs having died for love of Jesus, but even more remarkable to me is remembering that I have blood-relatives who are martyrs. The grace of God has been in my family from the beginning. My parents were already quite old to be having more children when they brought their ninth, and last child, into the world and named me Thien-An, which means God's grace. I have one older sister, who entered religious life while still quite young, and seven brothers. I have long thought about my baptismal name and its significance; there is little doubt that God's grace has always been a part of my family and has brought me into the spousal relationship I have with Christ today.

> There is little doubt that God's grace has always been a part of my family and has brought me into the spousal relationship I have with Christ today.

PINKY PROMISE OF GRACE

It is obvious in hindsight that God has been calling me to Himself from the beginning. When I was a small child, a close friend of our family, who was a seminarian, asked me, "Will you pinky-promise me to be a Sister when you grow up?" I had no idea to what he was referring; I knew my sister was a religious, but I saw her only when she came for her home visits. Even then, I never thought of asking about her life: what it was that she did all day, what it meant to be consecrated to God, and so on. So, I did what any young girl would do when asked to make a pinky promise and pinky-promised I would be a Sister. In hindsight, this was a small way that God revealed, when I was still very young, His desire to have me for Himself. Of course, it would not be until years later when I would agree to this with not just my heart, but my intellect and will as well.

FROM MIGRANTS TO IMMIGRANTS

In 1954, Việt Minh and the French ratified the Geneva Agreement, which split Vietnam into the North and the South. Because of the ensuing religious persecution and Communist oppression, my parents had a quick and private wedding. They and their respective families traveled approximately thirty miles on foot from northern Thanh Hóa to Phát Diệm in South Vietnam. During the travels, due to my father's young age and good health, the Communists chose him for work in their labor camps. They captured him and, while in bondage, he prayed to God for some miraculous deliverance from this captivity. Amazingly, that very night he was able to escape while the guards were sleeping. God was with him and, after a time, he and his wife were fleeing yet again from city to city.

My parents with their young daughter were finally able to settle in a small town called Tan Thanh, Bao Loc near Dalat in the southeast part of Vietnam. It was there that all the children would

---

The Vietnam War

When was it?
1954-1975

Who fought in it?
North Vietnam vs. South Vietnam & the United States

How was the USA involved?
The United States came to the aid of its ally, South Vietnam, in the efforts to stop North Vietnam from taking control of the South. However, due to casualties and lack of support back home, the United States withdrew from the war in 1963.

How did the war end?
The Vietnam War ended on April 30, 1975 when South Vietnam surrendered to North Vietnam. In 1976, the two countries were officially unified as the Socialist Republic of Vietnam.

eventually be baptized and confirmed while also taking active roles in Church-sponsored activities.

As the Vietnam War began, my parents began praying to discern whether they should send their sons to escape with people they barely knew to the United States of America. Knowing things were getting worse, some of my uncles who were in the South Vietnamese military warned that the USA would not be able to defend South Vietnam from the Communists. My uncles themselves attempted to leave the country as soon as they were able. My parents were hardworking folks, able to sell the coffee and tea they harvested to get the funds necessary to pay for my brothers' escapes. My mother and father contacted the people organizing the boat ride that would eventually carry my siblings to safety. Their faith in God was evident because they believed He would protect my siblings.

I remember clearly that six of my brothers, between the ages of fourteen and eighteen, were sent at different times, leaving by night so as not to get caught by the Communist police. One of my brothers was picked up by our father from school and was told, "Get your books. We're leaving." Thinking he was in trouble, he would later recall how he did not even know where he was to go. I still remember that when I was in the first grade, my dad sent all my brothers out of the country. He told me, "If your teachers ask where your brothers went, just say they went to Saigon [which is the big city] to study." I did not even know where they went. My parents did not say much, because they did not trust anyone around them; Communist spies were everywhere. To this day, I am still trying to piece together all of my brothers' stories. The faith of my parents was strong; they trusted in the Lord completely. If all this were to happen now, people might judge that my parents were negligent and led my brothers into danger. I look back and say that, in sending my brothers to a land where they could pray and worship God freely, my parents were like Saint Joseph and Mother Mary heeding the call of the angel to take baby Jesus to Egypt. In response to my parents' childlike trust, God protected my brothers and provided for their needs on the journey. One after another, all six of them made it to different locations in the United States, with the help of generous people. On my brothers' part, their cluelessness and innocence helped them to travel outside of our home country into a new land the Lord had prepared for us from all eternity. As I reflect on this, I realize that the lesson is that our trust in the Lord should be like that of a child: He will never abandon us. He said He will be with us until the end of the world. With God's help, my oldest brother sponsored the rest of the family, and we settled in Houston, Texas.

RESPONSE TO THE PROMISE

When I finished eighth grade, I fulfilled, without even knowing it, the pinky promise made long ago. That summer, my sister asked if I would like to come to Oregon for high school. Her religious community has a branch in Portland, Oregon, and when we left Vietnam together, she had joined them right away. I responded "yes", with the consent of my parents. During those years, I went to an all-girls private high school while living with the Sisters as an aspirant, the first stage in religious life. It might sound like a boarding school, but it was more than that, because we did everything with the Sisters. We prayed with them, we ate with them, we slept in the same corridor. At the end of the summer, we would go home and visit our parents for three months, then come back to school again. Living close to the Sisters, I felt

> "Therefore, behold, I will allure her, and bring her into the wilderness, and speak tenderly to her."
>
> Hosea 2:14

the call to religious life even more strongly. God had wooed me at an early age with the pinky promise and now, when I was a teenager living with the Sisters, He continued to send me different signs saying, "Come be my bride."

Every summer when I visited my family, I did not want to return to school, because I did not want to be a Sister like I had promised. I wanted to forget about what I had said to God, because I had a different plan. God did not want me to linger on that thought for long. My family on their part always bought a round trip ticket for me whenever I visited home. That was their way of saying, "You need to get back and finish school."

When I graduated from high school, the Sisters encouraged me to apply for college. They asked if I was interested in entering the novitiate, and I said yes. So I continued living with them and graduated from college with a teaching degree. I discerned that I wanted to continue living the religious life, if the Sisters would have me. They accepted my desire to live and profess the evangelical counsels for a year. Then, I renewed another year. The third year, a retreat priest from a Holy Cross community introduced silence during meals, a monastic tradition that is part of the Dominican life. I thought, "What a beautiful way to reflect on Scripture while being nourished bodily!" When I met with the priest, seeking advice, he inspired me to inquire more about religious life in other communities. That was the beginning of my journey toward a simpler and more austere way of life.

SIGNS FROM ABOVE

The Lord's ways are mysterious. As I look back, I can see the Holy Spirit working in me and in my surroundings. He nudged me with the question, "Would you be able to belong to this community for the rest of your life?" I voluntarily answered, no. But I wanted to make sure this answer did not come from me, that it was the prompting of the Holy Spirit. During my third year under temporary vows, I was sent to northern Virginia to take a teaching job at a Catholic elementary school in Alexandria. The community did not require the Sisters to wear the habit all the time. I asked permission to wear my habit to teach at the school because I wanted the children to see who and what a religious Sister is. In prayer, I asked the Lord to help me find the right community if it was His will, so that I could live the rest of my life as a religious, without second-guessing myself.

One day, a newsletter addressed to me came in the mail. I opened it, and it was a mailing from the Dominican Sisters of Mary, Mother of the Eucharist. I saw Mother Assumpta's letter about how the community was bursting at the seams and how they needed funds to build a larger foundation. I quietly tucked it away and prayed for vocations to their community, since I had taken the vow of poverty and did not have any money to send to support them. Later, the priest at the parish announced that the Vocation Directress from Mother Assumpta's community would come to visit and give a parish mission talk. I thought it would be a beautiful way of getting ready for Lent. I was reluctant to meet Sister Joseph Andrew, but she came into my classroom and gave a short talk about Saint Dominic and the Rosary. I was enthralled and convinced that God sent her just for me.

> "You will know your vocation by the joy that it brings you."
> Servant of God Dorothy Day

On another occasion, Father had an end of the year luncheon for the staff to enjoy. I was not wearing my habit, and Father did not recognize me when I greeted him. I reminded him who I was, and he lovingly reminded me that the habit set me apart and identified me with Christ. You could say that it was the final straw for me. I could not help but think that he was right.

How could I belong to Christ totally if I did not show that beautiful habit to the world?

I prayed a lot about whether it was God's will for me to leave my community. I still wanted to make sure it came from God. I asked for His peace to reign in me and in my superiors when the opportune time came to tell them. When I called the Regional Superior back in Oregon, she was understanding. She calmly said something like, "Sister, if you don't think this is the place for you, you are free to go." I could not believe what I heard. There was no "What's wrong; did something happen?" A deep sense of relief came over me, and I knew it was time. I said my goodbyes and left the community a month shy of fulfilling the vows for that year. My sister was devastated, but she respected my decision to leave. When I called my family, they were so gracious as to arrange the transportation needed for me to come home. My parents and siblings did not bombard me with questions about what had happened. I asked them to give me a month to continue living my religious life, fulfilling the commitments that I had made, and then I would tell them what was happening in my life.

As soon as the month was over, I told my family that I knew I was still called to be a religious somewhere else. My parents sighed with relief. I started looking for the next retreat held by a community for young women. I had three Dominican communities in mind: the Vietnamese Dominicans (whom my parents suggested), the Nashville Dominicans, and the Dominican Sisters of Mary, Mother of the Eucharist. The first two communities had their "come and see" retreats in the spring, the last community had one in November; it was then July. I was so excited; I signed up for the retreat and booked the flight for the retreat weekend in November.

Things moved quickly from there. I emailed the vocation directress, Sister Joseph Andrew, as Father Thomas Vander Woude suggested. The Directress's assistant inquired about my college background, and I gave her all the details of my past religious life. The Directress wrote back to me right away. She also spoke with my previous community. She then asked me to come up to Ann Arbor right away—instead of waiting until November—so that she could meet me and talk with me. I relied on Jesus' help. I asked Him again for another sign. Since I had already booked the flight for November, could the airline switch it so that I could fly out in August without extra charge? They said absolutely. The Lord is so mysterious in all His ways. Everything was going according to His plan. It was as though all the pieces of the puzzle came together in the nick of time. Whatever needed to happen, happened. I needed to see the doctor, check. Psychologist, check. Health checkup, check. Everything was completed within a week of August 28, entrance day. If that is not the grace of God, I don't know what is.

> "He has caused his wonderful works to be remembered; the Lord is gracious and merciful."
> Psalm 111:4

FOR ALL MY LIFE

With God's help, I entered my new religious family with much gratitude for my previous formation. God planted the seed through a friend, and He used all the means to help me get closer to Him. When I received the name Sister Christiana (*ana* meaning "grace" and *Christi* meaning "of Christ"), I finally understood that He wanted me to remember what it meant to live in His grace. With all my heart and soul, I belong to Him forever and ever in the religious community of the Dominican Sisters of Mary, Mother of the Eucharist.

> Women religious are a necessity in the world today. Their spousal love of Jesus Christ shows the world there is something greater than what the world has to offer. Each one of us are beloved sons and daughters of the Father and women Religious radiate this love. We need them to point us to the other worldly love of God and the promise of eternal life.
>
> —Father Sean Magaldi
> Vocation Director, Diocese of Rockville Centre

The Beauty Seeker

How I Left Boys, Beaches, and Ballet Flats for the Convent

Sister Gianna Marie Borchers, OP
Born in Santa Rosa, California

"No, Mommy, a dress. I want to wear a dress today!" Sighing, and with an exasperated smile playing on her lips, my mom put away the brightly colored tracksuit, so popular in the '80s and '90s, and reached into my closet for a dress. This exchange was a daily occurrence once I could speak, for "dress" had been one of my first words. My mom would pull out some cute and bright outfit, and I would persistently and flatly refuse to wear it unless it was a dress. I would only deign to wear pants if the shirt that accompanied them had some type of ruffle on the bottom, thereby fulfilling the essential requirement of a dress. Fast forward to the present: my mom now laughingly says this daily demand was an anticipation of my religion vocation when I would wear a "dress" for the rest of my life. Ironically enough, neither my mom nor I had any exposure to religious Sisters at this time, and thus this thought was far from our minds.

Unquestionably, the greatest gift of my life, after my vocation, is my family. I am the oldest of eight children, a homeschooler, and my dad, Keith, has worked for the Catholic Church in various catechetical positions and is founder of Evangelium Consulting Group. When I introduce myself and rattle off these facts, bright, idyllic images inevitably form in my listener's imagination. Surely, they presume, I must have known my vocation from a young age, due to my familial and personal piety; I must have been spared all suffering and strife; and in a nutshell, my life must heretofore have been a bed of roses. While it is undeniable that I have been spared many sufferings of my generation (particularly because my parents have a strong, loving, and holy marriage which did not dissolve into divorce) our family had its share of crosses and sorrow. This side of heaven, even roses have thorns; yet, in God's mysterious plan, these sufferings and pains mold and fashion the character and integrity of each Christian, if, *if*, they allow it. Suffering is often the crack in the heart through which grace slips. So I would not wish away these thorns. Looking back, both the roses and thorns that led to the discovery of my vocation are woven together beautifully into a tapestry that I will understand fully only in the next life.

> Suffering is often the crack in the heart through which grace slips.

When I was born, my parents were on the cusp of reversion. They had both been poorly catechized and thus their lukewarm faith was a product of ignorance, not malice. A pivotal turning point was when they decided to move to Steubenville, Ohio, in order for my dad to attend Franciscan University. While there, my parents began to live and love the Catholic Faith fully, thanks to their new knowledge of the Faith and the witness of their friends and the college faculty. With the support and friendship of Kimberly Hahn, my mom decided to start homeschooling me, since the schools in the area were far from ideal. This "only while we're in Ohio" plan would eventually turn into a several-decade endeavor, and my mom went on to homeschool all eight of her children. While my mom began homeschooling, my dad in turn began his studies in Franciscan's nascent catechetical program, led by the inimitable Barbara Morgan. My dad's deep love and passionate desire to teach and spread the Catholic Faith was born during these important years. Both the homeschooling and the formation and education received at Franciscan would have long-lasting ramifications in my family's life.

After this powerful reversion, my parents began in ways both big and small to incorporate the Catholic Faith and liturgical life into our family's daily life. It was only later that I realized how countercultural this was, when I discovered that other families generally did not pray together or discuss the Catholic Faith in heated debates around the dinner table. For me, it was the air I breathed. The traditions that materialized and blossomed as a fruit of my parents' reversion were seemingly simple, yet deeply impactful. We would have special desserts on feast days, put out stockings on the feast of Saint Nicholas, extend the celebration of Christmas for the entire octave by spacing out our gifts, and generally begin and end each day with family prayer time. I frequently witnessed my parents in personal prayer, usually in the early morning, and only if the house was on fire were we kids to disturb them during this hallowed time. Before any major decision, my parents spent many long hours in prayer and would ask us to pray as well. As each of us got older, it was not unusual to hear, "Have you prayed about it?" or "How is your prayer life?" from one or both of our parents.

While these traditions may sound as if they belong in a saint biography, rather than a modern story, the actual execution of many of these traditions was often far from perfect and extremely comical. Our family Rosaries were often a disaster, with one or more of my brothers dissolving into giggles, which would spread like wildfire, and inevitably disrupt the whole pious practice. I have many memories of my siblings lacing their plastic Rosary between their toes and then catapulting them across the room when my parents were not looking. Our "family huddle" after each Sunday Mass was a beautiful moment when we all would recite the Saint Michael prayer together, but the piety would soon fade as the bickering and teasing commenced immediately afterward. While the Catholic faith permeated and supported our chaotic family life, trips to the ER to stitch up gashes and set broken bones were also part and parcel of this "blessed chaos."

> "Soon we'll have the intimate happiness of the family, and it's this beauty that brings us closer to Him."
>
> —Saint Louis Martin
> Father to Saint Thérèse of Lisieux

When I was six, my dad took a job in Sioux Falls, South Dakota, to work for Bishop Robert Carlson. It was in South Dakota that I first met religious. They were a discalced Carmelite community and, after a few initial visits, at the wise age of eight I decided I would one day join them. This was hardly a surprise to my family, for my parents frequently shared their desire for each of us to discern prayerfully and intentionally our vocation and often remarked that they would feel blessed to have a priest and/or religious in the family. However, I was no Saint Thérèse, and my motives were hardly pure. Precocious child that I was, I had decided, after living with several younger brothers, that I had no intention to marry, since my husband would probably be as much a tease and a slob as my brothers were, and that I would avoid undue misery by becoming a nun. I am embarrassed to say that no love of God motivated me, for God was not even a Someone to me, but rather a something that I checked off my list. I was an obedient child and thus performed all acts of piety and religion with a sense of duty to my parents, whom I loved greatly, but not from an authentic love of God Himself. The Carmelites were very kind to me, allowing me to write them long letters filled with questions about the life of a nun, and even invited me to stay in their guest quarters for a few days to experience their life. I was convinced I would be another Saint Thérèse, enter young, and become a very great saint someday.

Shortly after meeting the Carmelites, I met the Dominican Sisters of Mary, Mother of the Eucharist. A close family friend entered this community and Sister Elizabeth Ann, as she became, won my undying love and admiration by giving me all of her Nancy Drew books (almost the whole series!) when she entered the order in Ann Arbor, Michigan. Our family attended her First Vows, and I felt greatly conflicted during the visit. Was I supposed to be a Carmelite or a Dominican? I settled on a Carmelite by the end of the weekend, since I did not particularly want to be a teacher. But, I secretly admitted to myself, the Dominican habit was quite lovely…and I needed to pick carefully which order to enter, since I would be wearing whichever habit for the rest of my life!

My desire to be a religious Sister did not last long, for around the age of twelve I became consumed with the pursuit and attainment of beauty and the desire to be loved and understood perfectly. All my actions and decisions revolved around these two goals: to be beautiful and to be loved. I cared much more about my hair and makeup than I did about praying the Rosary, and I thought more about my friendships with my peers than my friendship with God. The abundant love I received from my

Carmelites vs. Dominicans

Founders

The Prophet Elijah

While Elijah did not strictly found the Carmelite Order, the early hermits of the Order considered him their model and lived near Mount Carmel where Elijah heard "the still small whisper" of God. The Order was later reformed by Saint Teresa of Ávila.

Saint Dominic

Due to the rampant heresy of Albigensianism plaguing Europe, Saint Dominic founded the Order of Preachers (the Dominicans) to preach Truth. They consider themselves "contemplative apostles" seeking to share the fruits of their deep prayer with all they encounter.

Mottos

Zelo zelatus sum pro Domino Deo exercituum

With zeal have I been zealous for the Lord, God of hosts

Laudare, benedicere, praedicare

To praise, to bless, to preach

Some Saints of the Order

Saint Teresa of Ávila
Saint John of the Cross
Saint Thérèse of Lisieux
Saint Teresa Benedicta of the Cross (Edith Stein)

Saint Albert the Great
Saint Thomas Aquinas
Saint Catherine of Siena
Saint Rose of Lima
Pope Saint Pius V

parents and siblings was not enough—I was constantly seeking to make new friends and was determined to find the perfect soul mate that I had read about in so many books and seen in countless chick flicks. My Mr. Darcy was out there; I simply had to find him! I retained the habits and practices of a "good Catholic girl", attending Mass and Confession frequently and even making time for personal prayer, but it still was not motivated by love. My prayer time was a one-sided conversation: I told God my plans, presumed His approval, and left no time for silence to listen to His voice.

At the end of eighth grade, I was confirmed with several of my peers. Leading up the event, I was more occupied with studying for the grueling test, which involved extensive memorization, and worrying about what I would wear, than preparing to receive this fresh outpouring of the Holy Spirit. When I approached the Bishop to be anointed with the chrism, he looked at me long and hard and then said gravely, "Did you know that there was a time when the Church was considering canonizing the whole family of Saint Thérèse [my Confirmation saint] in one fell swoop?" Presuming the bishop was simply making conversation, I mutely nodded my head, waiting for the chrism, which undoubtedly would ruin my cute hairdo and clog my pores. "And what will this Thérèse do?" he asked, fixing me again with a probing look. Rather confused, and now thoroughly embarrassed, I looked up at him helplessly. Seeing my distress and inability to grasp his point, the Bishop put a strong hand on my shoulder and said with quiet command, "You will make your family saints." He then went on to finish the rite of Confirmation, but I could not forget his words, nor the deep peace that descended on me when he placed his hands on my head. I attempted to make light of the event with its piercing solemnity and subsequent responsibility and thus told my family about his words. They all laughed and said I would make them saints by testing their patience and forcing them to grow in virtue! I laughed it off, too, and ignored the small voice that said I was called to something different. Certainly, I would love and pray for my family, but I would do it within the context of my own plans. These plans were still materializing, but I was convinced I would get married to somebody extremely handsome, travel the world with him, and have some kids. We would immerse ourselves in culture, beauty, and the arts, and I would be deliriously happy and perfectly loved. In my youthful mind, I believed myself to be completely self-sufficient and my destiny something that could be plied and molded. I had only to stretch out my hand to grasp the glittering future that awaited. If pressed, I would have probably admitted that I controlled my happiness and my destiny, not God.

This seeming self-sufficiency was completely shattered when my mom had a life-threatening brain aneurysm a few months after my Confirmation. Shortly before the surgery that could have taken her life, my siblings and I filed into the hospital room to say goodbye—perhaps forever. I will never forget how my dad leaned down and kissed my mom before the nurses rolled her away, or the distinct smell of the hospital hallway where I paced back and forth with our neighbor, Julie Dahl. My mom epitomized much of what I hoped for and dreamed about: she was strikingly beautiful and was loved by my dad. We often joked that Hollywood could make a chick flick about their courtship and marriage, due to its rocky and comical start but nearly perfect finish. But no chick flick, except perhaps *A Walk to Remember*, has a tragic death. My mom had six kids and a loving husband—we could not lose her! I reeled under the realization that there were aspects of my life that I could not control. Life was fragile, and the more I grasped it, the more it was evident that it was not mine. I begged God with all my heart not to take my mom away; I could not live without her love and support. When she miraculously came out of the surgery without any side effects, I experienced euphoric gratitude, basking in the joy of answered prayer.

Yet even near-death experiences fade into faint memories, and by my junior year in high school, I was once again only outwardly Catholic but interiorly a pragmatic pagan. God had given me my mom back, but it was clearly my prayers and sheer effort that had won her back. I was again the master of my world and charter of my destiny. My continued quest to be loved and to be beautiful had only intensified, for we had moved back to northern California, and I once again was trying to make friends and fit in. Within a few months of our move, I had everything that a girl my age "needed" to be happy: a well-paying job; excellent grades and promising college opportunities; the newest version of the current technological fad, the iPod; a large group of lively, fun-loving friends; a cute and smart guy, who, I had reason to suspect, liked me; and, most importantly, a closet full of the cutest and most stylish ballet flats, which were all the rage. Yet I wasn't happy. I was utterly miserable, restless, and unable to make up my mind about college. Making decisions had never been difficult for me, and I was plagued by this lack of peace and total dearth of happiness. My mom, seeing my distress, recommended that I attend a discernment retreat with the Dominican Sisters of Mary, Mother of the Eucharist. I would be able to see our dear friend, Sister Elizabeth Ann, pray with the Sisters, and spend the weekend with other great Catholic girls. But my dreams of being a Sister were long past, and I questioned my mom's wisdom. A discernment retreat was the last thing right now that would help me! My unruffled mom continued to press her point: you did not attend a discernment retreat just if you thought you had a religious vocation. You could also take other discernment questions to the retreat, such as decisions regarding college, and take them to prayer. She reminded me that I was not going to be roped into the convent, and definitely not forced, so I had nothing to fear. Since I was

> You will make your family saints.

so desperate to find peace and answers, I finally agreed, and silently prayed, "Okay. God, are you listening? On this retreat, please tell me which college I'm going to attend. Thanks. Bye." As amusing as this seems, most of my prayers had sounded like this for the past ten years of my life.

I was met at the Detroit airport by two smiling, nearly glowing, Sisters. In their presence, I felt joy—not the fleeting happiness of the past few years, but deep, unshakeable joy. The Sisters made me feel perfectly at ease, as if I had known them for years, and I felt strangely at home in their presence. However, I convinced myself these emotions were simply ghosts of my childhood dream to be a nun, and I tried to pay the sensations no heed. Yet, the joy persisted and only grew with the passing hours. Vainly, I tried to focus on prayers regarding college decisions and instead felt more and more drawn to the Sisters and their life. On the second day of the retreat, I went to Confession in the afternoon and, for the first time, had the grace to see that I was not allowing God to be God in my life. Although I went to Confession regularly, it had become an insipid habit and I rarely prepared well. This Confession was quite different and, as I walked away, I felt as if actual scales had fallen from my eyes. With renewed clarity about my sins and with great gratitude for God's infinite mercy and patience, I heartily asked God for forgiveness and prayed for the courage to let Him be the true Lord of my life.

After Confession, I went to the chapel where the retreatants prayed Vespers with the Sisters. My heart was light after the transformative confession, and I felt as if I were on the brink of something wonderful. But what? Was God about to tell me in no uncertain terms where I would go to college? We all knelt to pray the Joyful Mysteries and I then experienced what I later dubbed a "spiritual two-by-four". Sometimes, I am rather slow; but the Lord in His mercy stepped in and made His love and His will very clear in the space of that unforgettable Rosary.

He so overwhelmed me with peace and joy that I no longer had doubts and no longer resisted. As my fingers slowly slipped over the Rosary beads and my mouth murmured each well-known prayer, I saw before my mind's eye the whole swath of my life and the golden thread of God's design beautifully woven into it. My persistent, aching desires to be loved and to be beautiful would only be fulfilled within my God-given vocation as a Sister. This vocation was not something that I could earn, let alone manufacture. God alone could love me as completely and as perfectly as I desired, and He alone could bestow on me His loveliness through His grace. This beauty would go even deeper than the lovely Dominican habit and would pierce my soul, where it would remain untarnished by age or sickness. Earthly perfection and beauty passes with time, but God's loveliness is an eternal beauty. This perfect, eternal love and beauty was what I had sought in all the wrong places. Overcome by this realization, I simply and sincerely gave my fiat to follow His will and learn how to love Him as a Person, as my Spouse. No longer was the Lord something to be checked off my list; He was the very rock of my existence and joy. I desired to be in relationship with Him and to entrust everything—my youth, my plans, my family—to His perfect will.

This explosion of grace was an undeserved, unexpected gift and still appears, thirteen years after the fact, too good to be true. Why in the space of just a few moments was I given such clarity and peace? Others must labor long and painfully before finding their vocation; yet, God in His mysterious plan saved me from such a circuitous path and made my way straight and clear. Unlike many other moments in my life, this event did not fade from my memory, and my life after that Rosary bears testament to the authenticity and power of the graces received. I returned home, was showered with support by my loving family, and finished my last year of high school before entering the community on August 28, 2008. Without question, it would have been difficult to remain steadfast in my resolve to enter after my senior year if not for my family's constant love, prayers, and support throughout the year. I now wear every day the lovely habit of the Dominican family, the mandatory "dress" of my toddler years, and have found Him whom my heart loves and will never let go. The path continues to be strewn with roses, which both pierce and pad my way. The thorn is a necessary reminder that I am not self-sufficient, and the petal is a promise of the eternal joy to come. *Deo gratias!*

> God alone could love me as completely and as perfectly as I desired, and He alone could bestow on me His loveliness through His grace.

How I Left Boys, Beaches, and Ballet Flats for the Covent

> Growing up in the 1960s in a mostly Polish South Suburb of Chicago I can honestly say I was partially raised by nuns! It was simply taken for granted that all teachers were Sisters! The impact of these dedicated women, who were extra "mothers" to us in so many ways, simply cannot be measured.
>
> How grateful I am for the education I received, both academically and in what it meant to be a child of God and a faithful son of the Church. These seeds were planted by those Sisters and nourished by my family—which made the pursuit of a religious vocation and my eventual decision to enter the seminary a reality. The radical "all or nothing" example of these women made them heroes. I am so very grateful.
>
> -Father David C. Downey
> Saint Clare Church, North Palm Beach, FL

When the Good Life Is Not Enough

Baptism, Beekeeping, and Becoming the Woman God Created Me to Be

Sister Irenaeus Schluttenhofer, OP
Born in Connorsville, Indiana

When people ask when and how I heard God's call to the religious life, I usually share my experiences in college. But, like most short answers to big questions, that oversimplifies the matter: my vocation did not spring up out of nowhere when I was twenty-one years old. Each vocation reflects fathomless graces from a faithful, persistent, and—as Scripture tells us—jealous God (see Ex 20:5, 34:14). Scripture clearly shows us that He will not accept a half-hearted or divided love; over time, the Lord showed me that He wanted it all. The story that He is continuing to write in my life is a story of learning how to give Him more and more of my heart. Here is a peek into that story.

My vocation story started in Baptism. Indeed, every vocation story starts there, for this sacrament bestows the graces necessary to gain heaven. To a wailing three-week-old infant came the indwelling Trinity. Although I have no recollection of the event, God came to dwell in my soul. He gave me faith to believe in Him, hope for the possibility of heaven, and love of both Him and neighbor. These incredible realities are true for each baptized person. The sacrament left a mark on my soul. It gave me a new family, somehow bigger than the Schluttenhofer clan. A distant homeland began to beckon: heaven.

But I was no cherubic child, just a normal one. I frequently instigated trouble with my two older siblings, talked back, and refused to clean my side of the room. For twenty years, I heard whispers of—and usually turned away from—the still, small voice (see 1 Kgs 19:12). In short, the Lord had serious work to do.

My family's attendance at Mass was probably the biggest factor in my vocation. Every Sunday, Holy Day of Obligation—or day that my dad thought was a Holy Day—my family and I were at Saint Joseph's Catholic Church in Lebanon, Indiana. As my siblings and I reached middle school and high school, the number of our classmates in Religious Ed dwindled. In our house, my brother, sister, and I sometimes complained about going to Mass, but we knew there was not really any point in arguing. My family was not terribly devotional; when we were at the table together, we prayed before meals, but usually not at other times. However, going to Mass was a non-negotiable. Although on a few occasions, I may have exaggerated symptoms to stay home "sick", my secret was that I actually really enjoyed going to Mass. As I grew older, I was an altar server and lector and attended our parish youth group.

My favorite time of the year was, and is, Christmas. At Christmastime, the traditions and joys of the season captivated my restless heart. I wanted to be better—not in a ploy to get more presents, but for Him. Each year, after decorating the tree and positioning the figures in the nativity scene, I would ponder over the lack of room in the inn, the angels, and the swaddling clothes. Linus's recital of Luke Chapter 2 in *A Charlie Brown Christmas* narrated my thoughts. At Mass on Christmas, I would sing at the top of my lungs that the Lord had come. At some point, the idea came to me: I wanted to give baby Jesus a home.

On Good Friday when I was about eleven years old, my family attended the Liturgy of the Lord's Passion; I cannot be sure, but I think we spent the trip to church complaining about the length of the Gospel. The time came to venerate the cross, and the lights dimmed. As we processed towards the cross, my mind was racing in typical middle-school fashion. I watched the other people: some parishioners kissed the cross, some people touched it or knelt down. How long were you supposed to stay there? What was normal? But as I got to the cross, the self-conscious thoughts faded away and other words started thumping in my head: "Crucify Him, crucify Him". The words of Jerusalem's crowds that the congregation painfully makes their own each Good Friday echoed as I touched the cross, and I was overwhelmed with a sense of shame followed by a present love. For the first time, I understood the reality of sin and the cost of salvation.

WHILE I WANDERED, HE WAITED

As high school arrived, however, a life focused on "an event a long time ago" and "heaven a long way off" simply could not compete with my very social life of friends, activities, and relationships. My family never talked about vocation, and I had never really seen religious life; it simply never crossed my radar. And if people were looking at my life, few would have thought me a likely candidate. As a teaching Sister today,

I laugh to think about my own lack of study skills: I usually did my homework the morning it was due! My world revolved around guys and friends.

Since this was a time in my life when I was not listening, God began to call a little louder. In high school, two events shaped my understanding of who God had created me to be. Since the time I was in elementary school, my family had "sponsored" a girl in Guatemala. In addition to my parent's monthly contribution, at least a few times each year, we would write letters or send a box of supplies. When I was sixteen years old, the opportunity arose to meet our sponsor child and experience the work of the missionary organization for a week. Miraculously, the trip was relatively affordable; my parents decided that we would all go to Guatemala. I was thrilled. I loved studying Spanish and had always loved to serve. As we worked with and listened to the stories of the people, I was struck by their simplicity and trust in God's providence. The country was also extraordinarily beautiful: volcanoes surrounded the Mayan town. One afternoon, I stood alone on the flat roof of the building. I started praying out loud, without even recognizing what I was doing or saying: "Lord, I want to give my life to you and to the Church."

To be clear: at that time, I had absolutely no personal prayer life. I prayed at Mass and youth group. But on my own? I almost always skipped the night prayers I knew I should say; when I did say them, my prayer was perfunctory. The only explanation for that day in Guatemala is that the Holy Spirit prayed through me. I did not know what my prayer meant. I hardly knew Him, and I had no idea what it meant to give my life to the Church.

The other important moment of my faith journey in high school occurred at the youth retreat for our diocese. I signed up to go, not knowing what to expect other than the advertised free t-shirt. On that cold February weekend in a high school gym, I met Jesus in Eucharistic Adoration for the first time. The priest carried the monstrance to each person around the

> "When the bee has gathered the dew of heaven and the earth's sweetest nectar from the flowers, it turns it into honey, then hastens to its hive. In the same way, the priest, having taken from the altar the Son of God (who is as the dew from heaven, and true son of Mary, flower of our humanity), gives Him to you as delicious food."
>
> —Saint Francis de Sales

gym. I felt immensely loved and immensely convicted of my sin. I wept, seeing my unworthiness, and resolved that I would start living for Him. The next day before the retreat ended, a Franciscan Sister gave a ten-minute vocation talk—the first I had ever heard. She passed around cards that allowed us to request more information and told us we could turn in the cards completed or blank upon leaving the gym. Hiding from my friends for a few minutes, I filled the card out and dropped it in the basket.

In the coming weeks, the joy of the retreat faded as I returned to my frenetic world of activities and relationships. Nevertheless, I now regularly checked the mailbox—not out of joyful anticipation, but rather to intercept what I already saw as a fatal error. Luckily, I retrieved the piece of mail before anyone else in the family spotted a letter from a convent with my name on it. After reading it cursorily, I tucked in the back pocket of a Bible cover and did not find it again until six years later.

When I started my freshman year at Purdue University, it followed the same pattern of my high school life. Although I still was not sure what I wanted to do, being at Purdue and studying environmental science fit perfectly, and I made friends quickly. Going to Sunday Mass was not an issue; my parent's stance on that obligation had formed a habit. A true extrovert, I even managed to bring friends to Mass! At church events, I felt truly alive and would want to live the Faith more deeply. However, I essentially lived two lives; who I was at church did not translate into the rest of my actions. At night, I would look up at the ceiling and think, "This cannot be all there is." My heart felt empty, and my conscience gnawed at me. The proverbial "Catholic guilt" told me that vice was not the answer; but to be honest, it was easier than virtue.

In February of my freshman year of college, a friend from Saint Tom's, the university parish, invited me to come on "a retreat with some Sisters in Ann Arbor". I did not know it was a discernment retreat, but I did know that I needed a retreat; I was at a very low point and looked forward to the happy feelings that had always followed high school retreats for me. But the Lord had something more in mind than just temporary happiness: He wanted to give me true joy.

I commenced a five-hour road-trip with women who truly loved Jesus. Upon our arrival at the school on Joy Road, a fleet of Sisters welcomed us with open arms. They grabbed our pillows and sleeping bags and swept us into a twenty-four-hour retreat that changed my life. That evening, the retreat master, Father David Meconi, SJ, preached about being beloved daughters of the Father. My heart burned at his words. Later, during Eucharistic Adoration, the Sisters made sure every young woman had the chance to go to Confession. In the confessional, Father asked penetrating questions and helped me to receive the Father's healing love. I wanted the joy the Sisters had, which clearly came from the Lord.

Upon returning to Purdue, I knew that my life needed to change if I wanted the freedom and the joy I had experienced on retreat. Slowly, I started finding myself more and more at Saint Tom's, where other students lived their faith fully and authentically. Peer pressure served as positive influence on my people-pleasing self! Over the next two years, I began living a sacramental life to the full. I had never known that someone might actually want to go to Confession! Going to the 9 p.m. Wednesday Mass became a new routine, and then somehow, I added the Monday, Tuesday, and Thursday Mass to my schedule. Suddenly, I could not imagine a day without Him.

> I wanted the joy the Sisters had, which clearly came from the Lord.

The Lord rarely lets me get comfortable. It seems to be His way to lead me to a place, help me see how good it is, and then to ask for something more, or take away the training wheels. In my college years, I grew in my faith, but He still wanted more. My relationship with Christ was still highly dependent on the social aspect; when I was tired, the factor spurring me to Mass or Bible study was still the fact that friends would be there or that others were counting on me. While small groups, events, and retreats build up one's faith, in the end, a firmly founded relationship with God has to be personal and not dependent on outside circumstances. During my junior year of college, God put this to the test.

WHEN THE GOOD LIFE IS NOT ENOUGH

During my junior year at Purdue, I took a semester off of college to work as a public spokesperson for the American beekeeping industry. I had been keeping bees since I was twelve years old and loved the industry; this was a dream job! The experience, which took me to more than half the states in the USA, pushed me out of my comfort zone in speaking with government officials and giving television interviews. It also reinforced my love of teaching. Still, although it was an

> **A Virtual Presence**
>
> Many religious orders, including the Dominican Sisters of Mary, Mother of the Eucharist have embraced the mission of "the world wide web" and have their own websites! Many women can learn more about our own community by visiting www.sistersofmary.org

amazing position, something deep within me remained unsatisfied. While traveling around the country promoting the importance of pollination and the benefits of honey, I still sensed a restlessness. I realized that I was made for something more, to tell people about something even better.

In the midst of this, I made sure to schedule in Sunday Mass everywhere I went, but I really missed the daily activities of Saint Tom's. Hotel television does not offer many good shows, so I started to pray and talk heart-to-heart with the Lord. I also started to Google "give your life to God", "becoming a nun", and "religious Sisters". The Dominican Sisters of Mary, Mother of the Eucharist continually showed up. Remembering my retreat experience, I perused the website. As I went through that year, I could not get the Sisters out of my head! While my life continued to be very busy, I now chose to let those busy events form me for Him, rather than distract me.

He showed me how to listen, especially through Mass and personal prayer. And as I started listening, the Lord "started" speaking! He spoke to me through the people I met, the places I went, and the desires of my heart. Around this time, I had a dinner conversation with a friend from Saint Tom's. It went something like this: "I just want to be happy and love Jesus." He responded, "Maybe you'll be a nun." At his semi-joking words, I spilled my water and choked on a piece of broccoli. Where Christ seemed to be leading was a 180-degree shift from all my plans! Other than the notecard-in-the-basket episode,

I had always assumed I would be a wife and mother. I never desired a fast-paced, high-paying job. I just wanted to love and be loved. My hopes and dreams included marrying a farmer or a beekeeper and, above all, being a mom. More than anything, I wanted to have a big Catholic family.

When I returned to Purdue, the Lord made it clear to me that I had to do something about my continuing restlessness. Although I had made progress in listening to the Lord, I still wanted to have control, to do what seemed logical or reasonable. I decided to change my major. Only months after starting classes in my new major, I realized that this career would not make me existentially happy, either.

SEEKING HEAVEN ON EARTH

So, I started to discern a religious vocation. I had heard that if you were going to discern officially, a spiritual director could be helpful. In the confessional, I asked my priest about it. After all, if I inquired during Confession and then did not follow through, the priest, bound by the seal of Confession, could not speak with me about it later! But the Lord outsmarted me. The priest gave me the best penance of my life. He told me to pray every day for a month, "Lord, help me to become the woman you have created me to be."

I did not even know a priest could give a penance that lasted a month. Still, I knew that Confession did not "count" if I did not do my penance. So each morning, I dutifully prayed to become the woman God had made me to be. That prayer changed my life. It changed my entire mindset on vocation. While I knew that I was seeking God's will, I was still thinking about it in terms of pros and cons.

> Lord, help me to become the woman you have created me to be.

> I knew what a vocation was and was asking the Lord which vocation He had called me to.

This prayer helped me realize that, if I did have a religious vocation, it was not something new. He was revealing a gift that had been waiting for me the whole time. I returned to visit the Dominican Sisters of Mary, Mother of the Eucharist at the end of my junior year of college. This time, I knew what a vocation was and was asking the Lord which vocation He had called me to. By the time I spoke with the Sisters' Vocation Directress, I told her that I was certain, more certain than I wanted to be, that I was called to religious life. She laughed, and then—to my surprise, horror, and amazement—agreed.

One of the elements of my prayer life that had been growing each day was a longing for heaven. Each of us is created for eternal life. Upon walking into the Motherhouse chapel, where the Sisters adore the Eucharist each day, I realized that if heaven is the beatific vision, seeing God face to face, then Eucharistic Adoration is the closest we can get to it on this earth. God showed me that to adore Him would be to start my heaven here. Even though I am far from perfect, and my Sisters are not perfect, and my students are not perfect, to be with the Lord each day, even if we only see Him dimly veiled in the Eucharist, is a taste of His infinite love and the glory of heaven.

While my heart longed at that moment to start immediately the Dominican life of praising, blessing, and preaching, I returned to Purdue to start my senior year of college. God calls each person differently, and in conversation with the Vocation Directress, Sister Joseph Andrew, I knew that I needed that last year to continue to receive His love and grow in trust. That year, the Lord taught me how to love His mother. In my twenty-two years as a Catholic, I had never managed a whole Rosary on my own. That year, I started praying one decade at a time between each class, and learned how to love my "Mama Mary" in a whole new way. The Rosary taught me how to meditate on the life of Jesus. To this day, whenever I am walking more than a few steps, I grab my Rosary and start to say a decade. I do not pray the mysteries in any particular order, and "decade" is a loose term of between eight and twelve Hail Marys. Still, I think there is something a mother must particularly love when a child comes to her as a complete mess!

And that word is a good summary of my vocation story: I was a mess, and I still am a mess! And that is okay. Because, trusting in His love, I know that He is not done with me yet.

NO SUCH THING AS A DO-IT-YOURSELF SAINT

My parents taught me to do many useful things. We froze and canned fruits and vegetables for the winter. I learned how to sew when I was in third grade. We were a do-it-yourself kind of family. Oil changes? Who would waste money to take the car to the shop, when one could do the job in the garage at home? I carried those lessons with me into adulthood, paying for college with scholarships and, at one point, as many as three part-time jobs. While this is a good habit in many respects—I have completed many DIY projects in the convent—it also has its pitfalls. Rather than see every circumstance of my life as a way to return love to the Beloved who has loved me "to the end" (Jn 13:1), I am tempted to think that I can become a saint by my own willpower or creativity. It is usually fear that fuels this disordered self-sufficiency; I want to keep control.

Here is an analogy. I am a passenger on an airplane. Jesus is the best pilot ever and He is preparing the plane for landing. I look outside, realize the ground is fast nearing us, and begin to experience fear. Yes, Jesus has clearly had this situation under control the whole time. I could enjoy that time with Him, trust that He knows what He is doing, and enjoy the adventure. On the other hand, I know that landing is potentially dangerous. Taking my eyes away from Him, I grab the parachute that I sewed "just in case." The seams look…decent. I have a choice. Maybe I should just leap out of the plane in my parachute, rather than potentially crash inside. It is easier to trust in my own shoddy work, rather than to trust completely in Someone else and place my life in His hands—where I do not have any control.

It is a ridiculous analogy with an obvious conclusion; however, as I have shared my vocation story with others, I have found that it is not uncommon. With DIY Saint Syndrome, we are tempted to a mediocre life of our own design, rather than taking the risk of free and loving trust in Him.

It is an age-old problem. After God led the Israelites out of slavery, through a wall of water and away from their oppressors, they started to worry about where their next meal would come from. In Egypt, they might not have been free, but they had onions. They could not worship the Lord, but they could make great stew (see Ex 16:3, Num 11:5). Following a pillar of fire and cloud into freedom is unpredictable. It is scary. Our temptation is to be safe, to cling to what we know and avoid losing the little we have.

> "The greater and more persistent your confidence in God, the more abundantly you will receive all that you ask."
> -Saint Albert the Great

In my discernment, and even after entering the convent, I have learned more and more to trust in Him. In the words of Saint Polycarp: "He has been my Lord and Savior, and has never done me harm." God has never let me down, even when He has brought me to the rough road of the cross. But it is hard to be vulnerable—in prayer and with my Sisters—and embrace my own weakness. It seems safer to keep checking my parachute and looking for the emergency exit. But that is not how He has created us to live. There is no such thing as a DIY saint. He has made us for Himself. He has made us for authentic freedom, joy beyond our small imaginings, and total self-giving love. He has called me to follow. It is scary, unpredictable. But, simply put: He is God. He can do all things, and I can do all things through Christ who gives me strength (see Phil 4:13).

> "He has been my Lord and Savior, and has never done me harm."
> -Saint Polycarp

Trusting in Him, I know that He will bring me safely home. Finding my vocation has truly been a journey of becoming the woman God has created me to be. He called me to be His bride. All the rest—the messy circumstances of my messy life—is within His loving providence. I may be a mess, but as I tell my Sisters and my students: I am His mess. Praise God!

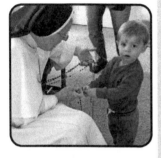

> More than ever the world needs the powerful witness of women dedicated entirely to Christ. What Saint Cyprian wrote of them 1,800 years ago is still true today: 'If we compare the Church to a tree, then they are its blossom. Virgins show forth the beauty of God's grace; they are the image of God that reflects the holiness of the Lord. ... They are the glory of mother Church and manifest her fruitfulness. The more numerous her virgins are, the greater is her joy.'
>
> When the Virgin gives birth to our Savior, do we not sing 'Joy to the World'? Thus through Christ's Bride, the Church, and especially through her consecrated daughters, will the world be reacquainted with the joy Jesus desires us all to possess (see Jn 15:11).
>
> —Father Jacob Boddicker, SJ

From South to North of the Border

Known, Loved, and Awaited

Sister Maria Francisco Molina, OP
Born in Mexico City, Mexico

It was the last day of my summer vacation before starting my freshman year in high school. My parents, my sister, and I had finished dinner and had gone down to the basement to watch some home videos. The past few years had held a series of moves from Mexico to England to Minnesota, and the thought of watching some home videos together and reminiscing about favorite memories seemed comforting. We picked a videotape out at random and began to watch it.

The video showed footage from the first time we had lived in England. My sister was three years old, and I was five. We were living in Leeds, England where my dad was getting his Master's degree in Economics at the University of Leeds. My mom was recording us while we were playing, and asking us questions about what we were doing and learning in England. She had intended to send this video to my grandma back in Mexico. As the video drew to a close, my mom asked us to come closer to the camera and say goodbye to our grandma. My five-year-old self ran to the camera saying, "Goodbye, Grandma. I love you."

Just as we had finished watching this scene, I heard the phone ring upstairs. I waited for either my mom or dad to get up and answer it, but neither of them heard it over the videos. The phone kept ringing, so I ran upstairs to pick it up. As I was running up the stairs, I got a feeling that something was wrong. I do not know how to explain it, but I knew that my grandma was dying. I picked up the phone, and it was my grandma's sister. She would not tell me what was wrong but just asked to speak to my mom. I called out to my mom and ran upstairs to my room, weeping. I started praying to God with my whole heart to save my grandma.

MY GRANDMA TAUGHT ME TO PRAY

Growing up in Mexico City, I had always lived with my grandma. She was a second mother to me. She had ten grandchildren, but I was her favorite, and she did little to hide it. She had been the one to pick out my name when I was born. Shortly after I was born, she had had a brain tumor removed, and after the surgery, she was no longer able to live by herself. My family moved in with her to take care of her. I loved living with my grandma. She would play with me, and every night before I went to bed, I would go to my grandma's room and say my prayers with her. Sometimes if I woke up at night, I would sneak out of my room and into my grandma's room, climb in her bed, and go back to sleep with her close to me. My grandma had been the one who taught me how to pray, and to have a devotion to the Sacred Heart of Jesus.

When I was five, we moved to England for the first time, and one of my aunts moved in with my grandma to take care of her. Once my dad had completed his Master's degree, we moved back to Mexico and resumed taking care of my grandma. My mom started to realize that my grandma was having problems with her memory. She was forgetting things like how to use utensils and button up clothes; she had even forgotten my name. The doctors said that there was nothing to be done and that we had to learn to accept the fact that her memory was only going to get worse. My mom asked

> "When you call me, and come and pray to me, I will listen to you. When you look for me, you will find me. Yes, when you seek me with all your heart, I will let you find me."
>
> Jeremiah 29:12-14a

me to pray for my grandma and I took her request to heart. I would pray for her every day but especially at Mass on Sundays. My family would go to the children's Mass at Saint Rose of Lima Parish, which was run by the Dominican friars. During the intercessions at Mass, I would always ask God to heal my grandma so that she would remember me again. One morning, my mom woke me up and told me to go to my grandma's room and ask her what my name was. I raced down the hall to her room to ask her. She not only remembered my name but also remembered that I was her favorite. I knew that God had heard and answered my prayer. I was so happy because God had given me back my grandma.

We continued to take care of my grandma until I was twelve years old, when we moved back to England the second time, this time for my dad's doctorate. This move back to England was much harder than the first because this time I was aware of being separated from my grandma. I did not want to move. I did not want to leave my grandma behind. Another one of my aunts had arranged to move in with my grandma and take care of her while we were gone. This did little to console me, because I loved taking care of my grandma and missed her terribly. After my dad had finished his coursework for his doctorate in England, we moved directly to Minnesota for his new job. As much as I missed my grandma and would have preferred to go back to Mexico, I could not fail to recognize that God had given my family the opportunity to live in the United States.

THIS NIGHT, I NEEDED GOD

The night my grandma's sister called us in Minnesota, I had closed the door of my room and had thrown myself on my bed crying. I could hear my mom talking on the phone with my great-aunt. I could not make anything out, but the long silence on my mom's part confirmed to me that my grandma was dying. The thought was unbearable. To me, death seemed like a separation from her that I could not bear. I knew that God had given me back my grandma before and that He could do it again if He wanted to. I pulled out a little book of daily reflections on the Mass readings that I kept in my nightstand drawer. Nightly, before saying my prayers the way my grandma had taught me, I would read the reflection for the day. Some nights I would be too tired to read them and would simply say my night prayers and go to sleep. This night, however, I needed God to save my grandma. I flipped to that day's reading, which was the first letter of Saint Paul to the Thessalonians, where he consoles those who have lost a loved one. The reflection said that when someone we love dies, we are going to be sad for a while. Nevertheless, because Jesus conquered death, we can no longer mourn like those who do not have the hope of the resurrection. I had just finished reading this when my mom came in and explained that my grandma had had a brain aneurysm and was on life

> "We do not want you to be unaware, brothers, about those who have fallen asleep, so that you may not grieve like the rest, who have no hope. For if we believe that Jesus died and rose, so too will God, through Jesus, bring with him those who have fallen asleep."
>
> 1 Thessalonians 4:13-14

support. She asked me to pray for a miracle. Even though I wanted a miracle, I somehow knew that I should instead pray for a holy death for my grandma.

Although I cried myself to sleep that night, I did not cry alone. I had never before felt God so close to me, and I understood He was more saddened by my grandma's death than even I. While I had always known that God was real, I now knew that He cared for me and kept me in mind. I kept replaying the scene from the home videos wherein I had said goodbye to my grandma and told her that I loved her. My thoughts turned to everything that had occurred so that moment could happen: I knew this was no accident. God had given me a chance to say goodbye to my grandma and consoled me in a way only He could have orchestrated. I realized that God had gone to great lengths to show me that He understood how important my grandma was to me. That night I knew without a doubt that I was known and loved by God.

My grandma died the next day. Sadly, we were not able to go to Mexico for the funeral. As painful as that was, I would not have wanted it any other way because I knew that God had given me a grace to experience His love and providence in a tangible way.

THE DREAM OF AN AMERICAN EDUCATION

Time eventually eased the pain. I did well in high school. I had seen the many sacrifices my parents had made for my sister and me to have this opportunity and felt a great responsibility to take full advantage of it. My parents would remind us that anyone back in Mexico would give an arm and a leg for the opportunity to receive an education in the United States. My dad would sometimes remind me to study hard because our education was the only inheritance that he could give us. I knew that America was the place where, if you worked hard, your dreams could come true. I took this opportunity as a confirmation from God for me to pursue the career I had always wanted, which was aerospace engineering. Flight and space had fascinated me as a child. I also enjoyed taking things apart and trying to fix them. When I found out that you could put these two interests together and make a living out of it, I knew what I wanted to pursue. It would have been next to impossible for me to fulfill my dream back in Mexico. I knew that working for this with all my ability would be the best way to show my parents and God my gratitude for all they had given me. My goal of going to college and studying aerospace engineering was one of the driving forces in everything I did.

RE-DISCOVERING GOD THROUGH CONFIRMATION

Academics and sports became the most important things to me when I was in high school, even more than my faith. But when I was a senior in high school, my sister asked me to be her Confirmation sponsor. I went to the meeting for the Confirmation sponsors, at which they explained that we, in a way, were responsible for getting those being confirmed to Heaven. My heart sank at this thought because I had not taken my own Confirmation seriously. I had skipped my Confirmation retreat and had just picked my grandma's name instead of choosing a Confirmation saint. I felt like a hypocrite telling my sister she had to go on the retreat, so I made a deal with her that we would go to it together. I had never been on a retreat so I did not know what to expect. All I knew was that I wanted to participate fully, to be a good example to my sister, and to make up for the retreat I had skipped.

> I believed God knew me and loved me; it was now my turn to know and love Him in return.

Before this retreat, I had never been to Eucharistic Adoration in my life. The retreat had all-night Adoration, and that night I could feel God's presence the same way I had felt Him with me the night that my grandma was dying. I recognized the same God who had consoled me that night, right there in front of me. He was there, no doubt about it. I realized that God was closer to me than I had ever imagined and that He had been expecting me for a long time. It was at this point that I realized that God wanted to be with me not only in life's sorrows, but always. He wanted a relationship with me. I understood that this kind of love required a response from me. I believed God knew me and loved me; it was now my turn to know and love Him in return.

After the retreat, my priorities began to change. The changes were very subtle at first. I did not fully recognize that my relationship with God had slowly become my priority until I was well into college. When I got to the University of Minnesota, I was happy to be actualizing my dream of studying aerospace engineering. This was still a major driving force in my college life, and I did very well. I applied myself to my studies and could see God's blessing my efforts. I had a successful college career. By my senior year, I had become the president of the university's chapter of the Society of Hispanic Professional Engineers.

> **Who is Our Lady of Loreto?**
>
> The title of "Our Lady of Loreto" refers to the Holy House where the Holy Family lived. While originally in Palestine, the house was transported to Loreto, Italy. Stories say that the angels themselves carried it to Italy, making Our Lady of Loreto the patroness of aviators.

I was a research assistant in the Unmanned Aerial Vehicle Laboratory of the aerospace department. I had interned for Eaton Corporation for three summers as an engineering intern and had saved up all of my internship money to get my pilot's license.

All throughout college, I was slowly coming to know more and more about God and His Church and to love Him more. The seeds of devotion to the Sacred Heart my grandma had sown in me were beginning to sprout. I had started going to Eucharistic Adoration every chance I could. I could not stay away. I looked forward to the First Friday Adoration nights in honor of the Sacred Heart held for college students at Saint Paul's Seminary in Minnesota. I consecrated myself to Mary on the Feast of Our Lady of Guadalupe and began to pray the rosary every day. I shared my life with her, and she drew me closer to Jesus. Mary helped me come to the realization that Jesus wanted to share not only in the hardships and failures of my life but also in my joys. So I told Him of my joys, particularly the thrill and freedom I experienced whenever I went flying. I felt especially close to God and Our Lady of Loreto any time I would fly the plane into God's heights!

FLYING HIGH IN AEROSPACE

The summer of my sophomore year in college, I moved out to Orange County, California, for an aerospace engineering internship. I had interned with Eaton's truck transmission department in Michigan the summer before and had thoroughly enjoyed it. I was on the systems engineering team, and we wrote the software to automate our transmissions. Our team was also in charge of validating and certifying our software, which meant that we got to test drive our software changes in our semi-trucks. I enjoyed driving the eighteen-wheelers around, but most of all I enjoyed my coworkers and the culture of the company. I expected a similar experience with the aerospace internship, but found it sorely disappointing. It was a very difficult work environment, and I dreaded going to work. I realized that I desperately needed God's help if I was going to get through that summer. I decided to start attending daily Mass before going to work every day and to ask Jesus to help me get through each workday.

After a couple of weeks of going to Mass, the woman who sat in front of me asked if she could speak with me after Mass. She waited for me, and what she had to say took me by total surprise. She did not introduce herself but grabbed me by the arm and asked me if I wanted to be an actress. I did not know how to respond, but before I could politely decline, she told me that the reason she was asking was that she thought I would make a good nun. This made even less sense, and I was beginning to think it was some sort of joke. Still, she assured me she was serious. She proceeded to explain that she was making a vocations video and needed someone to play a nun. She explained that, from the moment she saw me, she knew that I would make the perfect nun for her video and that she could put me in contact with the producer. Before I knew it, she was asking me for my phone number. I thought she was a little crazy and quickly put a stop to it. I thanked her for the opportunity, but told her that I could not act to save my life. She was very insistent but finally let me go.

The fact that someone thought I would make a good nun seemed very funny to me. I told my family about the incident and they all agreed with me: this could not be true. Each morning, when I would see this woman at Mass, I remembered what she had said. I still thought that the incident was humorous, until one day I caught myself thinking that maybe religious life would not be as bad as I thought. This thought shocked me, and as soon as I recognized it, I quickly rejected it. At that point in my life, religious life meant only one thing. It meant giving up everything I had worked for, and my happiness. How could I give up my aerospace degree, my pilot's license, my career after all God had done to give me these things? No, this could not be what God wanted of me; besides, He had given me every opportunity to pursue my plans for my life, and based on my success, He was blessing them.

God helped me finish off my summer assignment. As soon as it was completed, I requested to return to Michigan, which I did the following summer. I put this difficult assignment behind me and kept pursuing my plans but the thought of religious life never went away. By the time I was a senior in college I could not stop thinking about religious life. The thought was almost distracting, and I could no longer ignore it. Just before graduating from college, I realized that I had everything I thought I ever needed to be happy, and it was not enough.

THE RESTLESS HEART ONLY GOD CAN FILL

I went with a restless heart to my last First Friday Adoration night at Saint Paul's Seminary. I no longer knew what to think. God had given me everything I had ever wanted and more. Yet the happiness I had once found in my dreams now seemed empty. I began to wonder if I was being ungrateful for everything God had given me. I questioned why I was not satisfied. The thought of religious life kept coming back and at some point, much to my surprise, it became a desire. I did not understand how I could want this so intensely when in fact I knew so little about it. I had always been sure of what God wanted me to do with my life, but now this was no longer the case. I poured out all of these thoughts before Jesus in the Eucharist and finally told Him I did not know what to do any more. I told Him that He knew me and

> I told Him that He knew me and loved me better than I knew and loved myself and that I trusted Him to help. At this, I heard a voice in my heart say, "Be my bride."

loved me better than I knew and loved myself and that I trusted Him to help. At this, I heard a voice in my heart say, "Be my bride." I understood this to be a call to religious life, even though I did not yet know that a religious Sister was a bride of Christ. Having this sense of direction brought me a peace and joy that I had not experienced before. It brought my heart rest. I told Jesus that if this was what He wanted, He was going to have to make it happen, because I knew no Sisters nor communities and had no idea how to proceed. As soon as I had given Him this permission, God worked very quickly.

Upon graduating from college, I moved to Kalamazoo, Michigan, to work for Eaton's truck division as a systems and control engineer. Within a few weeks of moving to Kalamazoo, God gave me a faithful Catholic young adult community to help me grow in my faith and a spiritual director, Father Chris Ankley, who became a father-figure to me. The first time I met with Father Chris, I told him that I was discerning a vocation. The only Sisters I knew at that point were the Dominicans from my parish back in Mexico. Without really knowing what I was saying, I told Father that I was thinking about the Dominican Order. He quickly introduced me to his Director of Religious Education, Kathy Williams, whose sister was Sister Veronica Marie, a Dominican Sister of Mary, Mother of the Eucharist. It turned out that I already knew Kathy from playing Ultimate Frisbee with her in the Catholic Young Adult Sports League in Kalamazoo the previous day. Kathy told me all about her sister's community and encouraged me to go on the discernment retreat that November. I could see God's hand in all of this, so I went on the discernment retreat.

This was the only other retreat I had been to since my sister's Confirmation when I was in high school. At this retreat, I learned that a Sister is a bride of Christ. This explained the reason for the joy I saw in each one of the Sisters. It was the joy of being chosen by God Himself to be His and no one else's. I then understood the words God had spoken to me that night in First Friday Adoration before I graduated from college. I could not believe that this was what He had meant. It seemed too good to be true.

Like the retreat in high school, this retreat also had all-night Eucharistic Adoration. In Adoration that night, I experienced a sense similar to the one I had the first time I saw Him in Adoration five years before: that Jesus had been expecting me for a long time. However, this time it was different, because I knew the One who was awaiting me. It was the Friend my grandma had introduced me to when I prayed with her at night. The Friend who had always heard my prayers. The Friend who had consoled me the night my grandma was dying. The Friend who had shown me in Adoration that He wanted to be with me always. The Friend with whom I had shared my joys and sorrows. The Friend who had asked me to be His bride. The Friend who now awaited my reply. I realized that He was not asking me to give up the things I loved but was rather asking me to be His. Everything I had found hard to let go of before no longer seemed to matter. My only desire was to be His and spend the rest of my life with Him and for Him.

I requested and received application papers during that retreat and entered the community the following August. On the day of my first vows, I looked back on all that had led up to this long-awaited day. I was filled with awe and wonder at God's providence and love; my only

> God had wanted so much more for me than I could have imagined.

response was humble thanksgiving. I realized that God had wanted so much more for me than I could have imagined. It is said that you can know where you are going by looking back on where you have been. Looking back at God's providence in my life has convinced me that I am known, loved, and awaited by Him and that He will only continue to draw me deeper and deeper into His Heart.

Lived Experience

"Just as God once chose the Blessed Virgin Mary to manifest His glory and cooperate in the salvation of souls, so also He now chooses women for the religious life unto the same purpose.

-Father Sam Conedera, SJ
Saint Louis University,
History and Catholic Studies"

Finding the Pearl of Great Price

The World Is Not Enough

Sister Mary Aquinas Cheng, OP
Born in Galveston, Texas

"My soul proclaims the greatness of the Lord, my spirit rejoices in God my Savior. ... The Mighty One has done great things for me, and holy is his Name" (Lk 1:46-47, 49).

Mine has been what one might call a charmed life. Everything was handed to me: good health, better friends, and a far more loving family than I deserve. "I drew them with human cords, with bands of love; I fostered them like those who raise an infant to their cheeks; I bent down to feed them." (Hos 11:4).

The one thing I did not have turned out to be the most crucial of all: a relationship with Jesus Christ.

Sure, we attended Mass on Sundays. My parents even sacrificed non-existent funds to procure a Catholic education for my sister Marjorie and me. But like many cradle Catholics, they—and we—were poorly catechized. In middle school, I began to rebel, and by college graduation, I had fully embraced every lie our society sells and sunk into a life of sin, thinking this would make me happy.

One thing my parents did inculcate in me was our Asian cultural values, which included excelling in school and making tons of money in order to help the family.

All went as planned. Almost without effort, I got into the school I wanted, interned at NASA, graduated early, and landed my dream job as a consultant with a Big Four accounting firm. My colleagues were "white-hat" (ethical) hackers, whom our clients, mostly Fortune 500 companies, hired to try to break into their information technology systems. They always succeeded.

The new job brought me home to Houston, and since it entailed spending eighty percent of the time traveling, it only made sense to live with the family. While we were in college, my father entreated us to return home when possible. In my parents' native Philippines, sons and daughters traditionally fly the nest only upon marriage. Many couples linger long after that. My siblings and I grew up with all four grandparents in our home, which was an immense blessing for all of us.

In gratitude for our schooling, my sister Marjorie and I spent our signing bonuses on a bedroom set for our parents. But my employer paid so handsomely that plenty remained for a personal shopper, a trainer, and a white Mercedes-Benz f or myself.

Little did I suspect the Lord was readying "the twitch upon the thread" (G.K. Chesterton, *The Innocence of Father Brown*). "Put no trust in princes, in children of Adam powerless to save. Who breathing his last, returns to the earth; that day all his planning comes to nothing" (Ps 146: 3-4).

Before long, our parish youth minister, Charles, invited me to volunteer with the new Life Teen program. Though I espoused nothing of the Faith, it seemed like a good way to spend time with my younger brother Matt, who was starting middle school and consequently Edge, Life Teen's junior high curriculum.

The first "Edge night" was on the source and summit of our Faith: the Holy Eucharist. It was the first I had ever heard of the Real Presence! Here was Almighty God in the flesh, humbling Himself just to be with His beloved, unworthy creatures—with me.

I was hooked. The youth group kids and I read the Bible together. The Word of God came alive as one long love letter. Through the centuries, through different literary genres, through countless human authors, He who is Love reveals Himself always trying to draw near to His people: first in Eden, then in the Ark of the Covenant, and finally in the tiny white host that we receive into our very flesh. By this means, He plans to transfigure us from within and to draw us into the eternal ecstasy that is His own divine life.

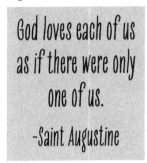

God loves each of us as if there were only one of us.

-Saint Augustine

Eight years elapsed. I enjoyed my job, made great Catholic friends, and dated The World's Most Perfect Boyfriend. We never even fought. In time, we started seriously discerning marriage. After an evening of planning for the future, I found myself inexplicably sleepless. The next morning, I phoned Marjorie as soon as I knew she would be awake. She listened and remarked, "It sounds like you two are looking for different vocations." It was as if a burden had been lifted. Later that day, I went to see him. He had come to the same conclusion. Our mutual feeling was, "I love you so much. If the Lord has something better for you, I want you to have that."

So, the romance ended, more peacefully than I thought possible—his grandmother even continued to write me later in the convent until she passed away. A chastity speaker I once heard claimed that breakups are more amicable in chaste relationships; now, I experienced it for myself. One reason unchaste breakups can be so messy is that, during the marital act, our brains release powerful bonding chemicals like oxytocin to keep husband and wife together for life. The human body is designed for monogamy.

IF YOU WANT TO MAKE GOD LAUGH, MAKE PLANS

After a year, I visited Marjorie and her new husband, Ken. A common refrain in vocation stories is, "I had everything I wanted, and it was not enough." It was certainly the case here. Marj could tell I was restless, so as the oldest, she nagged me about dating, "putting yourself out there", etc., etc. That did not sound appealing. Exasperated, she exclaimed, "I just do not understand why, if you know you are called to marriage, you aren't doing something about it!" To which I retorted, "I do not know if I am called to marriage! I have never really discerned my vocation! I haven't ruled out religious life..."

"Wait, you haven't ruled out religious life?"

"Please. Who do we know who has even thought about it?"

"Hmph. We will fix that."

And with that, she sat down at her laptop and signed me up for a diocesan discernment retreat.

Originally, I planned to cross religious life off the list directly upon arriving at the retreat. Lo and behold, the priests and religious there turned out to be normal human beings! To my chagrin, I could talk with them as I would with friends or family. What I did eliminate that weekend was remaining single forever: the Lord was calling me to commitment.

With that weekend, discernment commenced in earnest. When you want to know God's will for your life, the most important thing is, of course, to ask Him. Yet at first, my prayer went along the lines of, "Father, Thy will be done …but please don't ask me to do this…"

> My God, I am so in love with You! It would be an honor to be Your bride … if You would have me.

Six months later, I was in Adoration during my lunch break. Gazing at Him, I realized: "My God, I am so in love with You! It would be an honor to be Your bride…if You would have me." Suddenly, everything changed.

The question thus became where God wanted me to live as His spouse and in which community. A helpful online article had given two "signs" for finding the right community: 1) the Lord will put it in your path, and 2) it will feel like home. After befriending wonderful Sisters in several communities, it still was not clear which was to be mine. On the two-and-a-half-hour drive home from one such convent in Victoria, Texas, I begged the Lord to show me.

Within an hour of my return, my friend Fiona, on sabbatical in Nicaragua, Google-chatted to suggest a community she had met six months before: the Dominican Sisters of Mary, Mother of the Eucharist. Taking a leaf from Marj's book, I immediately registered for their next discernment retreat, slated for February 2012.

The retreat was eye-opening. There was all-night Adoration, and the Sisters gave short conferences on, among other themes, God's love, giving everything to Him, the Dominican charism, and praying for priests. With every talk, my heart burned within me (see Lk 24:32). It was not home per se; it was more like my soul was vibrating at a certain pitch and with the community struck a beautiful chord.

Elated, I met the Vocation Directress, Sister Joseph Andrew, applied for entrance, spent a week with twenty-plus others at the Motherhouse for pre-postulancy (a type of orientation), and was finally accepted to enter on August 28. Everything seemed perfect.

A SUDDEN CHANGE OF PLANS

During this period of preparation, Sister Joseph Andrew recommended we read the lives of the saints. The more I read, the more dissimilar their lives seemed to mine. They suffered immensely, all the while loving and praising God. I asked Him to make me love Him like that, to be more than a fair-weather friend…but then I got scared and told Him He could do it without making me suffer.

Well, He gave me my chance. On August 19, nine days before entrance, I was driving back to Victoria to witness the Final Vows of my friend Sister Louise Marie, IWBS. Road construction caused a half-hour delay, and I drove faster than I had ever driven in my life. Stupidly fast. Ten minutes from the convent, I encountered an overpass. Water had collected at the base from a brief shower earlier in the day. Upon reaching the puddle, the car began to hydroplane. Immediately I prayed, "Lord, I no longer have control over this vehicle. You just take it exactly where you want it to go." The car spun and crashed into the guardrail on the driver's side.

After the impact, I glanced down. My left hand was sliced open, my left hip in searing pain, and the same thigh horrendously disfigured. "That's going to take at least eight months of physical therapy," I thought. "So, You are telling me no convent next week. Okay." He may have been saying not now or not ever, and I trusted Him completely. "For I know well the plans I have in mind for you…plans for your welfare and not for woe, so as to give you a future of hope." (Jer 29:11).

Then the car flipped over the guardrail and proceeded to roll down the embankment. "People don't always survive this," I realized. Frantically I began calculating. My family had attended Mass the night before, and the day before that, I went to Confession. "Hey, I am golden," I thought. "Even if I go to Purgatory, at least I'll know where I'm ultimately headed. I might actually see Your face!" The prospect was exhilarating.

The car landed in a ditch, again on the driver's side. To my surprise, I did not die. While listening to the CD I had playing (interestingly, the Sisters' *Mater Eucharistiae*), I assessed the damage. A cursory scan in the rearview mirror revealed no obvious head trauma. My ribcage appeared intact, so probably no major organ injury. My toes wiggled just fine, so the spine seemed okay. Unsure whether anyone could see the car, I switched on the emergency flashers. The horn was already blowing. With my good hand, I felt around for my phone.

At this point you might think: Wow, that is some presence of mind. Anyone can tell you this is not normal for me. It must have been a special grace.

Meanwhile, the pain waxed intolerable. I began to pray aloud. At first, I tried the Our Father but could not remember the words. So I recited the Hail Mary over and over. She and the Holy Spirit felt particularly close. At no time did I feel the slightest fear.

> "Lord, I no longer have control over this vehicle. You just take it exactly where you want it to go."

After a few minutes, witnesses opened the rear passenger-side door. They hesitated to approach the vehicle, convinced that no one could have survived. An agile bystander named Tip clambered into the backseat and repeated the Hail Mary with me while we waited, first for the ambulance, then for firefighters to extract me with the Jaws of Life.

I suddenly remembered that during pre-postulancy, Sister Joseph Andrew had described "zeal for souls" as a driving force in a Dominican. Everyone else had seemed to agree; but at the time of this accident, I did not feel very zealous towards the people who would be trying to help me. All I could think of was Christ, with little regard for anyone else.

The accident threw everything into sharp relief. Our time here is fleeting; what matters is eternity. And the Lord still felt so close. As the paramedics wheeled me into the emergency room, my soul longed to proclaim His goodness from the rooftops (see Mt 10:27)!

The year that followed was a joyful one, full of innumerable serendipities. There is no way I could ever count, much less repay, the kindnesses shown me and my family by so many people; the Lord must do that Himself.

Words fail. Certainly there was physical suffering: I had a cut and broken hand, a dislocated elbow, a snapped femur, and a smashed hip – all on the left side. Yet even the pain felt like a crucible, slowly burning away the dross of my faults. Whether I actually was more charitable or patient is for my family and my caregivers to decide.

The surgical team, led by Doctor Dickson, ultimately performed three operations to repair the damage. The second and most critical surgery, repairing the hip, occurred August 23, the feast of Saint Rose of Lima. By yet another grace, the anesthetist was a family friend. He saved my life.

The hip had shattered into more fragments than the doctors hoped. Consequently, they did quite a bit of scraping, and I lost a lot of blood (over the next three days, they replaced all but one unit of blood in my body!) My blood pressure dropped precipitously. The protocol in such cases is to dial back the anesthesia, lest the patient slip into a coma and die.

The first thing I sensed was the hip feeling open and cold. It was excruciating. I tried to scream, but couldn't move. So, I just rested on this insignificant splinter of Christ's cross. It was the most palpably intimate moment of my life, save of course Holy Communion.

Nobody knew I was conscious. During surgery, the team monitors the patient's brainwaves, but mine indicated no increase in activity. My sister's theory is that my brain stayed calm because it was praying.

As my body gradually recovered throughout the year, I could feel my faults return. It was as if a wave of grace had carried me along, and exhausted itself as it neared the shore.

Naturally, people inquired about my future. The initial plan was to focus first on physical recovery, then start the discernment process over again. Yet, as my body grew stronger, so too did the desire in my heart. So, I resolved, "Lord, as long as the door is open, with Your help I will walk through it."

The Sisters kept in touch. Sister Elizabeth Ann, Sister Mary Theresa, and Sister Maria even traveled three hours from Austin to visit me in the hospital for forty-five minutes before driving back! After a year, Doctor Dickson deemed me physically fit for the convent. Two years and nine days after the accident, on the feast of Saint Augustine, August 28, 2014, I was among the fourteen happy postulants to join the community at long last. On July 27, 2017, we made first vows, and God willing, we will profess perpetual vows in 2022.

> "The greatness of our love of God must be tested by the desire we have of suffering for His love."
> — Saint Philip Neri

LIFE ACCORDING TO HIS PLAN

> "For everything there is a season, and a time for every matter under heaven."
> -Ecclesiastes 3:1

Religious life is no panacea. While your husband is perfect, on this side of heaven, His family—including yourself—are not. The Church dubs religious life a "state of perfection" not because those who live in it are already perfect, but because its plan of life offers all the helps necessary to attain Christian perfection over a lifetime. Woe to the Sister who squanders them!

When someone first joins a community or gets married, she labors to seem perfect, to live up to what she thinks is expected. Over time, living with another person reveals to her how selfish she really is. Yet she learns that, with God's grace, the other person loves her and forgives her even with all of her flaws. This frees her to be herself, to be patient with herself and with the other, and to hope that in Christ they can overcome their weaknesses together. "This is how all will know that you are my disciples, if you have love for one another" (Jn 13:35).

One difference that had concerned me was age: upon entering the community I was thirty-three, whereas the median age of all of the Sisters in the community was twenty-eight. At the February discernment retreat, I had felt out of place, a professional among teenagers. They were so pure; it pained me to recall my own wasted (as they seemed to me) years.

Religious life, however, ended up being a grand equalizer. Everything was so new, so different from our former ways of life, that we rarely felt the age gap. Virtually the only time it surfaces is when we discuss worldly matters. Such conversations become rarer the longer one is a Sister.

Like any relationship among fallen creatures, community life takes work. Then again, how many deeds worth doing do not? Together we fumble toward eternity, and every night we join the Church in Our Lady's song:

> **Magnificat**
>
> My soul proclaims the greatness of the Lord,
>
> my spirit rejoices in God my Savior
>
> for he has looked with favor on his lowly servant.
>
> From this day all generations will call me blessed:
>
> the Almighty has done great things for me,
>
> and holy is his Name.
>
> He has mercy on those who fear him
>
> in every generation.
>
> He has shown the strength of his arm,
>
> he has scattered the proud in their conceit.
>
> He has cast down the mighty from their thrones,
>
> and has lifted up the lowly.
>
> He has filled the hungry with good things,
>
> and the rich he has sent away empty.
>
> He has come to the help of his servant Israel
>
> for he has remembered his promise of mercy,
>
> the promise he made to our fathers,
>
> to Abraham and his children forever.
>
> — Luke 1:46-55

> When I think of my vocation discernment, and the people that helped shape my love for the priesthood, immediately my parish priests and the Sisters come to mind. For me, the Sisters represented the image and love of Our Blessed Mother in their holiness, joy, caring, wisdom, intelligence, and passion in teaching and sharing the true faith. They could identify potential vocations and nurture those early signs. We are sorely missing them in the world today.
>
> But religious women like the Dominican Sisters of Mary, Mother of the Eucharist give me great joy and hope. I know these Sisters and visited their house of joy. Seeing young and happy Sisters attract others to the Faith. Our world needs their spiritual motherhood now more than ever.
>
> —Father Paul Ugo Arinze
> Saint John Vianney Roman Catholic Church, Janesville, WI
> and Director of Vocations, Diocese of Madison, WI

Writing Straight with Crooked Lines

How I Lost a Tooth (And My Way) But Found My Vocation

Sister Maria Benedicta Bete, OP
Born in Dayton, OH

When I first thought about a vocation to religious life, I was a first-grader with a newly lost tooth, and I was in a moral quandary. Part of me felt a gentle tug on my heart calling me to be a religious; the other part of me wanted badly to be a mother. I had not spent all of preschool playing house for nothing! At Mass on Sundays, I had heard Bible stories about prophets testing God and decided, with typical first-grade aplomb, that asking God for a miracle was my only option. "Jesus," I prayed, "if you want me to be a Sister, make this tooth grow in by tomorrow morning. If you want me to be a mom, have it not grow in." The next morning, when I found that no miracle had occurred and I still had a wide, gaping hole in my bottom set of teeth, I concluded the obvious: I had a vocation to marriage.

The oldest of four children, I was born and raised in Dayton, Ohio. Throughout my childhood, my parents grew in their faith, eventually becoming devout Catholics and Third Order Carmelites. It was they who showed us how to live the Faith. All four of us siblings attended Catholic schools for twelve years and all of us are, I believe, the better for it.

From a very young age, I knew what a vocation was and, more importantly, that I had one. I wanted to know God's plan for my life and I wanted to know it immediately (hence the tooth bargain). However, as the previous incident might illustrate, I decidedly did not want my vocation to be religious life.

ACCEPTING THE CALL

After testing God with my lost tooth, I did not think further about vocation until I was in fifth grade. One day, while reading a biography of Mother Teresa, I was struck by the fact that she entered religious life immediately after high school. "Maybe real, normal, young people still become Sisters," I thought. "Maybe I could, too." The gentle tug on my heart that had always drawn me to God became all at once very evident, and I knew without a doubt that I had a religious vocation.

The next logical step involved finding a community. Since I had realized my call to religious life while reading a biography of Mother Teresa, I naturally thought I would join the Missionaries of Charity. "They teach sometimes," I told myself, "and I've

> **What is a Third Order?**
>
> Third Orders are usually in reference to the laity who are members of a religious order. Generally, these lay members also make promises to an Order (such as the Carmelites, Dominicans, Franciscans, etc.) and live the charism of their order in a way that is befitting to their state in life.

always wanted to be a teacher." And with that, I announced to my family that I would join the Missionaries of Charity—right after high school, of course.

My mother was not convinced that my vocation lay with the Missionaries. When I was in sixth grade, our family received a mailing from the Dominican Sisters of Mary, Mother of the Eucharist, a new religious community in Ann Arbor, Michigan.

"What about this community?" my mother asked me. "They're Marian and Eucharistic and they're even teachers. You seem much more like a Dominican to me than a Missionary of Charity."

As I looked at the letter—which told benefactors about the large number of young women entering every year—and at the smiling faces of the Sisters, I knew, irrefutably, that I would spend my life with these Sisters. I had never met them, but that did not matter to me. I knew that God was asking me to enter the Dominican Sisters of Mary, and to do it as soon as possible. I wanted to enter immediately! But God knew that, besides the fact that I was only twelve, I needed to grow a lot in His love and in human maturity before I would be ready for the adventure that is religious life.

PRAYER AND VOCATION

The rest of middle school was fairly conventional. I made friends, got into trouble with my parents, and read every book in the children's section of our local library. I loved school, my Faith, and my country, and was known throughout my grade at school as the girl who was going to be a nun. I did not mind; I was a little proud of it. But despite the fact that both my teachers and my peers often labeled me as some kind of particularly holy person because of my vocation, my prayer life was abysmal. I did not realize that a personal relationship with God is like any other relationship: it must grow and requires effort. As a child,

> I did not realize that a personal relationship with God is like any other relationship: it must grow and requires effort.

I was fairly devout, and I was pretty sure I could coast into Heaven on first-grade piety. When I realized late in middle school that I needed a massive overhaul in my spiritual life, I tried to pray consistently for a while, but it was just too hard. I did not feel anything and struggled to hear His voice. Besides, I was about to enter high school which would be full of things much more enjoyable than sitting around and praying. I still knew I was called to religious life—and I was still proud of it—but I never quite made the connection that this would involve prayer and a relationship with God.

In 2009, I began my freshman year at one of the three local Catholic high schools. From the start, I loved every minute: the wider social pool, the fun events, the Friday night football games, and the honors classes that challenged me academically for the first time in my life. Life was not perfect; but overall, I was happy. I loved my school, my friends, and my life.

That year, I met Miss Muhlenkamp. She taught my freshman Old Testament class, and my locker was right outside her classroom. A young, enthusiastic teacher, she taught us solid theology that challenged us to live Christian lives. A lot of the students did not like this and complained, but I appreciated her teaching the truths of the Faith.

Since I did not yet have my driver's license, my mother picked me up from school each day. On days when she was running late, or had to transport my brother and sisters places before she could come and get me, I chatted with Miss Muhlenkamp while I was waiting. I told her about my religious vocation and asked her questions. She was always very kind and gave me good advice about high school and about my vocation. The next year, she left the school and, during that year, I slipped farther and farther away from Christ, the Faith, and my family.

WALKING AWAY FROM CHRIST

The August before my sophomore year of high school, I walked into my mother's home office to find her staring somewhat dazedly at her computer screen.

"What's wrong?" I asked her.

"Aunt Maureen just emailed me," she said, "to tell us that Uncle Larry was just diagnosed with ALS."

My mother went on to explain that ALS, also known as Lou Gehrig's disease, is a terminal illness in which the muscles in the body slowly shut down until, finally, the heart stops. There is no cure.

I was stunned. Uncle Larry was my godfather. He and his wife had always been like second parents to me, and my best friend was one of their daughters. For the first time in a long while, I began to pray. I begged, cajoled, and bargained with God. He could not let Uncle Larry die; too many people needed him. My godfather was a holy man, a proponent of perpetual Adoration, and a strong supporter of the pro-life cause. God would not take a man like that, would He?

> "The most beautiful Creed is the one we pronounce in our hour of darkness."
> —Saint Pio of Pietrelcina

But only five months after my godfather's diagnosis, I received a text message from my best friend, Uncle Larry's daughter: "Please pray for my dad," it read. "He just died."

It was January 22, the anniversary of *Roe v. Wade* and the

National Day of Prayer for the Legal Protection of Unborn Children. Even his death was a witness to life, although I could not see that at the time. I only saw that God had taken away someone whom I, my family, and hundreds of good people had loved and needed. If prayer had been difficult before, it became nearly impossible now. If God is really good, I reasoned, why do good people die?

Slowly, I pulled away from my Faith. I stopped going to Confession and hardly prayed. I still attended Sunday Mass—non-negotiable in my family—but my participation was far from the "full, active, and conscious" participation desired by the Fathers of the Second Vatican Council. I thought more about what I was wearing and what I would do later that day than about the Holy Sacrifice taking place before my eyes.

A DESIRE TO BE LOVED

At the same time, I began to live only for myself. I did not want to pray because it was difficult, and this same sloth crept into other aspects of my life. I wanted desperately to be loved and became a chronic people-pleaser. Did my friends let others copy their homework? I would too. Did my friends date and gossip and wear too much makeup? I would too. At this time, if someone had threatened me with the classic adage, "If your friends jumped off a cliff, would you?" the answer would likely have been an honest, "Sure, if everyone else is doing it."

In her autobiography, Saint Thérèse—my Confirmation patron—wrote that, due to her own desire to be loved, she likely would have fallen into serious sin had God not preserved her from that fall beforehand. Similarly, God was extraordinarily merciful with me. Although I certainly was not living—or even trying to live—a virtuous life and had many sinful habits, my friends did not engage in drinking, drugs, or most of the other temptations common among high schoolers. Although

> "You cannot please both God and the world at the same time. They are utterly opposed to each other in their thoughts, their desires, and their actions."
>
> —Saint John Vianney

my friends and I made a lot of bad decisions, they were never of the "ruin-your-life" caliber, which was surely a grace from God.

But I was far from being a model student, daughter, or Christian. I spent most of my time talking with friends or watching brainless television shows in my bedroom. I hardly talked to my family and only emerged for meals or to go out with my friends. I was often angry with everyone and everything, especially myself. I picked fights with my parents and siblings; I found fault with my friends. Without a relationship with God, all my other relationships started to crumble. I was appalled by my own actions but could not seem to find a way out. And with the loss of my faith, my vocation fled, too. I began to think seriously about college and marriage again. After all, that was what everyone else was doing!

CHRIST CALLS ME BACK TO HIM

Toward the end of my junior year, I was chosen as part of a select group in my class who would attend senior retreat. The next year, when we were seniors, we would be the peer team to lead the first senior retreat of that year. No one was surprised that I was chosen; in the eyes of many of my teachers, I was still the good Catholic girl who wanted to be a nun. I agreed to go because many of my friends would be there.

Everything on the retreat went normally until the second night. There were the usual icebreakers, inspirational talks, and small group sessions. I went through the motions and had a good time hanging out with my friends. But that night, we celebrated the Sacrament of Reconciliation. Two priests drove to the retreat center to hear our Confessions. I sat in front of the Blessed Sacrament, along with my peers, fighting a moral battle far greater than my earlier quandary involving the tooth. I knew I needed God's healing love and mercy; however, humanly speaking, I was also scared to make myself vulnerable before God and His minister—the priest—in the Sacrament of Reconciliation.

> "Confession heals, Confession justifies, Confession grants pardon of sin, all hope consists in confession; in confession, there is a chance for mercy."
>
> -Saint Isidore of Seville

But the longer I sat, the more I wanted to be free from the selfishness and anger that was making me miserable. I forced myself to stand up, walk to the door, and step into the makeshift confessional. When I stepped out again, I felt like an entirely new person. For the first time in a long while, I was free! And I knew immediately, after returning to Adoration and meeting Christ's loving gaze, that I had a vocation to religious life and needed to do something about it.

GROWING IN PRAYER THROUGH ADORATION

Even though I knew I had a vocation, I still had not made the connection between prayer and religious life. I tried to be a better sister, daughter, and friend, but I certainly did not speak to God in prayer. He had healed me—and I was grateful—but prayer was still difficult, and I had a busy schedule! I was an avid actor and writer in high school and spent my time at rehearsals, with friends, and running a creative writing journal published by the school. What I failed to realize, in the midst of all the noise and bustle of my busy life, was that a vocation to religious life is not about finding your life's work; rather, it is a love story between Christ and the soul. You cannot marry someone you do not know, but that is exactly what I was planning to do. I wanted to enter the convent without knowing Christ—and loving Him—personally and deeply.

That summer, my mother told me about another retreat. This one was run by the Archdiocese of Cincinnati, my home diocese, and was a week-long event with twenty-four-hour Eucharistic Adoration. There was only one problem: it was the same week as a children's camp I helped with every year. I loved volunteering at the camp and did not want to miss it. In fact, I was usually so committed to helping with it, that my mother told me later she fully expected I would never miss the camp to go on the retreat. But the Holy Spirit had different ideas.

> A vocation to religious life is not about finding your life's work; rather, it is a love story between Christ and the soul.

When I heard about the retreat, I suddenly knew I had to attend. God was calling me to this retreat, and I knew I could not ignore His voice as I had been done for so long. I emailed the director of the children's camp, found a replacement for the week I would be gone, and signed up for the diocesan retreat.

When we arrived, I was shocked to recognize one of the adult coordinators of the retreat. It was my freshman theology teacher, Miss Muhlenkamp! I reintroduced myself to her and we caught one another up on the last few years.

"Are you still thinking about becoming a Sister?" she asked.

"Yes," I told her emphatically.

She nodded. "Ever since I met you during your freshman year, I've been praying that God would safeguard your vocation throughout high school."

Evidently, the Lord heard her prayers. I am certain that many of the graces won for me during my years in high school were a result of the prayers of my freshman theology teacher who never gave up on me or my vocation.

But the main impact of the retreat was not meeting Miss Muhlenkamp; it was meeting Jesus Christ in twenty-four-hour Eucharistic Adoration.

Meeting Him changed my life.

Throughout the retreat, I realized while in Adoration that there was a real Person in the room with me, One who was not just an article of Faith but who loved me. No wonder my friends, family, or hobbies never fully satisfied me. I was made for something far greater! In Christ's Presence, I was happy and totally at peace. He loves endlessly, and I had been yearning for His love for so long. For the first time, I began to love Him sincerely in return.

At the end of the retreat, I was a new person yet again. God used the first retreat to bring me back to Him; He used the second retreat to help me fall in love with Him. When we made resolutions at the end of the retreat, I determined to pray daily an abridged form of the Liturgy of the Hours—the prayer that

> "Prayer is being on terms of friendship with God, frequently conversing in secret with Him who we know loves us."
> —Saint Teresa of Avila

all priests and religious pray—as well as to attend daily Mass. Generally, I am hopeless when it comes to following through with resolutions. But this retreat was different. God, who had already given me so many graces, continued to pour them upon me, a good measure and overflowing (see Lk 6:38). For the first time in my life, I kept the resolutions and began to grow in my relationship with the Lord.

But while my prayer life improved, I was still full of selfish motives. I had a hard time getting up early for daily Mass and probably would have stopped going if it had not been for the desire to have my own car. I had recently taken the driving exam with a car I had borrowed from my grandfather because it was small and ideal for the parallel parking portion of the test. "Maybe," I thought, "if I just keep using the car, he'll forget to ask for it back." Then, inspiration struck. If I used the car to attend daily Mass, my parents probably could not make me return it to my grandfather! This was not the only reason I attended daily Mass, but it often got me up on mornings when it was still dark outside and the only place I wanted to be was back in bed. It was only later that I found out that my parents had always intended for me to use that car. But God used the misunderstanding—and my selfish desire for the independence provided by a car—to get me to Mass nearly every day of my senior year of high school.

FIRST STEPS TOWARD ENTERING

My prayer life was slowly getting in order, but what about my vocation? I was still fairly certain that God was calling me to the Dominican Sisters of Mary, Mother of the Eucharist. Several times throughout middle school and high school, I had attended the Sisters' First Profession ceremonies. The Mass of Religious Profession, in which the Sisters become the brides of Christ, made a big impact on me and cemented my conviction that this was the community where I belonged. But I had never spoken with the community's vocation directress or attended a discernment retreat. So in November of my senior year, I drove up to Ann Arbor for one of the Dominican Sisters' three annual discernment weekends. Immediately, I signed up to speak with Sister Joseph Andrew, the vocation directress. After I spoke with her, she asked me to look at other communities in the months between that retreat and the Dominican Sisters' February discernment retreat. "Come back then," she told me, "and if you still think God is calling you to our community, we'll talk more."

I was a little crushed. "What if this is not God's will for me, after all?" I thought. "What if He is calling me somewhere else?" But instead of leading me farther away from the Dominican Sisters, He only increased my desire to join their community. That Christmas, I visited a different Dominican community in Illinois and spoke with some religious Sisters in my hometown of Dayton. But nowhere drew me quite like the Dominican Sisters of Mary, Mother of the Eucharist.

In February, I went on retreat again and asked Sister Joseph Andrew for application papers to enter in the fall. When she gave them to me, I was ecstatic. After so many years of waiting—and so many twists and turns along the way—I was finally beginning the process to enter religious life.

CHRIST CONTINUES TO LEAD

At this point, the devil seemed to step in to do everything possible to keep me from entering. That summer, I was full of doubts. What if I was the one who wanted this and not the Lord? What if He was calling me to contemplative life? Had I really considered all my options? Maybe I was making a huge mistake.

Fortunately, I have an eminently practical mother who is also exceedingly wise. I might have been worried, but she certainly was not.

"I don't think you have a cloistered vocation," she said. "It seems to me that everything in your life has pointed toward this community. God makes very clear when something is not His will. If doors keep opening for you to enter, I would pursue it. He will close the doors if He does not want you there."

I scoffed. "Really, Mom...I'm not sure that's how a vocation works. What if this really isn't God's will? Or what if, for some reason, the community asks me to wait a year before I enter? What do I do then?"

"You practice obedience," my mother said. "If you are asked to wait, then joyfully be obedient to the community and wait. I really don't think you have anything to worry about. It seems very clear that God is calling you to this community and, I think, to enter now."

It took a while, but I finally realized that my mother—as she so often is—was right. Several times that summer she talked me off cliffs, but, come August, I was ready to enter. Past the surface anxieties and doubts, I knew deep down that the Lord was calling me to enter the Dominican Sisters of Mary, Mother of the Eucharist. Only later did I realize that He was the one who had planted the desire to be a religious in my heart and made it so strong that I could not wait; I had to enter right out of high school. A vocation, I slowly realized, does not arrive in a flash of thunder, or even in the miraculous growth of a tooth overnight; rather, it is the still, small voice in the depth of the heart that calls each of us to live for something greater than ourselves. God works with the desires He has given us, not against them. So in 2013, only months after my high school graduation, I arrived with my family in Ann Arbor, Michigan, to begin life as a postulant with the Dominican Sisters of Mary, Mother of the Eucharist.

My years in religious life have been wonderful ones. In the words of twentieth-century English Dominican Father Vincent McNabb: "If you want a truly exciting time all day and all night, for God's sake, become a Dominican!"

Time and time again, God has written straight with the crooked lines I have given Him. He has poured out many graces upon me and has loved me with a love far greater than I ever could have imagined or deserved. He has used the simple and the ordinary to draw me close to Himself: the advice of a mother, my own mistakes, and even a simple, first-grade request for a miracle involving a recently lost tooth. And I trust that He will continue to do so, until the day I see Him face to face.

> "There was a strong and violent wind rending the mountains and crushing rocks before the Lord—but the Lord was not in the wind; after the wind, an earthquake—but the Lord was not in the earthquake; after the earthquake, fire—but the Lord was not in the fire; after the fire, a light silent sound."
>
> —1 Kings 19:11-12

How I Lost a Tooth (And My Way) But Found My Vocation

> God is still calling women to courageously say YES to living as a witness to His love and mercy as a consecrated Sister. Our Church and world need more women to have And Mary's 'Yes' Continues as a beautiful and instrumental resource.
>
> —Rhonda Gruenewald
> Vocation Ministry

God is Ever Faithful

From Cajun Country to the Convent

Sister Mary Martha Becnel, OP
Born in Baton Rouge, Louisiana

Born and raised in southern Louisiana, I was surrounded by Catholic culture from my earliest years. In fact, Baton Rouge alone is home to over fifteen large Catholic parishes. Yet a historically Catholic culture often did not equate to a vibrant relationship with the Lord for many people I knew. I was blessed, however, to have parents who recognized the importance of raising their children Catholic. My mother realized that she could not rely solely on Catholic schools to teach her children the Faith, as her parents had done with her. Rather, she began to study the Faith diligently on her own, largely through reading various Catholic publications. And, in addition to sending us to Catholic schools, my mom resolved to pass on the riches of Catholicism to us personally, to ensure that her children would have the grounding in the Faith which she had not received.

One of the greatest gifts my parents gave to my three younger brothers and me was our annual attendance at our parish Church's Triduum liturgies. I loved participating in the Mass of the Lord's Supper on Holy Thursday, the Celebration of the Lord's Passion on Good Friday, and the Easter Vigil on Holy Saturday night, and I would look forward to this time every year. Although we unfailingly attended Mass on Sundays and Holy Days of Obligation, my family did not attend daily Mass. Thus, these services, calling us to church in a three-day immersion into the Paschal Mystery, thrilled me, because I deeply loved receiving Christ in Holy Communion. By the grace of God, I always believed and personally knew Him in the Holy Eucharist, and this grace was strengthened greatly through my family's participation in the Triduum liturgies each year.

> "By faith, man completely submits his intellect and his will to God."
>
> -Catechism of the Catholic Church, 143

One Easter Vigil in particular—when I was probably about eight or nine—I had a profound experience during the Mass. At that time, I was concerned, even scrupulously, that everything I said or wrote be the truth. Therefore, during the renewal of Baptismal promises, I suddenly thought, "I had better pay close attention when I'm saying 'I do': I need to make sure I really mean it, or that would be a lie." So, I listened attentively to each question in the baptismal promise formula, and I found that, with every article of the Creed, I could say confidently that I personally believed it. In hindsight, I realize this was the moment when I embraced the Faith fully and consciously as my own.

INKLINGS OF A VOCATION

When I was ten years old, I first started thinking about a religious vocation. I had read Mary Fabyan Windeatt's children's biography of Saint Catherine of Siena, who was my baptismal patron. Ironically—or, perhaps more accurately, providentially—Saint Catherine is also the most famous female Dominican saint in the history of the Church. As I read this book, I realized with a sudden inspiration that religious life was a possibility for me as well. Although I had very little exposure to Sisters and had never met a Sister in the habit, the idea was immediately attractive to me.

During middle school and throughout much of high school, I had very little idea of how to discern; I did not know how to begin discovering God's will for my life. In many ways, I wanted a mathematical formula so that I could plug myself in as the variable and see if "religious life" came out as the correct answer on the other side! It took me a long time to realize that God does not work like that—He works gently, individually, within the heart of each person.

ENCOUNTERING GOD IN HIGH SCHOOL

Another key moment in my developing spiritual life came during my freshman year of high school. That Lent, I attended the Stations of the Cross offered weekly in our school chapel during my lunch period. It occurred to me that since that I had this chapel—this access to the Blessed Sacrament—available to me, I should be taking advantage of it! So I made Our Lord a promise to try to visit the chapel at some point every day for

> "Our hearts are restless until they rest in Thee!"
>
> —Saint Augustine

the rest of my time in high school. Although this began mostly as a duty, it was not long before I was going to the chapel because I wanted, I longed to be there with Him. During these visits, I began to pray spontaneously from the heart and not solely with memorized prayers or prayers of intercession.

During my junior or senior year in high school, my parents received a direct mailing requesting donations from the Dominican Sisters of Mary, Mother of the Eucharist in Ann Arbor, Michigan. My mom, knowing that I had been thinking for years about religious life, and probably wanting me to know that an authentic living of religious life still existed, handed me the direct mailing. Surely at that time, she never thought I actually would move all the way to Michigan!

I was struck by the title on the outside of the envelope, "A Different Kind of Vocations Crisis", which referred to the community's urgent need for financial support because they were receiving such an abundance of young vocations! I read the mailing, poring over every word and delighting in all the pictures of brightly smiling Sisters. Interestingly, one week later, my parents received a second copy of the same mailing from the Sisters. Undoubtedly, we received the duplicate both by an accident on the part of the Sisters and by God's loving providence; I read—and relished—every word again! We remained on the Sisters' mailing list, and over the years, I enjoyed watching the increasing number of Sisters in this community. I saved each of the mailings: my mom told me later that, when she was cleaning out my room after I entered the convent, she found a whole drawer full of them!

The summer after high school, I worked at a young children's day camp run by my high school. One of the other camp counselors was having his own personal difficulties with the Faith, saying that he probably would not continue as a Catholic. This broke my heart! At the same time, I was seeing relatives who were not living in accord with the fullness of the truth taught by the Church, or who had decided to leave the Church altogether. I could not understand how anyone could be willing to exchange Jesus in the Eucharist for anything else in the world. I thought, "If only they had really come to know Christ the way I have known and encountered Him, then surely they would not be turning away from the Church." The necessity of teaching even young children the fullness of the truth—not in any watered-down version—became very clear to me. Thus I recognized a desire in my heart to save souls by teaching them the truth, especially the Truth Who is Our Lord in the Eucharist.

RUNNING AWAY FROM LONELINESS

After that summer of being set on fire with zeal to teach the truth, I attended Louisiana State University for college and studied education. LSU is a very large school; at that time, it boasted an enrollment of over 30,000. This was quite a change from my high school of about 800, where I knew all my classmates and several students in other grades. Although many of my high school classmates attended LSU (since it was located, after all, in our hometown) I rarely saw any of them on campus that first year. Also, I still was living at home, which meant that I spent less time on campus and had fewer opportunities to meet new people. All of these factors contributed to a feeling of deep loneliness during my freshman year in college.

> "And everyday, when your heart especially feels the loneliness of life, pray."
> -Saint Pio of Pietrelcina

At one point during this year, I convinced myself that

I felt called to a cloistered religious vocation. To be honest, this probably first occurred to me because of the thought that I would not need a college degree for that vocation and could leave the loneliness of college quickly to enter the cloister.

> A Holy Hour brings Heaven's choicest blessings on those who are faithful to their Hour.
> -Pope Saint Paul VI

How clueless I was about both discernment and religious life, and how easily we can deceive ourselves, even with the best of intentions! One day, I came across a postcard that one could send to a community of cloistered nuns in Louisiana to request information about their order. I filled it out, writing that I was beginning to think that I might be called to a cloistered vocation. But I made the mistake of putting it directly in our mailbox at home; my mother discovered the postcard and questioned me about it. The discomfort of that conversation was a grace that led me to realize that I had been seeking my own will rather than God's—that I was running away from loneliness, not running towards Christ.

Unlike the loneliness of freshman year, sophomore year at LSU found me blessed with good friendships at Christ the King Catholic Student Center on campus. I began to learn more about the Faith from these friends and was able to see a deeper intellectual side of the Faith that I had not known before, while also growing in prayer and the devotional life. These were truly Christian friendships that served to bring me closer to the Lord.

DISCOVERING A DOMINICAN HEART

In January of my sophomore year, I visited a Dominican religious community with one of my friends. The Sisters were joyful, and I loved the time I spent with them that week. But on that Friday, as the Sisters had Eucharistic Adoration in honor of the First Friday Sacred Heart devotion, I thought, "As beautiful as all this is, why couldn't they have Adoration every day, like the Dominican Sisters of Mary do?!"

After that visit, my prayer life deepened in several ways. I began praying personally to Saint Dominic. I would think of him and pray to him often, even referring to him as "Father." Additionally, I began to pray the Divine Office, also known as the Liturgy of the Hours. This prayer of the Church is prayed daily by priests and religious, as well as by many of the lay faithful. I loved being immersed in the Scriptures in this manner throughout the day. And, perhaps most importantly, I began attending Eucharistic Adoration more frequently at the perpetual Adoration chapel of a local parish. I remember thinking one day as I walked toward the Adoration chapel, "Whatever my vocation is, I want to have Eucharistic Adoration every day of my life." I had already formed the habit of going to daily Mass, and now I realized I wanted to adore Our Lord in the Blessed Sacrament daily as well.

LEARNING HOW TO DISCERN

Around this time, I asked a local priest to be my spiritual director and to help me with discerning my vocation. I knew Father Andrew Merrick because he had been assigned to my home parish when he was a seminarian. The greatest grace I received during those monthly meetings was to learn *lectio divina*, the method of prayer through meditation on the Scriptures. Each month, Father Andrew would give me a different passage to pray with for half an hour daily. Little did I know at the time how much this practice was preparing me for religious life, wherein we have a scheduled period of meditation of at least half an hour each day.

Praying this way with the Scriptures opened my heart anew. Gradually, without realizing it, I began to focus less on my need to figure out my vocation and more on Christ's personal love for me. I realize now that this is how discernment happens: not by looking at your gifts and talents as a checklist until you figure out God's will but—in quiet and stillness—listening to His Word and allowing Him to speak to your heart. Contrary to popular opinion, discernment is not a process of elimination, a matter of first trying out other things, such as a career or dating, to make sure you know what you are giving up. Authentic discernment of God's will can stem only from a deeply personal relationship with Him born from a life of prayer.

One of the passages that Father Andrew gave me for meditation was the account of the Samaritan woman at the well (John 4). Praying with this beautiful passage throughout the month, I suddenly realized that God was in love with me! I had known that He loved me and that I loved Him; I even had known for several years that I was in love with Him. But to realize that He was also in love with me was breathtaking!

---

5 Steps to Lectio Divina

Lectio (Reading): You take a short passage from the Bible, preferably a Gospel passage and read it carefully, perhaps three or more times. Let it really soak in.

Meditatio (Meditation): By using your imagination enter into the Biblical scene in order to "see" the setting, the people, and the unfolding action. It is through this meditation that you encounter the text and discover its meaning for your life.

Oratio (Prayer): asking for graces, offering praise or thanksgiving, seeking healing or forgiveness. In this prayerful engagement with the text, you open yourself up to the possibility of contemplation.

Contemplatio (Contemplation): is a gaze turned toward Christ and the things of God. By God's action of grace, you may be raised above meditation to a state of seeing or experiencing the text as mystery and reality. In contemplation, you come into an experiential contact with the One behind and beyond the text.

www.usccb.org/prayer-and-worship/prayers-and-devotions/meditations

From then on, I encountered His love in a fresh and deeper manner. He was loving me first; my love was merely a response to His.

Near the end of my junior year in college, I had an experience that opened my heart further to whatever God might will—yet in a wholly unexpected manner. I felt an attraction to a young man who frequented the Catholic Student Center at LSU, and I also thought he was attracted to me. I was confused and wondered how to find God's will in this situation. I did not understand fully that one could feel drawn to both religious life and marriage for the same reason—a response to Love! Today, I realize this makes perfect sense. It is essential for one to love both vocations and to seek which one belongs to her by God's design. But, before realizing this, I was worried that I would make the wrong choice and not find God's will. I prayed, and fretted, for months! Ultimately, I realized that God would not permit me to go astray from His will if I remained faithful to seeking Him and my vocation in prayer.

> "I sought Him whom my heart loves."
> Song of Songs 3:1

OUR LADY AND THE EUCHARIST

On August 15 of that year, I made Saint Louis de Montfort's Consecration to Jesus through Mary with a group of friends. I would learn later that this is the date on which my Sisters renew their Marian consecration every year! After we made the consecration, one of my friends observed prophetically, "I have heard everything goes faster with Mary." Was the same true for everyone? It was certainly true regarding my own discernment, at least. I would enter the convent just a year after making my Marian Consecration. Once I had given everything to Mary, my discernment ramped up to a whirlwind speed.

Further confirmation of my vocation came one evening during my senior year. While in Eucharistic Adoration at the Catholic Student Center, I heard in my heart, "Will you marry Me? Will you be My wife, My bride, My spouse?" My first inclination was to question whether this was from the Lord or just my own thoughts. After all, I had been seeking His answer regarding my vocation for eleven years at that point. Could it be possible that He was answering me now, so simply and clearly? Or was I deceiving myself? But I said, "If this is really You, Lord, then yes!"

After that experience, I continued to grow in my prayer life: attending daily Mass and Adoration frequently, praying the Liturgy of the Hours, praying the Rosary more often, reading spiritual books, and engaging in spiritual conversations with friends. I also began to feel called strongly to pray for, and be a spiritual mother to, priests. But still I did not feel sure if the words I had heard during Adoration that night were really from the Lord. Father Andrew had told me to pray about whether what I had heard meant specifically religious life or simply a spousal relationship with Christ in a general way.

> God speaks to us in the desires of our heart.

Praying the Rosary with my roommates one evening, I was meditating on the Fifth Joyful Mystery, the Finding in the Temple. I thought of the passage from the Song of Songs: "I sought Him whom my soul loves…Hardly had I left them when I found Him whom my soul loves" (Song 3:1b, 4a). It was as if Our Lady was saying to my heart, "You will find Him whom your heart loves in poverty, chastity, and obedience." When I told Father Andrew this, he said, "Okay, it's time to start visiting some religious communities." Later, I also realized while praying after Mass one Sunday that my heart's desire for religious life was so great that I knew it could not just be from me; it must be from the Lord.

DOMINICAN OR CARMELITE?

During my spring break, I visited a Carmelite religious community for a couple of days. I had felt for a few months—more genuinely this time—that the Lord might be calling me to a cloistered community, asking me to be willing to sacrifice teaching even as I was enjoying student teaching very much. In prayer, I had finally surrendered this desire. But, on the way to visit the Carmelite Sisters, I kept thinking about the Dominican Sisters of Mary and fretting about it all over again. Finally, I received the grace to realize that I did not need to worry so much about what I would do—teach or be cloistered—as about who I would be: a Dominican or a Carmelite. God would let me know.

During my visit at the Carmelite monastery, one of the Sisters told me, "If there is a thought that keeps coming up—not just a passing thought, but one that keeps coming up—it is something to pay attention to, because God speaks to us in the desires of our heart." As soon as she said this, I realized that the thought that kept coming back to me, no matter which religious community I was visiting or reading about online, was the Dominican Sisters of Mary, Mother of the Eucharist. I knew objectively that the other communities I had visited or learned about were also wonderful communities. But, somehow, for me, they could never match the Sisters of Mary. Finally, I thought, "I really need to go visit those Sisters!"

As I continued to pray that weekend with the Carmelite Sisters, the desire to bring the truth to souls came back to me. This desire, which had been strong after visiting the other Dominican community earlier in college, confirmed for me that the Lord was leading me toward the Dominican Sisters of Mary. But I was also confused because I still felt strongly called to be a spiritual mother for priests, and I knew that was a portion of the Carmelite charism.

> God gives us everything and takes away nothing.

After I returned home from the Carmelites, I decided to re-read everything on the website of the Dominican Sisters of Mary, which I had already visited many times. I found an article on the website that I had not noticed before which explained that part of the Sisters' charism was to be spiritual mothers for priests! I burst into tears: "God gives us everything and takes away nothing. I don't have to choose between my desires to bring the truth to souls and to be a spiritual mother for priests. It is all here in this community!"

"SOMEONE ELSE" DOESN'T WANT IT

After almost twelve years of discernment and many years of "stalking" the Sisters via the internet, I finally flew up to Michigan for a retreat. I left immediately after my LSU graduation to drive to the New Orleans airport, about an hour from Baton Rouge. On the way the traffic was terrible. My parents and I could see smoke ahead of us, which turned out to be from a blown tire on a semi-truck. In the stress of the stop-and-go traffic, my father said, "I don't know…maybe God doesn't want you to go there." My mother responded, "I think it's probably someone else who doesn't want it."

We finally arrived at the airport, and I literally ran to make it to my gate just in time. On board, however, we waited and waited, until finally hearing we would be rerouted due to weather conditions. The reroute was so long that we would need to stop on the way to refuel. Since the pilot did not want to stop, we ended up waiting yet another long stint in hopes that we would be able to find a third route that would not require refueling; however, that option eventually proved impossible. It was becoming very clear to me who it was who did not want this. But all the devil's attempts to stop my vocation were in vain. I arrived at Detroit Wayne County Airport at midnight. The good Sisters were there waiting for me, and they whisked me to the Motherhouse, where I could get a good sleep, instead of to the school where the retreat would be held the next day. As the Sisters took me into the chapel upon my arrival at the Motherhouse, I knew that the devil had lost this one big time! Sister Joseph Andrew confirmed this for me the next morning, as the Sisters were preparing to take me over to the school. She gave me a big hug and said, "Screwtape didn't want you here! But we all prayed for your safe arrival!"

"WELCOME HOME"

Later, when I met with Sister Joseph Andrew at the school, I told her my whole story. At one point as I was talking, she got up, came around the table, gave me another big hug, and said, "Welcome home, hon!" While I chose to wait until further into the retreat to decide about my application papers, I could not stop thinking about Sr. Joseph Andrew's warm, "Welcome home!" I had to wrestle with the idea of Michigan—and not Louisiana—being home. But I eventually realized that it was not so much that Michigan would be my home as that the Dominican Sisters of Mary, Mother of the Eucharist was home and family!

During the evening of the retreat, we watched a vocations video the Sisters had made. It was during this video that I realized that if I did not ask to enter then, I would regret it for the rest of my life. I asked Sister Joseph Andrew for application papers the next morning.

It was not all easy after that. There seemed to be a lot of tension between my mom and myself regarding my vocation, much of which, I realize now, actually stemmed from misunderstanding each other more than from a lack of support on my mom's part. But this was a cross for me leading up to entrance. It became difficult to tell my family goodbye as I was leaving to enter the convent, despite having longed so much for that day. So the actual day of my entrance, August 28, 2010, did not have the romantic feeling that I would have liked; rather, the loss and the sacrifice that are part of any gain were very present to me.

> I am loved infinitely and I am chosen by Infinite Love!

There are times when sufferings still show themselves: there is no authentic vocation that does not involve embracing the cross, because the cross is essential to our living of the Christian life. But there is an indescribable happiness, often deepened by the cross. The joy comes from knowing, in the depths of my being, that I am loved infinitely and that I am chosen by Infinite Love!

> The Religious Sister today is perhaps the single greatest counter-cultural sign, and thus one of the most powerful witnesses to Christ. Through her religious habit, which is the outward sign of her consecration, she proclaims to the world that she lives not for the false promises of our age but rather for Jesus Christ alone and the life of the world to come.
>
> —Father Patrick Fiorillo
> Chaplain at Harvard University

Aim High

From Combat Boots to ... Well, Actually the Shoes Didn't Change That Much

Sister Peter Thomas Burson, OP
Born in Fort Worth, Texas

How fast can you close an unwanted website? No, I don't mean because of inappropriate content or obnoxious ads. No filter or pop-up blocker would have caught this one. I mean a website that you do not want to see because its content is good—good in a way that is totally unexpected, immediately resonant, and utterly terrifying.

However fast you think you could do it, I'll bet I beat you the first time I closed it. I'm talking lightning speed! The second time took a little longer because I was confused and annoyed. How am I on this same website again? The link I just clicked had nothing to do with this! Stupid internet. *Click.*

The third time, I gave up because there were no parish events scheduled that night to occupy me in my occasional role as evening receptionist, because I had finished the research that had taken me online to begin with, and because, most uncharacteristically, I had forgotten to bring a book. So, I gave up and read every word on every page of the website. Then, I locked up the parish office, made my usual stop in the Adoration chapel on my way out, and drove home. And I assumed I would never think about what was on that website again.

Yeah, right.

My encounter with the website, to which I will return later, happened during the final weeks of my senior year of high school. Up to this point, the most important things in my life—the things that had shaped who I was and who I wanted to become—were my family, the military, and the Catholic Faith.

FAMILY

I have been immensely blessed with the gift of a loving, tight-knit, and also highly amusing family. My parents, sister and I have always genuinely enjoyed being together, and have always been able to make great fun out of almost anything. My extended family, especially my close relationship with my grandparents, gave me a strong sense of rootedness and a never-ending supply of stories. As is true for most people, my identity was first formed largely in my family; I cannot begin to express how much I received from them.

Among the many things that my parents instilled in me—often more by their example than by anything they said—was the notion that anything worth doing was worth doing well. This principle touched many aspects of my life, especially school. The public schools in Fort Worth were excellent, and I took challenging classes and pushed myself to excel. I loved to study; school was always a great joy. My parents taught my sister and me to treat school as our job, and without exerting any undue pressure, they held us to high standards. In short, from my family I learned to do my absolute best, to be of service to others, and to enjoy being with those I love.

MILITARY

My parents met when they were both US Air Force officers, and the military ethos was part of our family culture. Love of country, dedication to something bigger and more important than oneself, discipline and structure at the service of accomplishing a greater goal—these were values that I imbibed early on and loved. I was also always immensely proud of my parents' service and had a great desire to emulate them. Thus, it was natural for me to want to serve in the military, and that was my ambition from as early as I can remember. While normal childhood phases ("I want to be an astronaut!") came and went, even these transitory dreams were always framed in my mind within the context of the given: I was going to serve in the Air Force.

> **PATRIOTISM IS A VIRTUE!**
> Meaning: Paying due honor and respect to one's country with a willingness to serve.

Growing up, I read just about everything that I could get my hands on, including a lot that confirmed my attraction to the military life. In high school, I participated very actively in Junior ROTC, which is a military-sponsored program within a school. Here I had opportunities to wear the cadet uniform, learn about the structure and history of the Air Force, and experience military-style training in the summers. I spent all four years on the drill team (think marching while spinning rifles), had the chance to command the team for several years, and in my senior year, to command the cadet corps. All of this, especially the experience of teaching and leading others toward a shared goal of excellence, confirmed what I wanted to do with my life.

One of the great blessings of JROTC came during my last two years when my mom, a retired officer, redonned her uniform to serve as one of our instructors. She worked primarily with the cadet leaders, and I spent much of those two years in close consultation with her in a "professional" setting. Mom is a highly competent officer, though she does not conform to some people's stereotypes about women in the military. I had never gotten to see her in action before, and I found that she was both extremely good at her job and completely consistent with the warm, encouraging person I already knew as my mom. Her example confirmed that there need be no contradiction between what I wanted to do professionally and my commitment to faith and family.

At the end of my senior year of high school, my aspiration to serve in the military was close to becoming a reality. After a long application process, I was informed that I had received a particularly generous type of ROTC scholarship. This meant that for four years of college, I would be paid to go to school wherever I wanted, to study just about whatever I wanted, and then to do what I would practically have paid them to let me do: serve as an officer in the US Air Force. It could not get much better than that.

FAITH

Despite the prominent places that family, school, and preparation for the military held in my life, I would have said from early on that my Catholic Faith was the most important thing—even if my daily schedule did not always show it! I would not describe myself as pious, but I am told that when I was little, I would badger my mom to let us "do the Stations" after Sunday Mass. I was always really drawn to the realities of the Faith. Mom raised us Catholic and was an especially good example of faith lived in service. She was always volunteering for something, from organizing school fundraisers to taking lonely elderly folks grocery shopping.

When I was in middle school, my dad converted to Catholicism. This was obviously a blessing for our family and would prove to be a huge boon to my own appreciation of the Faith. While the witness of faithful living offered by my mom had prepared the way, the catalyst for Dad's conversion was largely intellectual. He read a great deal during the course of his conversion, and as he finished each book, he passed it to me. This immersion in the doctrinal and apologetic riches of the Church produced in me the deep conviction that our Faith is intelligible, reasonable, and ultimately true. While I would later need to mature by learning to ground and vivify my zeal for truth in charity, the knowledge I gained of the Faith at this time was invaluable.

In high school, I was deeply involved in parish life. Through the Life Teen youth program, I received solid catechesis and countless opportunities to encounter the Lord in prayer, especially in Eucharistic Adoration. I served as an altar server, which was an especially well-led ministry at my parish and very formative. My faith was further strengthened by summer adventures such as Steubenville retreats and weeks spent at Covecrest, a Life Teen camp in the Georgia mountains. For me, these experiences were always more peaceful than emotional or demonstrative. From each of them, I came away impressed by how the Church honors Jesus in the Eucharist, and this deepened my faith in the Real Presence and in the Lord's love for me. These encounters with Christ led me, and many other teens at my parish, to become daily Mass-goers whenever school was out of session.

As I looked towards my future, scholarship in hand, the Faith was a primary consideration in choosing where to go to school. I

> I came away impressed by how the Church honors Jesus in the Eucharist, and this deepened my faith in the Real Presence and in the Lord's love for me.

looked at many colleges, most of them Catholic; but when I visited the University of Notre Dame, I was sold. Much about the place attracted me, especially its love for tradition, but what really sealed the deal was the discovery that every dorm on campus had a Eucharistic chapel. The thought that I would be living under the same roof as the Blessed Sacrament was amazing! At Notre Dame, there was not only academic rigor and a strong ROTC program in which I could prepare for military service, but also a rich sacramental and faith life. Everything fit.

EXCEPT...

The only problem with all this was that I had not thought to ask God about it.

It was not as if I did not care what God's will was. I did, very much! I was just sure, without having really asked Him, that I was doing it. After all, what I wanted to do was a good thing, motivated by good intentions. I had seen from so many of my role models, especially my mom, that there was no contradiction between serving God and serving in the military. I figured that, like her, I would teach Sunday school on base as a young officer, hold myself and those I led to the highest moral standards, and raise a beautiful family. I was completely committed to living out my faith—wasn't that what it meant to do God's will? Besides, everything seemed to be working out beautifully; surely that was confirmation that I was on the right track!

> "I will attempt day by day to break my will into pieces. I want to do God's Holy Will, not my own!"
> —Saint Gabriel of the Sorrowful Mother

As for a religious vocation, I had never even considered the idea—not because I rejected it but because it was not even remotely on my radar. Though I have a very close relationship with my aunt, a Sister of Saint Joseph, I always assumed that a more traditional religious life was a thing of the past, and never gave it a thought.

MY PLAN VS. GOD'S PLAN

So, as my senior year of high school drew to an end, I was armed with my plan, and every door was opening to make it a reality.

Then came that pesky website.

The website, as you may or may not have guessed, was a site about religious life. More specifically, it was the website of the Dominican Sisters of Mary, Mother of the Eucharist.

Now, as I have said, I was not thinking about religious life. I was not looking up anything to do with religious life. The links I clicked looked innocent enough. They should not have taken me to the homepage of a religious community.

But they did; and I read; and the idea would not go away.

The reason I closed the web page so quickly the first two times it opened was that as soon as I saw the top banner—with a picture of young, smiling, habited nuns—something immediately, instinctively told me that this was a threat. Had I verbalized that thought, it would have sounded ridiculous, but I reacted nonetheless.

The third time, when curiosity overcame fear and I started reading, I was amazed. Sisters like this still existed? These Sisters wore habits and had "sister-y names," and their daily schedule was full of things I had come across in books, things like "vespers" and "spiritual reading" and "profound silence." They existed now? And they looked…well, happy! As I read more—about this community's Dominican charism of study, preaching, and devotion to truth; about their teaching apostolate and radical community life; about their particular devotion to the Eucharist and their communal practice of consecration to our Lady—I became more and more impressed. Not, of course, that this had anything at all to do with me. I had a plan, and a very good one, thank you. But it was nice, in a general sort of way, I told myself, to know that such women were out there. I remember thinking, "If I were going to be a Sister, which I'm obviously not, because that's crazy, nobody does that anymore, but if I were, which I am definitely not…then I would want to be like them! Everything about them makes sense to me! Well, that is nice. Moving on."

Despite my immediate dismissal of it, the idea of religious life, once planted, would not die. Baffled by the persistence of this new and uninvited thought, I tried to stifle it. All that summer, I successfully ignored it. In the fall, when I headed off to Notre Dame, and found I loved my classes and ROTC and all the other opportunities of campus living even more than I had expected, I could almost forget about it. Except when I tried to pray, that is. Then, it

> "Entrust yourself completely to My will saying, 'Not as I want, but according to Your will, O God, let it be done unto me.' These words, spoken from the depths of one's heart, can raise a soul to the summit of sanctity in a short time. In such a soul I delight. Such a soul gives Me glory. Such a soul fills heaven with the fragrance of her virtue."
>
> —Jesus to Saint Faustina

was always in the back of my mind: *You need to be open to religious life.* Always. It was so persistent that I eventually realized, "I'm either going to have to think about this or stop praying altogether!"

Well, somewhere along the way I had picked up the idea that I must not stop praying, and at Notre Dame I had more opportunities to pray than ever before. There was the tabernacle in my dorm chapel where I stopped frequently throughout the day. There were Sunday and daily Masses, readily available in any of the five dozen chapels on campus, but which most days I attended in the beautiful Basilica, a mere three-minute walk from my dorm. There were Holy Hours, retreats, praise and worship nights, talks and discussion groups hosted by campus ministry, reverent liturgies with beautiful music, and a quiet, peaceful chapel where the Blessed Sacrament was exposed for hours every day. I loved it all. But always, always, that quiet, persistent, voiceless whisper: *You need to be open to religious life.*

> I began to discover that the persistent nudge I had been fighting was not an external imposition on me, as I had thought. It was prompted by God, certainly, but it was also coming from my heart – from a place of deep, unspoken desires that I had no idea even existed.

When I finally decided to give this matter some attention, I honestly believed that it was just a test. You know the story of Abraham sacrificing Isaac? "And then God said to Abraham, 'Well done, you passed the test. I was just seeing if you loved Me; go back to life as usual now.'" There is a bit more to this passage than my paraphrase suggests, but that was my understanding of it at the time. When I begrudgingly decided to "be open to religious life"—whatever that was supposed to mean—I was convinced that it was a valuable but hypothetical exercise. If I could just work myself up to being "open" enough, then surely my faith would be strengthened and my love for God increased, and the Lord would pat me on the head and say indulgently, "You are a good girl, I knew you loved Me more than your plan. Now go on back to what you were doing, with My blessing."

But of course, if you give an inch, God takes a mile. "Being open" did not go at all as I had hoped. As soon as my wall of absolute opposition came down, I began to discover that the persistent nudge I had been fighting was not an external imposition on me, as I had thought. It was prompted by God, certainly, but it was also coming from my heart, from a place of deep, unspoken desires that I had no idea even existed. Despite my contentment with my classes and training, something within me expanded at the thought of a life radically given to God.

Slowly, it dawned on me that this might not be hypothetical: it might actually be my vocation. But it still seemed like a distant possibility, far off in the future. Then—and I can still remember the moment when this thought occurred to me, pulling into a hardware store parking lot while running errands for my mom over Christmas break—I realized very abruptly that I might be supposed to do something about this vocation question now. Now. Not in a decade or so, when my commitment to the Air Force would be complete; not after I had checked all the goals off my own list and decided to finally give God's plan a whirl. Now.

IT GETS REAL

Back on campus for the spring, and with all these thoughts swirling in my mind, I received an e-blast from campus ministry with the subject line, "The Sisters are coming!" It is indicative of my continuing obliviousness that I had not the slightest idea what this could be talking about. When I opened the email and read, "The Dominican Sisters of Mary, Mother of the Eucharist will be on campus next week..." my jaw just about dropped through the floor. I knew that name. Those were the Sisters from that website! Now they had followed me to college? Not fair, God! As I read through the email and found that their itinerary comprised campus ministry events that I regularly attended, a dispute broke out between the proverbial little angel and little devil perched on my shoulders. I do not want to go. *I should go.* I do not want to talk to them. *I should talk to them.* Eventually the little angel won me over, on the grounds that free food would be served at these events and that free food is something always to be accepted. This really profound reasoning on my part serves as proof that God can truly make anything work to His purposes. I would go, eat, and hear the Sisters out.

When I did, I was astonished. The Sisters who came were young, normal (except that they were Sisters), and beaming with joy. One of them had left Notre Dame just two years before to enter the convent. And they seemed so happy. These were women who had found something wonderful in life.

Also of interest: When I summoned up the courage to talk to the vocation directress, Sister Joseph Andrew, and chaotically spilled out all my jumbled thoughts of the past ten months, she did not think I was crazy. She seemed to find it perfectly natural for me to think I might have a vocation; in fact, she thought I might have one, too. She convinced me that I would need to find out more by coming on a retreat, held at the start of the summer.

Suddenly, things became immensely more real. "Discernment" had just changed from vague, hypothetical thoughts that I had discussed with absolutely no one, into plans to visit a very specific, not at all hypothetical community—the same community whose web page had gotten me thinking about this to begin with. Reluctantly, for I was still very unsure and shy about all this, I realized that concrete steps like buying a plane ticket meant I would need to tell those closest to me that I was thinking about a possible religious vocation. When I did so, they must have thought it was totally out of the blue. But I knew, if I was honest with myself, that it was not. Though I had worked hard to avoid, suppress, and reason my way out of the thought of a vocation, I had to admit that "being open" had gradually changed something in my heart. I had found a deep and unrelenting desire to do God's will, and it seemed very possible that this was it.

COUNTING THE COST

Nevertheless, I was terrified. There was still so much that was unknown to me, and the surge of fear and resistance rising in me showed just how attached I was to my plan. To consider relinquishing control over my life was very scary! Going into the military was comfortable, familiar; it would be challenging and demand self-sacrifice, absolutely, but I was eager for such a challenge and knew, or at least thought I knew, what such a life would look like. What is more, I was sure I would be good at it. Religious life? That was mysterious and unknown and posed a kind of challenge—to become a

> "Lord, teach me to be generous;
> Teach me to serve You as You deserve;
> To give and not to count the cost;
> To fight and not to heed the wounds;
> To toil, and not to seek for rest;
> To labor, and not to ask for reward, except to know that I am doing your will."
>
> -Saint Ignatius of Loyola

saint—that I was not so sure I was eager to embrace. I had no guarantee I would be good at any of it.

It is tempting for me to trivialize those months now that I know the rest of the story; but at the time, it was agonizing. Written into my ROTC scholarship contract was a clause that allowed me to walk away at any point during my freshman year—but not later. I could return for sophomore training, confirming my contract and committing the next eleven years to military service. Or I could disenroll—essentially guaranteeing that any future for me in the Air Force would be gone. I would have to make a decision, whether or not I had an answer from God about my vocation. I had wanted to be a military officer since before I could remember. I had worked toward that goal my whole life. If I walked away, and it turned out I did not have a vocation after all—then what?

It is one of the great graces of my life that God allowed me to make that decision myself, "in the dark"; it required faith I did not know I had. I prayed and prayed that semester, and when summer came I still had no certainty and no backup plan, but I did have peace in knowing that God was asking me to trust Him. I disenrolled.

GOD'S PLAN > MY PLAN

> The Lord let me leap into the dark, but in His kindness, He did not leave me there for long.

The Lord let me leap into the dark, but in His kindness, He did not leave me there for long. When I went on the retreat held by the Sisters just after making my decision about ROTC, I expected simply to gain a bit more insight into their life. I certainly did not expect certainty. But as soon as the Sisters squeezed themselves and all of us into the chapel of the school where the retreat was being held and began to chant Vespers, as they do every evening,

I knew. I knew. In a way totally unexpected, and totally unlike my usual analytical way of approaching things, I knew this was how I was supposed to spend my life: consecrated to God, a bride of Christ, living, praying, and preaching in service to Him and His Church. I had found peace—right there in that community with the ubiquitous web page.

(NOT) THE END

How I wish I had the space—and you, reader, the patience!—to tell you more of the story: about the friends who were absolute rocks of support; about that summer, spent working at Covecrest and how my newfound vocation was nurtured there; about the outpouring of encouragement from my parish during the year I spent at home preparing to enter. In heaven, you will get to hear the rest of my story of how God worked in my life, if you are interested, and I will get to hear yours!

Perhaps that is the best part of this and every vocation story: they do not stop where they seem to. By the nature of the genre, vocation stories tend to end with a culminating event like entering a convent, and that is only reasonable. But of course, that is not the end. That is only the beginning. I can testify from my own life that the graces God gave during my discernment have since been surpassed many times over, and that the joy I experienced in finding my vocation is nothing next to the joy I have been given in living it!

May each one of us live our vocation faithfully all the way to heaven, where we will not need websites to find God's will—where we will see Him as He is.

From Combat Boots to... Well, Actually the Shoes Didn't Change That Much

> Religious Sisters truly lift up the Church and the world by their prayer and presence. The communal life of religious Sisters has a power of impact seen and unseen. What Sisters 'do' truly no one else can because they embody individually and collectively the bride of Christ IN LOVE with their Spouse Jesus and His Body the Church. With their witness we have a Church that pops!
>
> – Father Ethan Moore
> St. Monica-St. George Parish, Cincinnati, Ohio

God Loves Us All—Even the Pranksters

Finding What Love Really Means

Sister Mary Perpetua Ha, OP
Born in Los Angeles, California

"Our Father, who art in heaven … forgive us our trespasses as we forgive those who trespass against us." From the age of six, I'd whisper the words of the Our Father each night as I tried to fall asleep, making sure I forgave any grievances from that particular day. I would closely examine my conscience: "Do I truly forgive this person for doing this to me? Have I stopped being angry at this situation?" It didn't matter if I was crying, scared, sad, sleepy, happy, or excited; it was always the same: forgive. The grace that filled my young soul allowed me to realize the power of forgiveness. It allowed me to open my heart to Christ and ponder His mystery that surrounded me so tangibly. My pure and childlike faith trusted this more than anything in life. God was real, and He was with me. In all this, God was preparing me for a lifetime of forgiveness, acceptance, and love; this in turn would become the path to my vocation. I clung to the words of the Our Father in an attempt to know God. It was all I had. It was hope in moments of confusion.

I grew up the daughter of Vietnamese parents: my father was a non-practicing Buddhist and my mother a Catholic who only infrequently attended Mass. I had a younger sister and brother, fraternal twins.

My Catholic grandmother lived only twenty minutes away, and it was she who taught me about the Catholic Faith. The Our Father was one of the two prayers I knew by heart, because my maternal grandmother prayed the Rosary three times a day. I often spent summer days at her home, which meant attending daily Mass and praying the Rosary with her. Even though most children would consider days with her boring, I loved them. She told me stories from the Bible, of Marian apparitions, of times when she knew God was present in situations. She made sure I prayed for my father and his conversion. Her words echo through my mind, "Never stop praying for your dad. Don't fear anything except God." She taught me that true strength is rooted in faith. Grandma would often tell stories of when she was a child. Christianity was looked down upon in Communist Vietnam. She and her family would wake up before dawn to pray by candlelight, when no one would see them.

> "Say the Holy Rosary. Blessed be that monotony of Hail Marys which purifies the monotony of your sins!"
> —Saint Josemaría Escrivá

Like all the women in my family, my mother was strong and selfless. As a young teenager in Vietnam, she had been a cross-country runner. During one meet she was sick with a fever and was forbidden to attend the race. She snuck out anyway and returned home with a first-place award. This was my mother: determined and resilient. She was a single mom for the first few years of my life. She graduated college and worked hard to support us. It was she who spent hours doing homework with my siblings and me. She nursed us back to health when we were sick. We were her life, and she loved us in the best way she could. Although her faith was weak at times, her virtues formed me into the person I am today.

My Buddhist paternal grandmother also shaped who I am. "Grandma, will you ever love Jesus?" I would ask her. To my child's mind, it was a little incomprehensible that anyone did not, especially someone I loved so much. I wanted her to go to heaven with me.

This was the grandma that my siblings and I came home to each day after school. It was she who took care of us most often. I am a lot like her: strong, determined, and funny. Her integrity is evident in her life story.

She had married one of the French soldiers who occupied Vietnam in the mid-1900s, and had four children. Even though she was a practicing Buddhist, she raised the children Catholic, her husband's faith. Her husband died young, and when the French left Vietnam in the 1950s, anyone with French descent had to leave the country too. Her children were deported, while she was left alone in Vietnam. Still, she remained strong and put her children through boarding school in France. She eventually remarried and gave birth to my father. She was another mother to me. As a child, I prayed each day that she would find God.

> I did not know anything about the Eucharist or that there was a tabernacle with Christ's Real Presence within, but I could sense Him there.

As my siblings and I grew up, my mom started to take us to Mass more frequently. My father was a hands-off father, so perhaps the daunting task of handling three young children alone was the reason we had not gone to Mass as often before. When we did go, we would attend a nearby parish, Saint Joseph. I remember feeling a sense of awe each time I walked in. I did not know anything about the Eucharist or that there was a tabernacle with Christ's Real Presence within, but I could sense Him there. As I watched people receive Holy Communion I would think, "I want to do that. I want Him." I just knew that the people were receiving God Himself.

A FATHERLESS CHILD?

Growing up, my relationship with my father was very strained. He always seemed distant. At first glance, our relationship was typical of an Asian father to his daughter. It was complicated by the fact that my father was the youngest son of a man with almost twenty children from three different wives in Vietnam. He was raised in a home that seemed affectionless and authoritarian. Although he cared for us in his own way, he was never taught how to love like a father.

After years of this distance, I began to tell myself, "He can't be your real father." When I was twelve, I devised a plan to prove this. I decided to sneak a look at the important paperwork when no one was around. I waited until the right moment. The day came when I had the house all to myself and could get in and out of the files quickly. I ran for the hidden keys and went to the files. I unlocked the box and slowly looked through each document. Then, I came upon my birth certificate. I took a breath and read it slowly. It did not have my current last name but rather my mother's maiden name. I continued looking until I reached the line that said "father." Right next to it was one word: "unknown." I was devastated that I was fatherless; there was no joy in my being correct, just confusion. I tried to bring up the subject with my parents, but the result was only silence.

As the years continued, my family life became increasingly complicated and disordered. I nurtured this confusion as an

> "It is not enough to love the young; they must know that they are loved."
> —Saint John Bosco

adolescent; pain and emptiness took over. Closeness and intimacy disappeared, even with God. I felt forsaken. I kept God at a distance. I was always ready for the worst to happen. My survival tactic became numbness: "Don't allow anyone to love you. Then no one can hurt you." I did not believe in love anymore; it was for the weak.

At crucial times, God would place someone in my life to love me and give me hope. These people would smooth out the cracks in my heart before I could fall apart. Yet, I never realized this because I was so emotionless. But they were there.

One of these people was my fourth-grade teacher. She recognized that I was struggling to find happiness and hope in life. I would sit with her and become lost in my own world of misery. She made it a point to show me that I was lovable and loved. She cared and asked probing questions, usually to no avail. She would sit with me in silence, wait, and wonder. I usually did not reveal anything about my life, but simply by being with me, she reminded me, "No man is an island." This was the beginning of chiseling away the walls I had put up around my heart. At the same time, I was resolved never again to let others see this side of me.

YOU ARE THE HAPPIEST PERSON I KNOW

One high school afternoon as I sat in a courtyard tutoring a friend, she looked at me as I laughed loudly at a joke. "You are the happiest person I know," said Shana. I smiled and continued joking. I played the part of a girl with the perfect life and a promising future. I had it all together. I was an honors student and in Student Council, Spanish Club, Peer Tutoring; sang in Woman's Ensemble; acted in musicals; planned school dances and pep rallies; and was an officer in French Club—and I did not even take French! The perfection that I exuded on the outside helped the girl who was crumbling on the inside keep it together. If I kept busy, I could fool everyone, including myself. I would make it in life, and do it as perfectly as I could. I did not need anyone; they would fail me anyway.

After years of not practicing the faith, my mother succumbed to my grandmother's unfailing pleas to put my siblings and me into Religious Education so we could receive the Sacraments. I was so far behind that I was a teenager in a class of second graders. Eventually, I was placed in a Confirmation class with young people my own age. During my years of Confirmation preparation, I was required to attend retreats. At fifteen years old, I asked my mother, "Mom, do I have to go? I'm going to waste a whole weekend. What's with this God stuff anyway?"

Throughout the retreat's talks and break-out sessions, I sat stone cold. When my group leader, Natalie, asked me to share my thoughts, I would shrug my shoulders and answer, "I think what she just said." Little did I realize that what I heard was slowly seeping into my heart. My persistent leader—who is still my friend today—kept chipping away at the walls around my heart.

Twenty-four hours into the retreat, each retreatant received a letter from her parents. I received one envelope. I went to the chapel where there was Eucharistic Adoration and sat in a corner. I looked at the envelope with anticipation but did not recognize the handwriting. I opened it. It was from one of the retreat leaders, because my parents had failed to write me. My heart tightened with pain. My leader knew I did not have a letter from my parents, and she sat with me. I sobbed as the pain from my life overcame me.

I thought, "Why doesn't anyone love me? Why am I alone?

I just want to give up." In the middle of the hurt, I felt God. He seemed to say, "You are loved and you are not alone. I've always been with you, carrying you in your suffering." I stared up at the monstrance. Love overflowed my being. I did not have to survive on my own; God was with me. In this moment, my childhood faith flooded back. Those words that I repeated from the Our Father each night returned. I forgave my parents for everything; I had found Love again.

> "And whenever you stand praying, forgive, if you have anything against any one; so that your Father also who is in heaven may forgive you your trespasses."
>
> Mark 11:25

Over the next few years my life at home became harder. There was discord among all the adults, and that trauma affected everyone. But this time, I no longer stood alone and disoriented. Instead of succumbing to darkness, I reached out to Christ in the difficult moments, calling His name every time I felt lost. Even when it was hardest to let go and forgive, I forgave.

YOUTH MINISTRY AND THE MILITIA IMMACULATA

At first, I did not know what to do with my newly discovered faith, so I just went to church. That is where God is, right? I made my mom drop me off at the first Mass on Sunday and pick me up after the fourth and last Mass of the day. In between Masses, I sat in the chapel trying to pray. This lasted a few weeks until I realized I could join the youth ministry at my parish. God was all I wanted, and I could not get enough of Him.

Youth ministry became my life and my haven away from home. No one knew the secrets I held inside. I still had a hard time

> ### Who was Saint Maximilian Kolbe?
> - Born in Poland in 1894
> - At the age of 10, received an apparition of our Lady, who offered two crowns: one red (martyrdom) and one white (purity). He chose to receive both crowns.
> - Entered the Order of Franciscans and was later ordained a priest in 1919.
> - In 1939, was arrested by the Nazis and was taken to Auschwitz death camp.
> - In 1941, offered to take the place of a man condemned to die and was sentenced to the starvation bunker. When he was found still alive two weeks later, he was killed by lethal injection.
> - Canonized by Pope Saint John Paul II in 1982, who declared him a "martyr of charity."
> - Patron of journalists, media communications, and the chemically addicted.

trusting people. They accepted that, however, and gave me my space. They knew something was not right, but they loved me. I did everything, like I always do, with creativity and full force. I attended every event and then began planning and running them with newfound, authentic, and lifelong friends at my side.

These friends unknowingly kept me strong through the next years. They and I liked to analyze the world while spending time together. This was often at Anni's home where her mom would cook us huge dinners. She loved having all the girls over and spoiled us as we sat around their cozy dinner table. We were her kids too. It was during times like this, and sleepovers at my friend Jen's home, that I saw what families could be like. There was so much joy and community. As my siblings entered high school, they too joined youth ministry and enjoyed these gatherings. We became known as the fun prankster-siblings. Through these encounters, we learned how to be part of a stable family.

During this time, I secretly harbored thoughts of religious

life in my heart. I told no one. I would often wake up overwhelmed by God's love. I sensed He was calling me to be a religious Sister. Then, fear would overcome me. "How?" I would ask. The only nuns I saw were in movies. They were usually portrayed as dark and apathetic. I would lie in bed and pray, "Okay, if you want me to be unhappy for the rest of my life, I'll do it because I love you." Then I would roll out of bed defeated, but secretly happy that He would want me.

As high school ended, I wanted to know God more and more. This led me to the Militia Immaculata (MI), a Marian movement started by Saint Maximillian Kolbe. The MI was a group of vibrant youth and young adults who were on fire with their faith. In 2002, I flew to Chicago to attend a Young Adults New Year's Retreat with the MI in Marytown, the national shrine of Saint Maximilian Kolbe. It was a beautiful week with talks, Adoration, and fellowship. There I met the Dominican Sisters of Mary, Mother of the Eucharist. Each morning, we would see two Sisters in the beautiful Marytown chapel attending Eucharistic Adoration and Mass. The Director of the Young Adults, Shevawn, jumped at the chance to have Sisters present at the retreat and invited them to give a talk. I was interested but not moved. I had given up my whim of becoming a Sister and was determined to get married. I even had a well-planned wedding binder and attended wedding shows. Sisterhood was in the past. I would not let myself consider it again. My plan was the only plan now.

MOTHER MARY HEALS HER DAUGHTER

As the years passed, I became more and more involved with Militia Immaculata. Though I spent so much time with these people, they still did not know my life story. They thought of me as the sweet and funny girl. In 2004, I went on a pilgrimage to France with a group from the MI. It consisted of mostly middle-aged adults as well as eight young adults. This trip was made possible through my parish community and my dad's generosity; giving money was the principal way he showed his love. The main part of the pilgrimage was spent in Lourdes, France. Late each evening, after the crowds had left, my friends and I would go to the Grotto to pray. I would sit there for hours, begging the Blessed Mother to let me grow closer to her Son and know His will for my life. Above all, I asked for healing and trust. It was easy for me to forgive everyone else, but I could not forgive myself for things over which I had no control. I was ashamed and feared the secrets I held from the past. In many ways, I was still a lost little girl. The only way I could be found was to trust God completely. I needed to let it all go each night. On the fourth night, after bathing in the Lourdes water, I sat in the Grotto again. Like the waters that freely flowed next to the Grotto, my tears of pain and surrender began to flow through me in deep sobs. Our Lady told me to give it all to her Son, and I slowly did.

> "I do not promise to give you happiness in this world, but in the next."
> —Our Lady of Lourdes to Saint Bernadette

Shevawn, the youth director, had a good sense of people. I always felt as though she looked at me with wonder, prayer, and love. She confided that she sensed something within me and desired to know about it. I did not tell her anything, but she encouraged me to discern religious life. I was reluctant.

WORLD YOUTH DAY AND A VOCATION – BUT WHICH ONE?

In 2005, I attended World Youth Day in Cologne, Germany, with the Militia Immaculata. As we prepared for the trip, Shevawn told me four of the Dominican Sisters of Mary, Mother of the Eucharist were coming with us. I did not act excited. The day we left from Chicago O'Hare, the first people I saw in the terminal were the Sisters. I was determined not to be distracted by them. Contrary to my usual friendly manner, I walked straight past the Sisters and headed for my friends.

But I could not stay away for long. I was assigned to sit next to Sister Ave Maria for our twelve-hour flight to France. As I sat next to her, I noticed how normal she was. She was kind, sweet, and funny. I even realized that she, too, was a prankster. At the same time, I watched as she stayed faithful to her daily meditation and prayers during the flight. My heart sped up, but I resisted any attraction to religious life.

> "Joy is a net of love by which we catch souls."
> —Saint Teresa of Calcutta

As I got to know the Sisters, I stopped avoiding them. However, I still resisted the gentle call and prodding of God. I told myself to follow the plan, my plan, which was perfect. My children could become priests and nuns if they wanted.

As part of our pilgrimage, we went to Auschwitz-Birkenau, the most deadly concentration camps during the Holocaust. I was deeply affected by the stories and scenes, especially the starvation cells in Auschwitz and the gas chambers in Birkenau. I separated myself from the group and wandered around Birkenau alone, walking the railway tracks that had herded millions to their death. A deadening sorrow crept over me. I stopped at one of the gas chambers and prayed as grief overtook my heart. I turned to exit the camp as I prayed, "God, all these people had a purpose and a plan for their lives but they were not able to fulfill Your plan. They had no choice, but I do. What is Your will for me?" I knew he wanted me to be a Sister. I promised God, "I will fulfill your will." I left the concentration camp with my resolve.

Still, I resisted letting anyone see what was in my heart. On the last night of our trip, in Paris, we planned a girls' pampering night. As I walked with one of my friends, Sister John Mary walked beside me. She asked, "Will you come to one of our discernment retreats?" I responded, "Why would I do that?" She said she thought I would like it. I panicked and blurted out, "If you let me paint your toenails, I'll come!" In Sr. John Mary's gentle fashion, she declined my proposal, but persisted in inviting me to visit the Sisters. Again, I panicked and tried to change the topic, "Does Mother ever see your toes?" She answered, "No." I replied, "So, let me do it and I'll come." I thought my ploy had worked, as Sister John Mary dropped the topic.

The pilgrimage changed me, but I was not free enough to respond to God's invitation to the religious life. I jumped into teaching in an inner-city middle school and started a Master's program. I continued volunteering at church. I helped at RCIA. Soon I became very close to one of the other volunteers, a green-eyed, handsome young man and we became inseparable friends.

He told others that he would marry me one day. I never had a man love me as he did. In profound ways, he taught me how to trust others again. He would do anything for me and loved me unconditionally. Eventually, I had to admit that I could not love him that way in return. My heart was divided. Why did God bring someone to love me in this manner if He wanted me to enter a convent? Perhaps He was showing me that I had the choice of marriage and could be wholly and deeply loved by other people. If I chose religious life, it was not going to be because my human relationships had failed. It would be my own free choice.

In honesty, I told my boyfriend that I was discerning religious life and needed to give it a chance. He was supportive, but not thrilled. He was willing to lose me only if it was God's will and made me happy.

During this time, Shevawn would tell me the Sisters were

inquiring about me. I would retort, "Why? There were a hundred other people on that trip." Secretly, I began reading everything on the Sisters' website. In May, I flew to Seattle for a Militia Immaculata event just because I knew the Sisters would be there. At dinner, the Sisters surrounded me, and I was overjoyed. I spent every moment I could with Sister John Mary and, as we parted, she asked me again to come to their May retreat. I told Sister I was seeing someone. She smiled, gave me a knowing look, and left. My heart was torn out of my chest until I finally decided to humble myself and go on this retreat. The rest is history. I entered the Dominican Sisters of Mary the following August.

God amazes me each day as grace continues to abound in my life. I am now under final vows and love my vocation. But the story does not stop there. God is working in my family. Within the last year, my father mentioned God for the first time. His heart has grown soft with love for his grandchildren. He is learning how to express what he truly feels. My mother has been faithful to the Church for years now with her rich prayer life. My little sister met her husband in our youth group. They have a holy marriage and two little boys. My brother lives in Seattle and is thriving in his career. He says his life is Mass, his girlfriend, running, and his work. Often, I tell people that my siblings are examples to me because they are a lot holier than I am. They have the biggest hearts because they dwell in God. When I reflect on my past, my present life is a miracle. People who know my whole story ask, "How did you and your siblings turn out so normal?" With smiles on our faces, our answer is always the same, "God's grace." I am excited to see what my Spouse has in store for the future. Love endures all things, forgives all things, and heals all things. God is Love.

> God amazes me each day as grace continues to abound in my life.

> We are living in a most extraordinary time; the present moment provides a tremendous opportunity to help souls. The gift of women's religious vocations is one that magnifies the presence of Christ Jesus in our world, for it is the Lord who invites us to contribute to his mission to heal and transform our world. Women religious are essential in our Church's striving to contribute to the upbuilding of 'on Earth as it is in Heaven.'
>
> —Father Casey Beaumier, SJ
> Director of the Institute for Advanced Jesuit Studies at Boston College

An Invitation to Love

Discovering the Double-Dominican-American Dream

Sister Mercedes Torres, OP
Born in Brooklyn, New York

"*Tú va ser monja?*" shouted a bright-eyed five-year-old living in an orphanage in the Dominican Republic. "Are you going to be a nun?" the little boy questioned happily as he bounced about clapping his hands in mine, as I repeatedly chuckled "No", while guiding him to the table where the Sisters were laying out lunch for the dozens of other children.

I had graduated from high school three days earlier. While many of my classmates were bouncing around Mediterranean beaches to honor this great occasion, I got onto a familiar flight from New York's JFK airport to Santiago, Dominican Republic. I had taken this four-hour flight many times before with my family, but this time I went alone. I had decided to spend some of my summer with my grandparents who lived there. It seemed like the perfect reset before heading to college.

I did not initially plan to stop at the orphanage on my way to my grandparents' ranch, but went upon the recommendation—with a touch of gentle force—of my aunt. She knew that I loved children and thought I would enjoy a few days helping the Sisters. Playing with the children for a few days seemed like it would be great. Spending a few days with the Sisters seemed like it would be awkward. Hence the need for "gentle force". It *was* great and it was *not* awkward. I was surprised by all the joy I encountered upon arriving at the orphanage. A peaceful, honest, and pure joy prevailed among the Sisters, the volunteers, the visitors and, most beautifully, the children.

A FAMILY GROWS IN BROOKLYN

My parents are from the Dominican Republic. Green hills rolling endlessly, one into the other, interrupted by thin brown stalks bursting in green palms and dotted sparingly with brightly colored houses roofed with red tin. The quiet, uneven, dusty, brown roads carved into these hills, trodden by mules carrying joyful men in Panama hats, were the roads that eventually brought my parents out of the countryside and to America and to Brooklyn.

My parents did everything they could to secure the American Dream for their two children. This entailed all the necessary loving sacrifices and care to instill a deep love for their old home, while ensuring a way for us to make our future in our new home. They did it all in tandem with my uncles and aunts and cousins. My father is number fifteen of eighteen children, born on a simple ranch nestled in the mountainous Cibao region of the Dominican Republic. By the time I was born, most of his siblings had come to America, along with many of their cousins, their cousins' cousins, and the cousins-of-the-neighbors-who-live-on-the-other-side-of-the-river.

It is common for families from a particular region in one country to immigrate together to the same region in the United States. Such was the case for the Torres-Estévez family and many others who were leaving the San José de Las Mata region and landing in Bushwick, Brooklyn. And they all settled in a several-block radius of a parish. This built-in community meant that walking down the street I would be instantly recognized as *"hija de Geno"* (Geno's daughter) or *"nieta de Juanico"* (Juanico's granddaughter). I loved it. It just fit.

Going to Mass on Sundays was like going to a mini family reunion. Only the next Mass could end our visiting time. Every Sunday I prepared myself to spend at least thirty minutes losing my parents to various packs of adults chatting enthusiastically. I would spend the time sticking with my brother, scanning the crowd and reuniting with cousins, while being hugged by the same people who called me "Geno's daughter" and told me how much I had grown, even though I was almost positive I had seen them last week.

This outdoor session moved indoors to a nearby aunt's house with company-kindling food like plantains, rice, beans, or other Dominican fare. Various family members cycled through, always leaving with a foil-covered plate in hand.

My brother and I were very close growing up. We were close in age and companions in all we did. We felt like we had extra siblings in our cousins and always enjoyed getting to see them, which sometimes was multiple times a week. This bond with our cousins deepened when

> "Love begins in our home by praying together."
> —Saint Teresa of Calcutta

we spent weeks over the summers with them, staying with our grandparents in the Dominican Republic. These summers allowed us to have our own stake in the hills and country roads that our parents called home.

Our family gatherings also often included prayer, especially when my grandparents were involved. Prayer began and ended their day, and if you were with them, it did the same for yours. This was the lens through which I saw my faith: family and community. We prayed the rosary together. We went to Mass together. We said our devotions together. I sang in the church choir, but only because my cousins were there. I looked forward to Mass, mostly because it involved more time with my cousins and family. I never saw faith as a personal experience; rather, it was embedded in my beautiful Dominican and family culture that was the foundation of my identity.

THE AMERICAN DREAM?

Part of securing the American Dream involved a heavy emphasis on academic success. Success in school improved our chances for a successful American future. My brother and I were very fortunate to be tracked into challenging classes from elementary school onward. Most of my cousins went to the Catholic parish school, but my brother and I went to public schools, bearing the classic New York names: P.S. or I.S. followed by a string of numbers.

When I was in seventh grade, I began a program that selected Hispanic and Black students from New York City to receive full scholarships to attend top boarding schools in the Northeast. After rounds of IQ tests and interviews, I began the fourteen-month intensive classical schooling designed to prepare me for the education I would soon receive; all of this was in addition to my normal schooling.

The moment came when I was about to begin boarding school. My brother had completed the program three years before I did and was already attending a boarding school in Connecticut. I was now ready to begin my adventure at a school in New Jersey. This was a great academic achievement and an incredible opportunity for both of us. It was also a major break with tradition. Typically, in Latino culture, a daughter does not leave the home until she gets married. It was still unusual for a young woman to go away for college, even in my family. Now, I was about to go away for high school. Still, this was an unparalleled academic opportunity; I was mature enough and up for the challenge and my parents could not let it pass unheeded.

I loved my new school. I loved the academic challenge, the dorms, the tight-knit community of the school within the House System and great friendships.

However, the faith that was tied to my family easily and naturally unraveled. Two "chapel credits" were required each trimester. It was not a Catholic school, but Catholic Mass was offered every Sunday. But, over the course of my four years at my boarding school, I never once attended Mass.

> "The great thing to remember is that though our feelings come and go, God's love for us does not."
> —C.S. Lewis

There was just no room for Catholicism in my life at boarding school. Upon my return to New York, my faith that had been founded upon the family and Dominican culture was no longer a part of my daily experience. Whatever I had of my faith limped along; yet it revived when I returned to my family on breaks. Additionally, by my senior year, my literary interests went the way of Camus and Kafka; thus, my values were shifting, too.

With virtually no foothold in my faith and all of my attention on academic and social success, I then headed to a large university in California. My life became controlled by putting forth the "perfect" image. I played the worldly game of a life painted "beautiful." And I was good at it. My portrait was meticulously maintained in eyes perfectly shadowed, clothes patterned and matched to perfection, veneered smiles, and a walk that radiated self-confidence. I was seen in the right places and knew the right people. It was a life that many pursue as an ideal today, but it masked a self-destruction and empty dissipation. It was a search for truth and dignity that only had one answer.

NEW BEGINNINGS IN OLD PLACES

I later found myself back in New York with my dream job. I worked for a non-profit based in Manhattan, which brought medical donations, pharmaceutical companies, and delegations of doctors down to Cuba and Nicaragua. I was doing exactly what I had hoped I would do. I loved getting to help plan and join the trips and interact with the companies, doctors, health ministries, and families we served.

Although I was back in New York, my Los Angeles life came with me. Upon my return to New York, I lived with an aunt and uncle in Queens. Their youngest daughter, Christy, was also living at home, working on her Master's and teaching in Queens.

> "God sends us friends to be our firm support in the whirlpool of struggle. In the company of friends, we will find strength to attain our sublime ideal."
>
> -Saint Maximilian Kolbe

In true Torres family fashion, I always considered Christy to be an older sister. We always got along and enjoyed each other's company. We shared a common sense of humor and pure enjoyment of our family and Dominican culture. The one thing that I could never understand was her passion for her Catholic faith. I always knew her to be very active in her faith and the Church. After a deep encounter with Christ in her early teens, she was joyfully dedicated in service to Him and the Church in Brooklyn. She was part of the youth group of our local parish, which I always strategically avoided, and moved on to wider ministry throughout New York. She had a beautiful singing voice, which she generously returned to the Lord in ministry. There was much that we understood and enjoyed about each other, but why she had such a strong faith always escaped me.

We could never calmly get through discussions regarding abortion or any moral or social teaching that put the Church at odds with the prevailing culture. It was incomprehensible to me that someone that I loved and with whom I saw eye-to-eye on so many topics, who had similar experiences and educational opportunities, could be so wrong. Religion was for our parents and grandparents and, frankly, it belonged in the Dominican Republic, or at least stopped at the doorstep of our Dominican parish.

She regularly invited me to join her and her ministry friends for events or just spending time together. I always declined. I had zero interest and made sure that came across. I would much rather spend my time going into the City with my friends, living my worldly life.

> Perhaps these people who lived their faith were normal after all.

A LIFE TRANSFORMED

It began with conversations and hospitality. Christy often brought some of her ministry friends over to the house. On off nights when I happened not to go out, I would, hesitantly, enter into the conversations and the laughter. The realization soon dawned on me that perhaps these people who lived their faith were normal after all.

Soon I moved into an apartment and was busy with work, my boyfriend, and sustaining the perfect portrait of my social life. Time passed. I had not seen Christy's ministry friends in a while.

Then, one of them reached out and invited me to a retreat she was running. For some reason, I felt that I should go. I did not tell Christy about these plans. I changed my mind several times on the way to the retreat, even at one point doing an about-face back to the subway station. But I knew I had to go and so I eventually got myself there. I did not know how I ended up there or what I was doing there. After all, I was not one of "these people". I did not go on retreats. But there I was.

> "Enjoy yourself as much as you like if only you keep from sin."
>
> -Saint John Bosco

On Saturday afternoon, I suddenly felt the need to go to Confession. I tried to slip in unseen. I walked out spiritually, physically, and visibly lighter. Mass on Sunday completed what began in Confession the day before. It revealed to me Christ as Savior; Christ as a person; my need for Him above all things. I received the great gift of His mercy. I was "found again and 'restored to value'" (John Paul II, *Dives in Misericordia* §6). I walked out forever changed on that Divine Mercy Sunday.

The vibrant and loving framework of the cultural faith I learned and lived as a child came alive in the person of Christ. I knew immediately my need for knowledge of Him and His Church. I purchased a Catechism, attended daily Mass and prayed the rosary I learned with my grandparents years ago. The "perfect portrait" no longer took the shape of nights out and a focus on "being seen." I was free to live and free to love—in Christ. I moved forward, happily spending my evenings and free time with Christy and her friends, finally allowing myself to enter fully into the conversations and laughter.

Throughout this time, I also accompanied this new group of friends to events with the Franciscan Friars of the Renewal (CFRs). We helped at soup kitchens and retreats, attended the monthly Catholic Undergrounds, and helped at their friaries. This was my first time seeing young habited religious. I had already seen a life joyfully lived by the missionary Sisters I had known in the Dominican Republic, but to my knowledge, no one did this in America. It could not be done by someone who was "normal" and my age. I suddenly realized that it *was* done by young people right here in New York. They did wear habits, they were joyful, and they had a genuine love for all those whom they encountered.

Later in September, I walked up the stairs to my apartment and saw a few white envelopes waiting for me on the wooden steps. My Catholic mail was amping up because of a recent purchase of *True Devotion* to accompany me on the Saint Louis de Montfort Marian Consecration journey I was about to complete.

I could see the various appeals for financial support that peered at me from five steps away. I scooped up the envelopes with a half-glance and saw a long line of young women dressed in blue vests and skirts, with smiles all the way down the line. Those real smiles were now familiar to me from the religious I knew in New York. The envelope declared, "We have a different kind of vocations crisis!"

The timing was comical. I was just coming back from spending some time with Christy and another friend, Alverlis. Inspired by a documentary we had watched, we imagined how "crazy it would be if we became nuns". We discussed possible names—I proclaimed mine would be something with "mercy"—and wondered how we would look in veils. It was all with a light-hearted air. We knew it would never actually happen.

I thought this vocation-rich envelope had such amusing timing that I took a picture and sent it to Christy and Alverlis so that they could enjoy it along with me. We all laughed as I tossed the mailing from the Dominican Sisters of Mary, Mother of the Eucharist into the trash.

There were moments in the month following the "envelope encounter" that the possibility of considering a vocation at some point in the future crossed my mind. These moments came whenever I worked with the CFRs or encountered the Sisters of Life. They came in the form of a subtle butterfly-in-the-stomach lift in my heart, accompanied by a deep, sudden sense of joy. However, there was no real chance of having a vocation, of course. I was not called to be a Franciscan or even a Sister of Life. To my knowledge, these were the only religious orders that fit the bill of young, normal, habited, joyful communities. Thus, any possible need for discernment was over. I could continue along, enjoying my friends and planning my next trip to Cuba for work.

A LIFT IN MY HEART

At the end of January I found myself at the March for Life in Washington, D.C. Christy and I had come full circle. A topic that had once caused such tension between us now united us so beautifully and genuinely. In some ways, I could hardly imagine how I could have ever been "on the other side".

While spending time with Christy and some other cousins and while handing out fliers, I noticed a group of young postulants dressed in blue and a couple of Sisters dressed in white among them. I had never seen these Sisters in white habits before. What community was this? I weaved through the crowd to read their banner, trailed by Christy. I had no intention of speaking with the Sisters since, to my mind, once you decide to speak to the Sisters, you become a Sister, and that was not the plan.

I read the banner waiting to be displayed during the March. "Dominican Sisters of Mary, Mother of the Eucharist". The name instantly gave me the same deep rush of joy I had felt months before. I loved everything about the name. "Dominican": I could obviously get on board with that; "Sisters of Mary": Marian devotion was sown deep in my Torres heart; "Mother of the Eucharist": Eucharistic Adoration, fueled by daily Mass, had increasingly become the center of my devotion. It all fit. My eyes continued to the next line of the banner: "Ann Arbor, Michigan". I stopped there. There was no way I was going leave New York, presuming I was "going" anywhere, let alone to the Midwest. That was enough for me, so I walked away. My cousin Christy was clearly watching my progression of emotions. She grabbed my arm quickly, and swiftly reminded me, "Isn't that the community that sent you the mailing in the fall?" I stopped, speechless, and looked her in the eye as I nudged passed her.

> "Take delight in the Lord, and he will give you the desires of your heart."
> -Psalm 37:4

I spent the next two days clicking through the Sisters' website, engrossed in their life of prayer and community. There were three retreats a year: the February retreat fast approaching, a May retreat, and a November retreat. The February retreat was too soon, and it was my birthday weekend. I had plans! I was going to be in Nicaragua for work in May. The November retreat seemed like the obvious option. I knew a few young women who were discerning, and I knew it took time to pray, think, and visit communities. Besides, I was not even discerning.

I spoke to Christy and Alverlis constantly about the community. It soon became obvious I needed to take the next step: contact. I emailed Sister Joseph Andrew, trying to sound very aloof and simply requesting more information. She replied with a loving embrace—one that you could only receive from one of Sister Joseph Andrew's emails. She encouraged me to attend the February retreat. This seemed crazy to me. It was two weeks away! But, a few exchanges of emails and a plane ticket half-covered by a benefactor led me to cancel my birthday plans and go on the February retreat. I knew I needed to go.

When I arrived, I was still reticent. I was not like these other women; I was not "discerning". *Why was I here?* However, as I settled in, I could not escape the sense of "home" that came over me. I could not put words to it, nor did I feel the need to do so. I began to open my eyes to what was around me.

Seeing the Sisters with the retreatants made me realize that yes, I could love others like that. Seeing them with each other made me realize that, yes, I could love my Sisters like that. Seeing them pray in community and in Eucharistic Adoration made me realize that yes, I could pray like that. I could love Him like that. I could live for and with Him like that. What is more, I was supposed to. I had to say "yes."

> My vocation was an invitation to love.

It was clear that this was how I had been created to love. I was created to love Christ through this consecration. To love Him first and to have the privilege to love others through Him, in His love. My vocation was an invitation to love. A challenge to give myself entirely and fully to Him and thus to be given to all. This was what I had been created for: to live this love as a Dominican Sister of Mary, Mother of the Eucharist.

It all came together in a conference with Sister Joseph Andrew and my request for application papers. This was an entirely unexpected decision for me, but there was no fear or unrest. It was a decision of peace and a decision of love.

This knowledge is what I carried with me as I brought the news to my family and friends. Christy was surprised but joyful as she picked me up from the airport. She was supportive and ready to help as needed. I needed to figure out a way to tell my parents. I wanted them to know before anyone else. Fortunately, we had already arranged to meet briefly in Miami while I returned from a trip to Cuba and they returned from a trip to the Dominican Republic. I told them of my new plans to enter in six months. They were stunned. My father repeated, *"Piensalo bien"* (Think this over well). I had, of course. All I could do was to let the news sink in.

I later called my brother who, understandably, had a similar reaction to my parents. This was something that was never remotely discussed as an option. This was certainly something that no one expected from me, of all people. Only one year before this, I had brought my boyfriend to the Dominic Republic to meet my parents. I had gone to the right schools, I had studied abroad in Europe and South America, and I now had a great job and apartment in New York City. I had only recently showed signs of conversion, and suddenly this conversion was infinitely more than just a shift

> "Holiness consists simply in doing God's will, and being just what God wants us to be."
> —Saint Thérèse of Lisieux

in friends and my daily routine, as my family observed from a distance. Nobody in my family had done such a thing. But, my call was unmistakable.

Once the acceptance letter came, I went ahead and let everyone know. It was happening, and I was happier and at greater peace by the day. That peace has prevailed over the course of my religious life. My family has been able to enter into my joy as the years have drawn on, and it has been a gift for all of us.

There is no greater joy than accepting the invitation, the challenge, to love God more each day. He calls me to draw nearer to Him continually in my community as His spouse. This is religious life: an invitation to love. How could I ever be worthy of such an invitation? Only by His great mercy and love.

> Thank you, consecrated women! Following the example of the greatest of women, the Mother of Jesus Christ, the Incarnate Word, you open yourselves with obedience and fidelity to the gift of God's love. You help the Church and all mankind to experience a "spousal" relationship to God, one which magnificently expresses the fellowship which God wishes to establish with his creatures.
>
> Thank you, every woman, for the simple fact of being a woman! Through the insight which is so much a part of your womanhood you enrich the world's understanding and help to make human relations more honest and authentic.
>
> —Pope Saint John Paul II

Put Out Into the Deep

The Dominican Sisters of Mary Mother of the Eucharist

Updated for Second Volume

Sister Joseph Andrew Bogdanowicz, OP
Born in Oak Ridge, TN

T he founding of the Dominican Sisters of Mary, Mother of the Eucharist is a captivating love story that began more than twenty years ago with a challenge from Pope Saint John Paul II. *Vita Consecrata,* the Holy Father's 1996 Apostolic Letter to religious throughout the world, summoned religious communities to send out their members to begin anew in efforts to revive this vocation. This call resounded in the hearts of four professed Dominican Sisters living in a convent in the Deep South of the United

Four Foundresses with John Cardinal O'Connor

States. Subsequently, they left all—for the second time!—to answer the Holy Father's exhortation and God's call.

The first year of 1996-1997 found the Sisters living in a converted barn on an estate in Purchase, New York. Under the direction of John Cardinal O'Connor, then Cardinal Archbishop of New York, they prayed to the Holy Spirit, studied, and labored. In time, their love bore fruit in the Constitutions of a new community. The Holy Father blessed the establishment of the community and approved their Constitutions, and the Church bade the Foundresses to "go forth and multiply". Upon the invitation of Bishop Carl F. Mengeling of Lansing, Michigan, they traveled west, arriving in Ann Arbor on the evening of April 4, 1997.

Bishop Carl F. Mengeling

Immediately, they converted a regular house into a convent and, by year's end, needed more cells—the monastic term for the Sisters' very small rooms. They traded beds for bunk beds as the space quickly filled again with new young women entering the community.

By 1998, their little convent was bursting at the seams, and construction began on a Motherhouse, which would be built in three phases due to financial constraints. Each time a phase was finished, the community had already outgrown its new quarters before even moving into them.

Built on the dreams and sacrifices of our first Sisters and the generosity of many benefactors, the Motherhouse is now too small for the community's more than one hundred and fifty Sisters. All the cells are occupied, and halls, storage rooms, and kitchenettes are variously commandeered as makeshift sleeping areas when the entire community is home. In the chapel, the Sisters perform elaborate maneuvers to reach their kneelers without bumping into one another. At table, elbow-room is a long-forgotten luxury. When the Sisters dispatched around the country and to Rome come home to Michigan for Christmas and short periods of the summer, the Motherhouse is filled to overflowing. More building is being planned across the U.S. to accommodate our growing family. In the twenty-third anniversary of the community's history, we now gratefully have built the first phase of a Priory in Georgetown, Texas to hold, eventually, another one hundred and thirty Sisters.

What is it that attracts so many young women to this community? Why has God blessed such humble beginnings? The simplest answer is that the Spirit moves wherever He wills. The longer answer is that love always demands a response. The foundation of this community required a great response of love and heroic sacrifice. Early on, the Foundresses believed God's gift in this new community would be blessed by both life and Divine love!

A EUCHARISTIC AND MARIAN SPIRITUALITY

The four original Sisters were united by a deep hunger for the Eucharist, for God-with-us and within-us, and a desire that He be the heart of all they did. Consequently, from the very beginning, they combined a very active apostolate with contemplation, daily Mass, a daily Eucharistic Holy Hour, and fidelity to the Divine Office. Quite literally, they wrote their hunger for Christ's Body and Blood into the Constitutions of the community. The Foundresses firmly established  that to be a Dominican Sister of Mary, Mother of the Eucharist, was to have the Eucharistic Heart at the center of one's being.

Perhaps no less important to these Sisters would be contemplating the face of Christ through the eyes of His mother, Mary. As one Foundress expressed it, "It is the Marian response of total self-donation that we have been called to utter, and by which we too, like Mary, will become icons of Christ." The Foundresses wanted this self-donation to be expressed in three concrete ways. The first is the response of Mary the *Virgin*, the one who waits for the Spirit's coming and whose whole being becomes an empty vessel open to receive God's Word. The Sisters, too, are called to embrace this paradox of emptiness and fullness. Secondly, the Sisters reflect Mary, *Spouse* of the Spirit. Marian receptivity is an active response, a perpetual and never-ending "yes" to Love. Similarly, the vocation of each Sister is a single affirmation, continuously expressed in each moment of the day.

Finally, Mary's response is lived as *Mother*, especially as Mother of the Eucharist. In recent years, many searching theological minds have attempted to plumb the depths of Pope Saint John Paul II's remarkable "Theology of the Body". Mary understood and lived that theology in one single word: motherhood. This is love that encompasses the whole person, a real and tangible love that is not afraid to reach out to the other. It sees beauty in every life, including the life still hidden in the womb. Its vision penetrates beyond appearances to the human dignity rooted in God's image, just as the adorer of the Eucharist penetrates the veils to know Christ's Real Presence. Pope Francis expressed this movingly in a meeting with sick children in Assisi in 2013:

> On the altar we adore the Flesh of Jesus; in the people we find the wounds of Jesus. Jesus hidden in the Eucharist and Jesus hidden in these wounds. But there is something else that gives us hope. Jesus is present in the Eucharist, here is the Flesh of Jesus; Jesus is present among you, it is the Flesh of Jesus.[1]

A mother's love gives and bears another's burdens as her own. She stands at the cross, a witness to the beauty behind the gift of Christ's Blood. A mother is always faithful: even after her child has disappeared from sight, and only empty, bloodied cross-beams remain, a mother waits with faith and hope. The Eucharistic mother reflects this in a very special way. In his Apostolic Letter *Salvifici Doloris*, Pope Saint John Paul II reflects that, on the cross, Christ is consumed by the intensity of His own love; but He is not alone: a mother's love stands at the heart of His consummation—and therefore at the heart of the Eucharistic mystery that re-presents that consummation moment by moment on altars throughout the world.

Such motherhood is required of a Dominican Sister of Mary, Mother of the Eucharist. These Marian elements, like the Eucharistic ones, find explicit mention and explanation in the community's Constitutions. Not simply the desire to be conformed to Mary, but also the actual pursuit of this goal, forms part of the formation of every young woman called to this way of life.

IN THE DOMINICAN TRADITION

Tradition relates that Saint Francis used to walk the streets of Europe crying, "Love is not loved, Love is not loved." Saint Dominic told his brethren that it was up to them to teach the world how to return love for Love. In fact, the first Dominican novices had only just arrived when Saint Dominic sent them back out into the world, fired with zeal for souls and eager to spread the Truth. Our Dominican community of Sisters, in its turn, was endowed with the Dominican missionary zeal in two unique ways.

The first is the Sisters' charism for teaching. After the Second Vatican Council, teaching became, among charisms, the forgotten stepchild. Many communities turned from this traditional apostolate to social work and initiatives for social justice. Our Foundresses felt that the world today suffers most acutely from ignorance and spiritual hunger. Consequently, they established the Sisters as a teaching order within the Dominican family.

The second unique expression of Dominican zeal is a boldness for expansion. Knowing that religious life is essential to every diocese, the Foundresses would not be satisfied with a single large convent and mission houses in the surrounding area. Rather, they desired that religious life, faithfully renewed and animated by the Second Vatican Council, would once again be visible throughout the United States. They sought to respond to the needs of the Church in our time. In the twenty-first century, as in the thirteenth, Dominican zeal for souls requires each religious to be both a true contemplative, guarding prayer with monastic practices such as silence and the cloister, and a true apostle, engaging the culture and accompanying her Spouse into the public square.

> The Sisters cannot simply live a consecrated life; they have to be able to understand, defend, and communicate it to others in an increasingly secularized society.

Furthermore, the community was founded as a unique response to Saint John Paul II's call for the New Evangelization, which he said would come through evangelization that was "new in its ardor, in its methods, in its expression."[2]

The Sisters cannot simply live a consecrated life; they have to be able to understand, defend, and communicate it to others in an increasingly secularized society. In short, the Foundresses had truly audacious goals that will continue to be lived out by their spiritual daughters; to be a Dominican Sister of Mary, Mother of the Eucharist, means working toward nothing less than the re-evangelization of the world.

THE CROSS

In addition to these principles, which have drawn so many young women to give their lives to God in this community, one final essential ingredient remains. Just as the Church can never forget her founding on Calvary, this new community cannot cease to be marked by the cross in which it is rooted. When the Foundresses responded to God's call, they gave the community not merely the right ideology or a solid structure but their very selves. This self-gift, faithfully learned and practiced through the years of their religious life before God's call in 1997, attains its fullest expression in the founding and continued nurturing of the community. Their visible witness of sacrificial love is a powerful attraction to many. Young Sisters come and stay because they witness the cross lived in love.

The Foundresses' self-offering was, and continues to be, joined by the gifts of many others: the bedridden mother who offered her sufferings; the priest who remembered the Community daily in his offering of the Holy Mass; and the white-haired man whose last years became a continual Rosary, the decades limited only by his limitless love as the beads slipped ceaselessly between his fingers. The spirit of the Cross runs through the heart of this community and, because of that, so does joy—overflowing, abundant, radiant joy!

SEND FORTH YOUR SPIRIT

Since the four Foundresses set out "into the deep" in 1997, the single convent has expanded to over twenty missions. Our Sisters live and teach in California, Florida, Illinois, Arizona, Ohio, Michigan, Texas, and elsewhere. One can even spot several Dominican Sisters of Mary, Mother of the Eucharist in Rome, where they serve as librarians at the North American College as well as in administration at Santa Sabina, the mother church of the Dominican Order.

In continuing fidelity to John Paul II's call for the New Evangelization, the community has also embraced new apostolic endeavors. Alongside their primary work of teaching, the Sisters catechize at hundreds of other sites and events throughout the year, including vacation Bible schools, conferences and retreats, youth groups, parish missions, and high school and college campus ministry events. The community has opened its doors to secular media such as Oprah; recorded three chart-topping CDs; published their *Disciples of Christ, Education in Virtue*® series, along with several books; and even hosted a concert of popular Christian musicians, designed to unite Christians in prayer. The community has built its own studio from which it launches Catholic podcasts, videos, and educational materials via the website *goledigital.org*. From the newest postulant to the busiest teaching Sister, every Dominican Sister of Mary, Mother of the Eucharist, seeks, like Mary, to bring Jesus Christ and His Gospel to the world.

Truly the Spirit moves where He wills. Even as the

The Dominican Sisters of Mary Mother of the Eucharist

Foundresses toss and turn in the still hours of the night, pleading for benefactors, wondering where to house the young women waiting to join them, and prayerfully keeping vigil over the Sisters' needs and concerns, God must laugh heartily to Himself. He knows what He is about. He is answering many prayers in this humble beginning. This is His gift, and He means to bring it to fruition.

Notes

1. Francis. "Address to the Sick and Disabled Children Assisted at the Seraphic Institute," Vatican, October 4, 2013, https://w2.vatican.va/content/francesco/en/speeches/2013/october/documents/papa-francesco_20131004_bambini-assisi.html.

2. During his pontificate, Saint John Paul II repeatedly called for this New Evangelization, which aimed to proclaim the faith to "entire groups of the baptized (who) have lost a living sense of the faith, or even no longer consider themselves members of the Church, and live a life far removed from Christ and his Gospel" (*Redemptoris Missio*, 33). That is, he intended the New Evangelization to reach those who live in historically Christian countries, such as the United States. John Paul II, "Address to the CELAM Assembly," trans. Dominican Sisters of Mary. Vatican, 1983, http://w2.vatican.va/content/john-paul-ii/es/speeches/1983/march/documents/hf_jp-ii_spe_19830309_assemblea-celam.html.

And Mary Said "Fiat"

Growing in Your Spiritual Life & Prayers

"Draw near to God, and He will draw near to you" (Jas 4:8).

Part I
Growing in Your Spiritual Life

If you are considering a religious vocation, you should make an effort to grow in your prayer life. In order for God to speak to your heart, you need to take time to listen to Him. Whatever your vocation is, a deeper prayer life will strengthen you to be the woman you are called to be. Women, in particular, are drawn in prayer to follow the example of Mary, who said, "Behold, I am the handmaid of the Lord. May it be done to me according to your word" (Lk 1:38) in response to God's invitation of love.

Every baptized person is called to holiness, and to heavenly life with the Blessed Trinity. Consecrated life anticipates that union and becomes a spousal bond here on earth. If you are called to religious life, there is nothing better you can do than come to know Christ—your potential Spouse—better. If that is your vocation, your relationship with Him today is the beginning of your relationship with Him in the convent, the same way that the relationship between a married couple began the day they met. If prayer seems difficult, or God seems far away, remember that He is close to you, inspiring in you the very resolution to pray better.

This chapter will provide some general guidelines on prayer and building that relationship. The second part of the chapter will provide you with prayers and devotions that may be helpful as you discern your vocation.

The Basics

There are certain "levels" to a flourishing spiritual life. Before focusing on prayers and devotions specially directed towards helping you discern your vocation, you will want to make sure that you have all of the basic pieces in place. The Catholic Church gives us certain regulations that all Catholics are required to follow. **Church law tells us to attend Mass every Sunday and Holy Day of Obligation, to confess our serious sins at least once a year, and to receive Holy Communion at least once a year.** In her wisdom, the Church realizes that these

> ### The Precepts of the Church
>
> The precepts of the Church are set in the context of a moral life bound to and nourished by liturgical life. The obligatory character of these positive laws decreed by the pastoral authorities is meant to guarantee to the faithful the indispensable minimum in the spirit of prayer and moral effort, in the growth in love of God and neighbor.
>
> *CCC 2041*

practices are the bare necessities for the spiritual life. They provide a firm foundation for a prayer life that goes far beyond them. To fall below this minimum is a sin.

Going a Little Deeper

Along with the practices required by the Church, there are some other spiritual practices that should be part of every Catholic's life. Incorporating these practices will support your vocational discernment.

Begin every day by offering your day to God with a morning offering. Starting your day in this way directs all of your works, prayers, sufferings, joys, and sorrows to God. We want every moment of our lives to be lived in union with Christ.

End every day with an examination of conscience in which you look back over the day and try to recognize God's presence in every circumstance, thank God for the good you have done, and repent of your sins. As this daily examination becomes a habit, you can start to think about the patterns of sin you see in your life and make concrete plans to break those patterns. Pray for God's help to avoid sin and serve Him. Receive the sacrament of Confession regularly, at least every month. If you are examining your conscience every day, you will not find it difficult to confess your sins frequently.

Spend around fifteen minutes every day reading the Bible or other spiritual books and reflecting on what you have read. Read slowly and carefully. Think of the words you are reading as God speaking to you. Pause occasionally to turn to Him and ask questions or reply. Reading Scripture and other spiritual books helps us get to know the ways of God and thus, hear his voice in our own lives.

> "It is simply impossible to lead, without the aid of prayer, a virtuous life."
>
> -Saint John Chrysostom

Saint Catherine of Siena stated that "knowledge must precede love"; that is, getting to know more about Christ—and our true selves—should lead us to love Him more.[1] Scripture and other reading can help us understand that we can be ourselves before God. For example, we see in the lives of the saints a tremendous variety of personalities and backgrounds. Within Scripture, the Psalms sometimes sing joyfully, but they also freely express tiredness, discouragement and anger, even though they always end with a prayer of trust. God doesn't want us to pretend to be pious and perfect, but honest.

Try to make a retreat every year. Many parishes and dioceses offer special opportunities to take time away from your regular schedule for God. Many religious communities also offer retreats. These may be retreats seeking to help you grow in your relationship with Christ more generally, or a vocation discernment opportunity specifically to ask God to help you discover His plan. Our community provides three weekend retreat opportunities for women discerning their vocation and one weekend for married women.

Pray with your family. A loving family that attends Mass together and shares other devotions such as the Rosary or reading Scripture is one of the greatest incubators of vocations. If you are reading this book because you want to support the vocation of a daughter or friend, know that fostering a prayerful, happy, Catholic home environment provides fertile soil for the seed of religious and priestly vocations to flourish. A young woman who has left home may find support in prayer in a young adult group, a Bible study group, or just a good group of faithful friends.

Praying through Discernment

According to the *Catechism of the Catholic Church*, prayer is an elevation of the mind and heart to God in praise of His glory

(*CCC*, Glossary). Prayer can be vocal, with exterior words and actions; meditation, where the mind and heart seeks—usually using Scripture, art, or other methods—to understand more of God and what He asks; and contemplative prayer, which can be described as "a gaze of faith," fixed on Jesus, or simply "being" with the Lord (*CCC*, 2700-2719). While it may help to set aside times for various kinds of prayer, there is no formula for perfect prayer. Above all, humbly ask God to give you the grace to love Him more.

As you grow in your prayer life, here are some basic devotions that we recommend to deepen your discernment.

Attend daily Mass and receive Communion. At Mass, you bring all of your trials, fears, hopes, joys and sufferings to offer to the Father along with Christ's sacrifice. In return, you are given the body of Christ as the "food for the journey" of your life. If you find praying at Mass difficult, you might pick up a book explaining its meaning. A good place to start is the teaching in the *Catechism of the Catholic Church* about the liturgy. Scott Hahn's *The Lamb's Supper: The Mass as Heaven on Earth* is a good book to help you begin to appreciate the depth of the Mass.

> "As far as possible, you should pray in quiet and silent devotion. Try to have a favorite topic of prayer, such as a devotion to the passion of Jesus, the Blessed Sacrament, awareness of the divine presence; go directly to Jesus without too much fuss."
>
> -Saint Peter Julian Eymard

Make a Eucharistic Holy Hour every week or even every day. The Blessed Sacrament is Jesus' Real Presence here with us. He wants to welcome us and fill us with the light of His presence. Sometimes it is good just to sit or kneel before the Blessed Sacrament, quietly basking in His love. Tell Him all of your troubles. Go through a list of all of those whom you love, asking Him for His blessings for them. Many people find that thoughtfully reading the Scriptures in front of Jesus in the Eucharist is a powerful experience, reading "the Word before the Word." A final idea regarding Eucharistic adoration comes from another Sister, who recalled choosing to go and spend time with Jesus in the dorm chapel when her roommate was spending time with her boyfriend. She thought she should give as much time to developing her relationship with Jesus as the roommate did with her future husband.

Mary is the model for every woman Religious as well as for every mother of a family. She looks on you as her daughter. She wants to help lead you along the path which Jesus has planned for your life. There are many ways to cultivate devotion to Mary. Some of these are: praying the Rosary, making a pilgrimage to a Marian shrine, and attending Mass on Saturday in her honor. There is a tradition of praying three Hail Marys every day for the light to know your vocation and the strength to follow it.

> "Let us run to Mary, and, as her little children, cast ourselves into her arms with a perfect confidence."
> —Saint Francis de Sales

Many Catholics deepen their relationship to Mary by consecrating themselves to her. **Marian Consecration** is a way of uniting oneself more closely to Christ and is often called "consecration to Jesus through Mary". Mary is the Mother and foremost member of the Church, so consecrating yourself to her is a way of entering more fully into the family of the Church. It involves making a deeper commitment to living your baptismal vows in imitation of Mary's immaculate holiness and total availability to God. There are several books that can guide you through a Marian Consecration, including Father Michael Gaitley's *33 Days to Morning Glory,* Saint

Louis Marie de Montfort's *Preparation for Total Consecration*, and *Totus Tuus: A Consecration to Jesus through Mary* by Father Brian McMaster.

It may be helpful for you to devote some of your spiritual reading time to the **history and spirituality of different religious communities**. Choose books about saints from the religious communities that interest you, or about holy men and women who shared the challenges that you are experiencing. Several Sisters in our community who were drawn to Dominican life by the figure of Saint Dominic. Try to meet the great religious saints. Ask for their intercession while you read about their lives. In addition to asking Jesus what path He has in store for your life, you are also asking the founders and saints of the religious orders to help you become a member of their families. Saint Catherine of Siena realized that she had a Dominican vocation after a dream in which Saint Dominic offered her the habit!

It can also be helpful to read **the lives of modern women who gave their lives to Christ**. For example, Mother Angelica is a recent influential figure in the Church who had to fight for independence from her mother so that she could follow God's call. She also wrote her mother some beautiful explanations of the spousal nature of religious life.

Making the Stations of the Cross is a beautiful way to deepen your love of Christ. Meditating on Christ's passion will give you strength to follow Him. It will help you see the value your sufferings have when they are united to His. You can make the stations with a visual focus, by walking around a church which has the images of the fourteen stations, spending a

> "The remembrance of the most holy Passion of Jesus Christ is the door through which the soul enters into intimate union with God, interior recollection and most sublime contemplation."
> – Saint Paul of the Cross

few moments gazing at each one.

You can also use a prayer book, which offers meditations to read. No Religious who has a faithful love of the passion of Christ will ever stray from her vocation.

As you come to feel connected to a religious community or tradition, **allow your devotion to be shaped by the charism of that community.** If you enter a community, you will be joining a family. Take an interest in the customs and traditions of your future family. Usually the spiritual heritage of the community to which you are called will "match" your prior devotions in some ways, but will also give you many new treasures. Be open to these. Many Sisters had never or very only rarely prayed the Divine Office before entering our Dominican community, but fell in love with the Dominican way of chanting the prayers. Now they can scarcely imagine life without it!

Part II
Prayers

As you learn how to pray and deepen your relationship with Christ, you will often just have a conversation with Him, telling him about your desires, your joys, your struggles, and your fears. There are no wrong words in prayer; and God knows your heart and the gifts that He has given you. However, the Christian tradition has also given us many "tried and true" prayers—including many to Mary, our Mother—that may help you establish a consistent prayer life, which will serve you well when you are distracted or can't seem to find the right words.

Prayers to the Most Holy Trinity

Come Holy Spirit

Come Holy Spirit, fill the hearts of Your faithful and kindle in them the fire of Your love. Send forth Your Spirit, and they shall be created, and You shall renew the face of the earth.

O God, Who by the light of the Holy Spirit, did instruct the hearts of the faithful, grant that by the same Spirit, we may be truly wise and ever rejoice in His consolation, through Christ our Lord. Amen.

Morning Offering

O Jesus, through the Immaculate Heart of Mary, I offer you my prayers, works, joys, and sufferings of this day for all the intentions of your Sacred Heart, in union with the Holy Sacrifice of the Mass throughout the world, in reparation for my sins, for salvation of souls, and the intentions of my relatives and friends, and in particular for the intentions of the Holy Father.

(This prayer has many variations. In general, they all focus on giving the entire day to God and allowing Him to use your sacrifices for His glory and the salvation of souls.)

Anima Christi

Soul of Christ, sanctify me.
Body of Christ, save me.
Blood of Christ, inebriate me.
Water from the side of Christ, wash me.
Passion of Christ, strengthen me.
O Good Jesus, hear me.
Within your wounds hide me.
Permit me not to be separated from you.
From the wicked foe, defend me.
At the hour of my death, call me
And bid me come to you,
That with your saints
I may praise you forever and ever.
Amen.

Fatima Prayer

My God, I believe, I adore, I hope, and I love You. I ask pardon of You for those who do not believe, do not adore, do not hope, and do not love You.

(This prayer was taught to the three Fatima Children by an angel. The children were told to repeat the prayer three times while kneeling with their foreheads touched to the ground.)

The Divine Mercy Chaplet

1. **Make the Sign of the Cross and pray one Our Father.**

   Our Father, who art in Heaven, hallowed be Thy name. Thy Kingdom come, Thy will be done, on earth as it is in heaven. Give us this day our daily bread, and forgive us our trespasses, as we forgive those who trespass against us. And lead us not into temptation, but deliver us from evil. Amen.

2. **Pray one Hail Mary.**

   Hail Mary, full of grace; the Lord is with thee. Blessed art thou among women, and blessed is the fruit of thy womb, Jesus. Holy Mary, Mother of God, pray for us sinners, now and at the hour of our death. Amen.

3. **Pray the Apostles' Creed.**

   I believe in God, the Father Almighty, Creator of heaven and earth; and in Jesus Christ, His only Son, our Lord, Who was conceived by the Holy Spirit; born of the Virgin Mary; suffered under Pontius Pilate; was crucified, died, and was buried. He descended into hell; the third day He rose again from the dead; He ascended into heaven, and is seated at the right hand of God, the Father Almighty; from there He will come to judge the living and the dead. I believe in the Holy Spirit, the Holy Catholic Church, the communion of Saints, the forgiveness of sins, the resurrection of the body, and life everlasting. Amen.

4. **To start each decade, pray the Eternal Father.**

   Eternal Father, I offer you the Body and Blood, Soul and Divinity of your dearly Beloved Son, our Lord Jesus Christ, in atonement for our sins and those of the whole world.

5. **On the ten small beads, pray:**
   For the sake of His sorrowful Passion, have mercy on us and on the whole world.
6. **Repeat steps four and five for each decade.**
7. **After completing the fifth decade, pray the Holy God three times.**
   Holy God, Holy Mighty One, Holy Immortal One, have mercy on us and on the whole world.

Prayers to Our Blessed Mother

Vita Consecrata tells us that "A filial relationship to Mary is the royal road to fidelity to one's vocation and a most effect help for advancing in that vocation and living it fully." 2 Mary will always lead us to Jesus; she is also a model for every woman's heart. Here are some prayers to the Blessed Mother you may want to memorize, or use this book to pray.

The Rosary

How to pray the Rosary

Although different groups pray the Rosary with slight variations, here is the most common method for praying the Rosary:

1. **Make the Sign of the Cross and pray the Apostles' Creed:**

   I believe in God, the Father Almighty, Creator of heaven and earth; and in Jesus Christ, His only Son, our Lord, Who was conceived by the Holy Spirit; born of the Virgin Mary; suffered under Pontius Pilate; was crucified, died, and was buried. He descended into hell; the third day He rose again from the dead; He ascended into heaven, and is seated at the right hand of God, the Father Almighty; from there He will come to judge the living and the dead. I believe in the Holy Spirit, the Holy Catholic Church, the communion of Saints, the forgiveness of sins, the resurrection of the body, and life everlasting. Amen.

2. **Pray an Our Father:**

   Our Father, Who art in Heaven, hallowed be Thy name. Thy Kingdom come, Thy will be done, on earth as it is in heaven. Give us this day our daily bread, and forgive us our trespasses, as we forgive those who trespass against us. And lead us not into temptation, but deliver us from evil. Amen.

3. **Pray three Hail Marys:**

   Hail Mary, full of grace; the Lord is with thee. Blessed art thou among women, and blessed is the fruit of thy womb, Jesus. Holy Mary, Mother of God, pray for us sinners, now and at the hour of our death. Amen.

4. **Pray the Glory Be:**

   Glory be to the Father, and to the Son, and to the Holy Spirit; as it was in the beginning, is now, and ever shall be, world without end. Amen.

5. **Announce or think about the first Mystery (see below); then pray the Our Father.**

6. **Pray ten Hail Marys while meditating on the Mystery.**

7. **Pray the Glory Be.**

8. **Announce the second Mystery, and the Our Father. Repeat steps six and seven, and continue with the third, fourth, and fifth Mysteries in the same way.**

9. **After completing the fifth Mystery, pray the *Salve Regina*, or Hail, Holy Queen:**

   Hail, holy Queen, Mother of Mercy! Our life, our sweetness, and our hope! To thee do we cry, poor banished children of Eve. To thee do we send up our sighs, mourning and weeping in this valley of tears. Turn then, most gracious advocate, thine eyes of mercy toward us, and after this, our exile, show unto us the blessed fruit of thy womb, Jesus. O clement, o loving, o sweet Virgin Mary.

   Pray for us, O holy Mother of God, that we may be made worthy of the promises of Christ.

Mysteries of the Rosary

The Five Joyful Mysteries

  The Annunciation (Lk 1:26-38)
  The Visitation (Lk 1:40-42)
  The Nativity (Lk 2:8-7, Mt. 1)
  The Presentation (Lk 2:22-35)
  The Finding of Jesus in the Temple (Lk 2:41-52)

The Five Luminous Mysteries

  The Baptism in the Jordan (Mt 3:13-17)
  The Wedding at Cana (Jn 2:1-2)
  The Proclamation of the Kingdom (Lk 7:48-49)
  The Transfiguration (Mt 17:1-8)
  The Institution of the Eucharist (Mt 26:26-28)

The Five Sorrowful Mysteries

  The Agony in the Garden (Lk 22:39-46)
  The Scourging at the Pillar (Mt 27:26)
  The Crowning with Thorns (Mk 15:20-21)
  The Carrying of the Cross (Lk 23:26-32, Jn 19:16-17)
  The Crucifixion (Jn 19:25-30)

The Five Glorious Mysteries

  The Resurrection (Jn 20:1-9)
  The Ascension (Acts 1:9-11)
  Pentecost (Acts 1:13-14, 2:1-4)
  The Assumption (Lk 1:46-49)
  The Coronation (Rev 11:19-12:1)

The Memorare

Remember, O most gracious Virgin Mary, that never was it known that anyone who fled to thy protection, implored thy help, or sought thine intercession was left unaided. Inspired by this confidence, I fly unto thee, O Virgin of virgins, my mother; to thee do I come, before thee I stand, sinful and sorrowful. O Mother of the Word Incarnate, despise not my petitions, but in thy mercy hear and answer me. Amen.

Praying with Scripture

Lectio Divina

Lectio divina is Latin for "sacred reading." Rather than just reading, however, it is a meditative and contemplative prayer using a text, most often Sacred Scripture. Many people start *lectio divina* by using the Gospel of the day's Mass; these readings can be found online.

Begin by asking the Holy Spirit to open your heart to receive the Word. *Lectio divina* traditionally has four steps, and we've included some questions that may help you enter into the prayer.

Step 1: Reading (*Lectio*)

Slowly read a short scripture passage. You might go back and read it more than once.

What does the biblical text say in itself?

Step 2: Meditation (*Meditatio*)

Ponder the scripture passage. Consider the passage from different angles.

What does the biblical text say to us?

What does the Gospel passage reveal about the Person of Jesus Christ?

Step 3: Prayer (*Oratio*)

Talk to God about what He is saying through the Word. Ask Him what it means for you.

What do we say to the Lord in response to His Word of mercy and love?

Step 4: Contemplation (*Contemplatio*) and Action

After spending time in silence and receiving, consider how God is calling you to act.

What conversion of mind, heart, and life are You asking of me?

How is my life a gift of self for others in charity?

Surrender Prayer

Given by Jesus to Father Dolindo Ruotolo (1882-1970)

Surrender to Me does not mean to fret, to be upset, or to lose hope, nor does it mean offering to Me a worried prayer, asking Me to follow you and change your worry into prayer. It is against this surrender, deeply against it, to worry, be nervous and to desire to think about the consequences of anything. It is like the confusion that children feel when they ask their mother to see to their needs, and then try to take care of those needs for themselves so that their childlike efforts get in their mother's way. Surrender means to placidly close the eyes of the soul, to turn away from thoughts and tribulation and to put yourself in My care, so that only I act; saying, "You take care of it."

Aspiration: O Jesus, I surrender myself to You, take care of everything! (10 times)

A Prayer for Vocations

O God, you sent your Beloved Son, Jesus Christ, to bring eternal life to those who believe. The harvest is ready; send forth laborers, O Lord, for the salvation of souls. May your Holy Spirit inspire men and women to do the Father's will within the heart of the Church through the priesthood, diaconate, religious life and lay ministry. Please, Holy Spirit, make Your will known for my life and give me the courage to live it with love and fidelity. Mary, Mother of Vocations, pray for me. Amen.

A Final Word: Pray as You Can

When you are having difficulty praying, it might simply be a time of dryness, but you also might need to make some changes. A Benedictine abbot, Dom Chapman, coined the saying: "Pray as you can and do not try to pray as you can't."[3] If you are starting the beautiful adventure of a life of prayer, but can't get through a whole Rosary, pray a decade between each class or task. If you can't sit still for an entire Holy Hour, start by making quick visits at the Newman Center, or stopping into the church for fifteen minutes at the end of the work day. If you are struggling to just "be" with the Lord, bring a book or pray a litany slowly. God desires even your weakness.

> "Prayer is an aspiration of the heart, it is a simple glance directed to heaven, it is a cry of gratitude and love in the midst of trial as well as joy; finally, it is something great, supernatural, which expands my soul and unites me to Jesus."
>
> –Saint Thérèse of Lisieux

Although God may give special graces and a burning desire for prayer, for many people, it takes a long time to build up that relationship in self-giving prayer. Trust that He loves you and desires your holiness, far more than you know.

Notes

1. Catherine of Siena, "A Treatise of Divine Providence," *The Dialogue of St. Catherine of Siena*, trans. Algar Thorold, 1906, https://www.ewtn.com/library/SOURCES/CATHDIAL.HTM

2. John Paul II, *Vita Consecrata*, 28, Vatican, http://w2.vatican.va/content/john-paul-ii/en/apost_exhortations/documents/hf_jp-ii_exh_25031996_vita-consecrata.html,

3. Dom John Chapman, *The Spiritual Letters of Dom John Chapman, O.S.B.*, (New York: Sheed and Ward, 1935), 109.

Glossary of Religious Terms

Assembled by Sister Elizabeth John Wrigley, OP
Born in Kingsville, TX

Apostolate: This refers to the work one does as a Religious. Apostolates are as varied as there are needs in the Church, and include teaching, preaching, nursing, and, for strictly cloistered Religious, prayer.

Asceticism: All Christians are called to practice asceticism, or self-discipline through practices of self-denial. This call to asceticism is especially urgent for Religious.

Benedictines: A monastic order founded by Saint Benedict of Nursia in the fifth century. Saint Benedict's rule of life famously revolves around *ora et labora*, or prayer and manual labor.

Breviary: Sometimes called an "office book", the breviary contains all of the Psalms, readings, and prayers of the Liturgy of the Hours.

Canon law for Religious: Canon law contains the juridical norms which govern the practices of the Church. Specific laws are addressed to consecrated Religious, such as the requirements for the vow of poverty and necessary spiritual practices.

Carmelites: Later reformed by Saint Teresa of Avila in the sixteenth century, the Carmelites trace their history to a group of monks who established the eremitic life on Mount Carmel in the Holy Land around the year 1200. Carmelite nuns and friars claim the prophet Elijah as their spiritual father and lead a life dedicated to prayer and contemplation.

Cell: The monastic cell is the private room of a Religious, simply furnished, where he or she can pray to the Father in secret.

Chastity, vow of: By the vow of chastity, the Religious freely foregoes marriage and the goods of marriage for the sake of a deeper spousal relationship with Christ. For women Religious, this union flows into a spiritual motherhood toward those whom she serves.

Charism: Refers to a specific grace given to an individual or group for the building up of the Church. Examples include preaching, teaching, and healing.

Cloister: An area within a convent that is reserved for the sole access and use of Religious. The cloister serves as an invaluable safeguard both for the vows and for the spirit of prayer and recollection.

Common life: Also referred to as *community life*. A Religious shares her day-to-day existence with her fellow Sisters. Typically, this includes common times of prayer, meals, and recreation.

Consecration: An object or person becomes consecrated when set aside for a sacred purpose. In the case of the Religious, this takes place at the moment of profession of vows.

Constitutions: The governing documents of a religious congregation. Constitutions articulate how a particular charism is to be lived with integrity. Religious profess their vows in accordance with the Constitutions of their specific institute.

Contemplation: Deep union with God in prayer. Canon law for Religious identifies contemplation as the "first and principal duty" of all Religious (CIC §663).

Convent: The house where Religious reside, typically placed under the patronage of a saint or named after a title of the Blessed Virgin Mary. A Dominican convent includes a chapel, a refectory, cells, and gathering spaces.

Discernment: The process of hearing and understanding God's will in any particular instance. Above all, discernment is necessary to know and accept one's vocation.

Dominicans: Established by Saint Dominic de Guzman in the thirteenth century as the Order of Preachers. Dominican friars, nuns, and Sisters live a life dedicated to the contemplation and preaching of divine truth.

Enclosure: Whereas all religious houses have cloistered portions, the practice of enclosure is exclusive to contemplative communities, whose entire convent or monastery is cloistered. A classic image of enclosure is the "grille" or grated screen which separates a nun from guests in the parlor.

Evangelical counsels: The evangelical counsels are poverty, chastity, and obedience. These counsels are lived in imitation of Jesus Christ, who was the first to live poor, chaste, and obedient to the Father.

Extern: In communities with the practice of enclosure, one or two Religious may be given charge of temporal affairs and interactions with the world outside the enclosure. These Religious are called externs.

Formation: The program and process by which a Religious learns and internalizes her identity within the spirituality and charism of her specific institute.

Formation, human: The particular aspect of religious formation aimed at developing the character of the Religious. While not imposing a mold, human formation acknowledges that "grace builds on nature", and that our fallen human nature often needs purification through guidance and experience.

Formator: The formator is the individual Religious who holds chief responsibility for the direct formation of the young Religious entrusted to her. This term is typically applied to those working with Religious not yet perpetually professed. Examples include the Novice Mistress and Postulant Assistant.

Franciscans: Perhaps the best-known religious order, the Franciscans were established by Saint Francis of Assisi in the 13th century. The sons and daughters of Saint Francis live a life in imitation of the Poor Christ.

General chapter: Periodically, a religious congregation holds a general chapter at which major superiors are chosen and significant matters of the congregation are discussed and determined. The frequency of these meetings is set by the congregation.

Great/profound silence: The practice of many religious institutes, especially those of monastic origin, to observe absolute silence for a determined number of hours each evening. In most cases, this begins in the late evening and ends early in the morning.

Habit: The outer garment of a Religious, which reflects his or her identity as belonging solely to God. The habit's appearance differs from one religious community to another.

Institute, religious: Any entity in which members publically profess the vows of poverty, chastity, and obedience lived out in a common life.

Institute, diocesan: A religious institute placed under the authority of a particular bishop, rather than the Holy Father directly.

Institute, pontifical: A religious institute placed under the direct authority of the Holy Father.

Liturgical cycle: The feasts and seasons which make up the Church's prayer life. Religious especially seek to enter into the liturgical cycle through the observance of feasts and solemnities as well as the liturgical seasons of Advent, Christmas, Lent, and Easter.

Liturgy of the Hours: Also known as the Divine Office, the Liturgy of the Hours is the official prayer of the Church. Made up of hymns, psalms, readings, and intercessions, the faithful recitation of the Liturgy of the Hours is a privileged duty for all priests and vowed Religious.

Mendicancy: Referring to the practice of begging for one's daily sustenance, the mendicant life became widespread in the 13th century with the birth of the Franciscan and Dominican Orders.

Mission: A satellite house of any religious congregation, apart from the Motherhouse. Mission houses are typically smaller both in size and in number of Religious in residence.

Monasticism: The monastic life originated with the desire for a life apart from the world, dedicated to God. Monasticism is accompanied by a variety of external practices, such as silent meals and custody of the eyes, aimed at fostering a greater spirit of prayer.

Motherhouse: As the name suggests, a motherhouse may be the founding house of a religious congregation or the official residence of the major superior.

New Evangelization: The call of Saint John Paul II for Christians to re-evangelize their own lands and nations. Many younger Religious institutes were established as a response to this call, including the Dominican Sisters of Mary, Mother of the Eucharist.

Novice: From the Latin word for "new". A novice is in the initial stages of Religious formation and is typically focused on the study of the vows and integration into the spirit of the institute.

Novice mistress: The individual Religious who is tasked with guiding the novices.

Novitiate: The residence wherein the Novice Mistress resides with the novices. The novitiate may be attached to, or separate from, the Motherhouse.

Nun: The term *nun* properly refers to enclosed, cloistered Religious but is sometimes used colloquially to describe any Religious Sister.

Obedience, vow of: By the vow of obedience, the Religious binds herself to carry out all legitimate requests of her lawful superiors, in imitation of Christ who was obedient to the Father. By this means, the Religious has the certainty of accomplishing God's will.

Perfectae Caritatis: The title of a document from the Second Vatican Council; its English title is "Decree on the Adaptation and Renewal of Religious Life." In this document, the Council Fathers invited Religious institutes to exercise a creative fidelity in returning to the original charism of their founder or foundress.

Priory: A convent owned by the Community where at least twelve professed Sisters reside.

Postulancy: Sometimes called an aspirancy, this is the time before an individual becomes a novice. A time of transition from the world and of deeper discernment, the postulancy may last from a few months to up to a year.

Poverty, vow of: By the vow of poverty, a Religious renounces the right to dispose of material goods and possessions. All items received by the Religious are considered the goods of the Community.

Profession, of vows:

The act of binding oneself to the practice of the evangelical counsels. In religious institutes this is done as a public act, witnessed by the Church. Profession may be temporary or perpetual.

Profession, Temporary:

The profession of vows for a temporary and explicitly stated amount of time. The duration of temporary vows may differ by religious institute.

Profession, Perpetual:

The profession of the evangelical counsels in perpetuity.

Religion, virtue of:

The virtue of religion is the disposition to give God what is His due. Some acts that fall under the virtue of religion include prayer and adoration, gratitude to God for His many gifts, participating in the Holy Sacrifice of the Mass, and the fulfillment of vows by those who profess them.

Rule:

The founding charter and chief governing document of a religious order. All Constitutions have their origins in the specific Rule of the religious institute.

Scapular: A garment consisting of two long rectangular pieces of cloth attached over the shoulders. Often blessed, the scapular is a reminder of the obedience which the Religious has professed.

Superior, local: The individual Religious invested with authority by the major superior to govern a smaller house of the institute.

Superior, major: A Religious whose authority extends over the entirety of the institute.

Spouse of Christ: By professing the evangelical counsels, the woman Religious exchanges intimacy with a human husband for a spousal union with Christ.

Veil: The garment worn on the head by women Religious as a sign of their consecration. In many cases, a white veil indicates that the woman is a novice, while a black veil indicates she has professed her vows.

Vita Consecrata: A post-synodal exhortation promulgated in 1997 by John Paul II after the Synod on Consecrated Life, in which religious life is viewed through the icon of the Transfiguration.

Vocation: From the Latin word for "call," one's vocation is the unique, loving way in which God calls the individual to achieve holiness in this life. Like the pearl of great price, one's vocation is freely given and yet hidden. A listening heart hears and responds to this call.

Vow: A deliberate, free, promise made to God regarding a higher good that is possible to attain. Once a vow is professed, its fulfillment binds according to the virtue of religion.

Acknowledgments

Any given moment is but a snapshot of the full picture of our lives. It is my belief that this book, following four years after Volume 1 of *And Mary's 'Yes' Continues*, is yet another snapshot of our religious life—and already I sense my desire to begin work on Volume 3! Why? So that more amazing vocational discernment stories can be shared! God works uniquely in the heart of each young woman who comes to religious life. And it is He who, in His infinite goodness and mercy, showers our Community with so many wonderful vocations! While many may be interested, it is not every young woman who makes it through the strenuous process of application and is accepted for entrance. Other young ladies may discern out of the Community, or are helped to discern this, if need be, up until the time of Final Vows (which takes place a full eight years after entrance). However, the vast majority who enter as postulants find themselves, on some glorious day of their dreams, vowing poverty, chastity, and obedience in our particular Dominican community and thus becoming Brides of the God-Man, Jesus Christ!

Founded on the cusp of the New Millennium under the inspiration of the saintly Pope John Paul II, the Dominican Sisters of Mary, Mother of the Eucharist have tremendous devotion to this modern-day saint, who is believed to have had the gift of reading hearts—even miles and oceans away. Pope John Paul II is the Sisters' most commonly quoted saint, so allow me to quote him now: "Remember the past with gratitude. Live the present with enthusiasm. Look forward to the future with confidence." Fittingly, this saint offered these words to the world in his Apostolic Letter *Novo Millennio Ineunte* at the close of the Jubilee Year 2000. As I look upon the book you now hold in your hands, I pray always to do just this: to remember the twenty-four years of our Community's history with deepest gratitude; to present this book, our music, and all our efforts on the website *goledigital.org* with greatest enthusiasm; and to look forward to the future with the confidence that Christ is the Victor of all battles and that we can rest well if our greatest desire is to live within His Heart.

Regarding gratitude, the list of those who have made this book possible is seemingly endless. We include not only every priest who ever gave us the Eucharist, heard our confessions, and offered us his wisdom and friendship, but also the many religious women outside our Community whose own lives and spiritualities enrich our own. We are grateful for our families and the many people who share our whole-hearted devotion to Mary, Mother of the Eucharist, and who have looked on us with favor—spiritually, materially, and personally—in their own love and devotion. Each young woman who has made one of our vocational discernment retreats or has read this book or contacted me by email or phone or text—and the list seems as vast as the oceans, including, as it does, young women from most continents—has my personal gratitude for helping to shape this book through your own lives, struggles, and joys, and each story and blessing you have shared with me.

In particular, I offer immense gratitude to our beloved Mother Assumpta Long, OP, and to the other Foundresses of our Community, including Sister Mary Samuel Handwerker, OP, and also Sister John Dominic Rasmussen, OP, whose endless efforts with both our Education in Virtue program and digital media studio bring so many spiritual riches to you, your families and/or parishoners, and young people. If "hiddenness" in untiring work is a valuable virtue, Sister John Dominic excels in this! Also, I thank my vocation assistants—in particular, Sister Mary Avila Corpany, OP—whose own creativity and consistency in her obedience of assisting in the vocation office amazes me daily! Along with those listed as authors of chapters in the Table of Contents, I thank the many Sisters who assisted in proofreading, especially Sister Maria Benedicta Bete, OP, and Sister Peter Thomas Burson, OP.

A host of others deserve many blessings from God for their generous gifts offered when I most needed them. Allison Barrick ranks high for her reading, her assistance with the layout, and her constant enthusiasm, devotion, and energy, even as she continues to discern her own vocation and serve as layout manager for our Community's newsletter, and design and content specialist for our Mission Advancement Office. Rebecca W. Martin discerned, married happily, and then returned to lead the charge as copy editor for this work! And our talented Lauren Stefanov excelled both in charity and in "finding her Saint Joseph," as she carefully propelled the layout of this book to its completion!

As is always the case, there are many more people who remain unnamed in this litany of thanksgiving but whom God will bless most specially—and that is what counts most. I am in debt to each priest who generously contributed his thoughts to our book and whose own life inspires and enlivens our consecrated life, to each family and friend with whom God's providence has so generously given us to interact in this life, to each of my beautiful Sisters whose daily "yes" to God brings a continuum of new graces to us all, and to each and every young person who offers an open heart to Christ with the Marian dimension of "be it done unto me according to Thy Will." But how glorious to be in debt to those with whom one hopes and trusts one will spend eternity! May God, the Giver of all good gifts, bless all of us and bring us together some day, in that one perfect moment of the beatific vision! Mutual prayers and inspiration along the Way!

Dominican Sisters *of* Mary
Mother *of the* Eucharist

The Dominican Sisters of Mary, Mother of the Eucharist is a Roman Catholic community of women religious based in Ann Arbor, Michigan. Our community was founded in the Dominican tradition to spread the witness of religious life in accord with Saint John Paul II's vision for a New Evangelization.

Through profession of the vows of poverty, chastity and obedience, along with a contemplative emphasis on Eucharistic adoration and Marian devotion, our community exists for the salvation of souls and the building of the Church throughout the world. As Dominicans, our primary apostolate is the education and formation of young people. We remain open to engaging the modern culture with new forms of evangelization in order to preach the Gospel and teach the Truth.

Discerning Your Vocation?

And the Truth Shall Set You Free **Podcast**

What does the path to discovering a possible religious vocation look like? For many, a life of chastity, poverty, and obedience is a vocation that has not been modeled in modern-day America. But you're in for a surprise! Join Sister Joseph Andrew Bogdanowicz, OP, as she dives into the beautiful and unique stories of Sisters who answered that call.

Learn more at:
www.goledigital.org/vocations

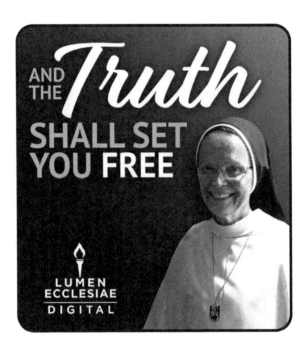

And Mary's 'Yes' Continues (Vol. 1)

By popular demand comes a beautiful book written by the Sisters themselves providing a much-needed inside view to vocation discernment entitled *And Mary's 'Yes' Continues*. It finally fulfills a longing by many hearts for an intimate resource and generous sharing of the journey into a beautiful vocation. Recognizing a need to provide discerning individuals, families, and loved ones accompaniment along the special call to religious life, under the direction of Sister Joseph Andrew, OP, Co-Foundress and Vocations Director, the Sisters created and now offer *And Mary's 'Yes' Continues*.

For more information about our community, vocations, and our various apostolates, please visit our websites:

www.goledigital.org   www.sistersofmary.org   www.golepress.com